Connected  Mathen

D0406715

Bits and Pieces II

Using Rational Numbers

Teacher's Guide

Glenda Lappan
James T. Fey
William M. Fitzgerald
Susan N. Friel
Elizabeth Difanis Phillips

Prentice
Hall

Glenview, Illinois
Needham, Massachusetts
Upper Saddle River, New Jersey

Connected Mathematics™ was developed at Michigan State University with financial support from the Michigan State University Office of the Provost, Computing and Technology, and the College of Natural Science.

This material is based upon work supported by the National Science Foundation under Grant No. MDR 9150217.

This project was supported, in part,
by the
National Science Foundation
Opinions expressed are those of the authors
and not necessarily those of the Foundation

The Michigan State University authors and administration have agreed that all MSU royalties arising from this publication will be devoted to purposes supported by the Department of Mathematics and the MSU Mathematics Education Enrichment Fund.

Photo Acknowledgements: 5 (sneaker sale) © The Photo Works/Photo Researchers, Inc.; 5 (cutting our prices) © Dion Ogust/The Image Works; 10 © Barbara Rios/Photo Researchers, Inc.; 12 © Rhoda Sidney/The Image Works; 20 © Voller Ernst/The Image Works; 21 © Dion Ogust/The Image Works; 27 © Topham/The Image Works; 40 © NASA; 44 © Steven Gottlieb/FPG International; 54 © Matthew Klein/Photo Researchers, Inc.; 58 © E. Alan McGee/FPG International; 71 © Tim Davis/Photo Researchers, Inc.

Copyright © 2002 by Michigan State University, Glenda Lappan, James T. Fey, William M. Fitzgerald, Susan N. Friel, and Elizabeth D. Phillips. All rights reserved. Printed in the United States of America. This publication is protected by copyright, and permission should be obtained from the publisher prior to any prohibited reproduction, storage in a retrieval system, or transmission in any form or by any means, electronic, mechanical, photocopying, recording, or likewise. Student worksheets and tests may be duplicated for classroom use, the number not to exceed the number of students in each class. Notice of copyright must appear on all copies. For information regarding permission(s), write to: Rights and Permissions Department.

Prentice
Hall

ISBN 0-13-053096-4
5 6 7 8 9 10   05 04 03 02

The Connected Mathematics Project Staff

Project Directors

James T. Fey
University of Maryland

William M. Fitzgerald
Michigan State University

Susan N. Friel
University of North Carolina at Chapel Hill

Glenda Lappan
Michigan State University

Elizabeth Difanis Phillips
Michigan State University

Project Manager

Kathy Burgis
Michigan State University

Technical Coordinator

Judith Martus Miller
Michigan State University

Collaborating Teachers/Writers

Mary K. Bouck
Portland, Michigan

Jacqueline Stewart
Okemos, Michigan

Curriculum Development Consultants

David Ben-Chaim
Weizmann Institute

Alex Friedlander
Weizmann Institute

Eleanor Geiger
University of Maryland

Jane Mitchell
University of North Carolina at Chapel Hill

Anthony D. Rickard
Alma College

Evaluation Team

Mark Hoover
Michigan State University

Diane V. Lambdin
Indiana University

Sandra K. Wilcox
Michigan State University

Judith S. Zawojewski
National-Louis University

Graduate Assistants

Scott J. Baldridge
Michigan State University

Angie S. Eshelman
Michigan State University

M. Faaiz Gierdien
Michigan State University

Jane M. Keiser
Indiana University

Angela S. Krebs
Michigan State University

James M. Larson
Michigan State University

Ronald Preston
Indiana University

Tat Ming Sze
Michigan State University

Sarah Theule-Lubienski
Michigan State University

Jeffrey J. Wanko
Michigan State University

Field Test Production Team

Katherine Oesterle
Michigan State University

Stacey L. Otto
University of North Carolina at Chapel Hill

Teacher/Assessment Team

Kathy Booth
Waverly, Michigan

Anita Clark
Marshall, Michigan

Theodore Gardella
Bloomfield Hills, Michigan

Yvonne Grant
Portland, Michigan

Linda R. Lobue
Vista, California

Suzanne McGrath
Chula Vista, California

Nancy McIntyre
Troy, Michigan

Linda Walker
Tallahassee, Florida

Software Developer

Richard Burgis
East Lansing, Michigan

Development Center Directors

Nicholas Branca
San Diego State University

Dianne Briars
Pittsburgh Public Schools

Frances R. Curcio
New York University

Perry Lanier
Michigan State University

J. Michael Shaughnessy
Portland State University

Charles Vonder Embse
Central Michigan University

Field Test Coordinators

Michelle Bohan
Queens, New York

Melanie Branca
San Diego, California

Alecia Devantier
Shepherd, Michigan

Jenny Jorgensen
Flint, Michigan

Sandra Kralovec
Portland, Oregon

Sonia Marsalis
Flint, Michigan

William Schaeffer
Pittsburgh, Pennsylvania

Karma Vince
Toledo, Ohio

Virginia Wolf
Pittsburgh, Pennsylvania

Shirel Yaloz
Queens, New York

Student Assistants

Laura Hammond
David Roche
Courtney Stoner
Jovan Trpovski
Julie Valicenti
Michigan State University

Advisory Board

Joseph Adney
Michigan State University (Emeritus)

Charles Allan
Michigan Department of Education

Mary K. Bouck
Portland Public Schools
Portland, Michigan

C. Stuart Brewster
Palo Alto, California

Anita Clark
Marshall Public Schools
Marshall, Michigan

David Doherty
GMI Engineering and Management Institute
Flint, Michigan

Kay Gilliland
EQUALS
Berkeley, California

David Green
GMI Engineering and Management Institute
Flint, Michigan

Henry Heikkinen
University of Northern Colorado
Greeley, Colorado

Anita Johnston
Jackson Community College
Jackson, Michigan

Elizabeth M. Jones
Lansing School District
Lansing, Michigan

Jim Landwehr
AT&T Bell Laboratories
Murray Hill, New Jersey

Peter Lappan
Michigan State University

Steven Leinwand
Connecticut Department of Education

Nancy McIntyre
Troy Public Schools
Troy, Michigan

Valerie Mills
Ypsilanti Public Schools
Ypsilanti, Michigan

David S. Moore
Purdue University
West Lafayette, Indiana

Ralph Oliva
Texas Instruments
Dallas, Texas

Richard Phillips
Michigan State University

Jacob Plotkin
Michigan State University

Dawn Pysarchik
Michigan State University

Rheta N. Rubenstein
University of Windsor
Windsor, Ontario, Canada

Susan Jo Russell
TERC
Cambridge, Massachusetts

Marjorie Senechal
Smith College
Northampton, Massachusetts

Sharon Senk
Michigan State University

Jacqueline Stewart
Okemos School District
Okemos, Michigan

Uri Treisman
University of Texas
Austin, Texas

Irvin E. Vance
Michigan State University

Linda Walker
Tallahassee Public Schools
Tallahassee, Florida

Gail Weeks
Northville Public Schools
Northville, Michigan

Pilot Teachers

California

National City
Laura Chavez
National City Middle School

Ruth Ann Duncan
National City Middle School

Sonia Nolla
National City Middle School

San Diego
James Ciolli
Los Altos Elementary School

Chula Vista
Agatha Graney
Hilltop Middle School

Suzanne McGrath
Eastlake Elementary School

Toni Miller
Hilltop Middle School

Lakeside
Eva Hollister
Tierra del Sol Middle School

Vista
Linda LoBue
Washington Middle School

Illinois

Evanston
Marlene Robinson
Baker Demonstration School

Michigan

Bloomfield Hills
Roxanne Cleveland
Bloomfield Hills Middle School

Constance Kelly
Bloomfield Hills Middle School

Tim Loula
Bloomfield Hills Middle School

Audrey Marsalese
Bloomfield Hills Middle School

Kara Reid
Bloomfield Hills Middle School

Joann Schultz
Bloomfield Hills Middle School

Flint
Joshua Coty
Holmes Middle School

Brenda Duckett-Jones
Brownell Elementary School

Lisa Earl
Holmes Middle School

Anne Heidel
Holmes Middle School

Chad Meyers
Brownell Elementary School

Greg Mickelson
Holmes Middle School

Rebecca Ray
Holmes Middle School

Patricia Wagner
Holmes Middle School

Greg Williams
Gundry Elementary School

Lansing
Susan Bissonette
Waverly Middle School

Kathy Booth
Waverly East Intermediate School

Carole Campbell
Waverly East Intermediate School

Gary Gillespie
Waverly East Intermediate School

Denise Kehren
Waverly Middle School

Virginia Larson
Waverly East Intermediate School

Kelly Martin
Waverly Middle School

Laurie Metevier
Waverly East Intermediate School

Craig Paksi
Waverly East Intermediate School

Tony Pecoraro
Waverly Middle School

Helene Rewa
Waverly East Intermediate School

Arnold Stiefel
Waverly Middle School

Portland
Bill Carlton
Portland Middle School

Kathy Dole
Portland Middle School

Debby Flate
Portland Middle School

Yvonne Grant
Portland Middle School

Terry Keusch
Portland Middle School

John Manzini
Portland Middle School

Mary Parker
Portland Middle School

Scott Sandborn
Portland Middle School

Shepherd
Steve Brant
Shepherd Middle School

Marty Brock
Shepherd Middle School

Cathy Church
Shepherd Middle School

Ginny Crandall
Shepherd Middle School

Craig Ericksen
Shepherd Middle School

Natalie Hackney
Shepherd Middle School

Bill Hamilton
Shepherd Middle School

Julie Salisbury
Shepherd Middle School

Sturgis
Sandra Allen
Eastwood Elementary School

Margaret Baker
Eastwood Elementary School

Steven Baker
Eastwood Elementary School

Keith Barnes
Sturgis Middle School

Wilodean Beckwith
Eastwood Elementary School

Darcy Bird
Eastwood Elementary School

Bill Dickey
Sturgis Middle School

Ellen Eisele
Sturgis Middle School

James Hoelscher
Sturgis Middle School

Richard Nolan
Sturgis Middle School

J. Hunter Raiford
Sturgis Middle School

Cindy Sprowl
Eastwood Elementary School

Leslie Stewart
Eastwood Elementary School

Connie Sutton
Eastwood Elementary School

Traverse City
Maureen Bauer
Interlochen Elementary School

Ivanka Berskshire
East Junior High School

Sarah Boehm
Courtade Elementary School

Marilyn Conklin
Interlochen Elementary School

Nancy Crandall
Blair Elementary School

Fran Cullen
Courtade Elementary School

Eric Dreier
Old Mission Elementary School

Lisa Dzierwa
Cherry Knoll Elementary School

Ray Fouch
West Junior High School

Ed Hargis
Willow Hill Elementary School

Richard Henry
West Junior High School

Dessie Hughes
Cherry Knoll Elementary School

Ruthanne Kladder
Oak Park Elementary School

Bonnie Knapp
West Junior High School

Sue Laisure
Sabin Elementary School

Stan Malaski
Oak Park Elementary School

Jody Meyers
Sabin Elementary School

Marsha Myles
East Junior High School

Mary Beth O'Neil
Traverse Heights Elementary School

Jan Palkowski
East Junior High School

Karen Richardson
Old Mission Elementary School

Kristin Sak
Bertha Vos Elementary School

Mary Beth Schmitt
East Junior High School

Mike Schrotenboer
Norris Elementary School

Gail Smith
Willow Hill Elementary School

Karrie Tufts
Eastern Elementary School

Mike Wilson
East Junior High School

Tom Wilson
West Junior High School

Minnesota

Minneapolis

Betsy Ford
Northeast Middle School

New York

East Elmhurst

Allison Clark
Louis Armstrong Middle School

Dorothy Hershey
Louis Armstrong Middle School

J. Lewis McNeece
Louis Armstrong Middle School

Rossana Perez
Louis Armstrong Middle School

Merna Porter
Louis Armstrong Middle School

Marie Turini
Louis Armstrong Middle School

North Carolina

Durham

Everly Broadway
Durham Public Schools

Thomas Carson
Duke School for Children

Mary Hebrank
Duke School for Children

Bill O'Connor
Duke School for Children

Ruth Pershing
Duke School for Children

Peter Reichert
Duke School for Children

Elizabeth City

Rita Banks
Elizabeth City Middle School

Beth Chaundry
Elizabeth City Middle School

Amy Cuthbertson
Elizabeth City Middle School

Deni Dennison
Elizabeth City Middle School

Jean Gray
Elizabeth City Middle School

John McMenamin
Elizabeth City Middle School

Nicollette Nixon
Elizabeth City Middle School

Malinda Norfleet
Elizabeth City Middle School

Joyce O'Neal
Elizabeth City Middle School

Clevie Sawyer
Elizabeth City Middle School

Juanita Shannon
Elizabeth City Middle School

Terry Thorne
Elizabeth City Middle School

Rebecca Wardour
Elizabeth City Middle School

Leora Winslow
Elizabeth City Middle School

Franklinton

Susan Haywood
Franklinton Elementary School

Clyde Melton
Franklinton Elementary School

Louisburg

Lisa Anderson
Terrell Lane Middle School

Jackie Frazier
Terrell Lane Middle School

Pam Harris
Terrell Lane Middle School

Ohio

Toledo

Bonnie Bias
Hawkins Elementary School

Marsha Jackish
Hawkins Elementary School

Lee Jagodzinski
DeVeaux Junior High School

Norma J. King
Old Orchard Elementary School

Margaret McCready
Old Orchard Elementary School

Carmella Morton
DeVeaux Junior High School

Karen C. Rohrs
Hawkins Elementary School

Marie Sahloff
DeVeaux Junior High School

L. Michael Vince
McTigue Junior High School

Brenda D. Watkins
Old Orchard Elementary School

Oregon

Portland

Roberta Cohen
Catlin Gabel School

David Ellenberg
Catlin Gabel School

Sara Normington
Catlin Gabel School

Karen Scholte-Arce
Catlin Gabel School

West Linn

Marge Burack
Wood Middle School

Tracy Wygant
Athey Creek Middle School

Canby

Sandra Kralovec
Ackerman Middle School

Pennsylvania

Pittsburgh

Sheryl Adams
Reizenstein Middle School

Sue Barie
Frick International Studies Academy

Suzie Berry
Frick International Studies Academy

Richard Delgrosso
Frick International Studies Academy

Janet Falkowski
Frick International Studies Academy

Joanne George
Reizenstein Middle School

Harriet Hopper
Reizenstein Middle School

Chuck Jessen
Reizenstein Middle School

Ken Labuskes
Reizenstein Middle School

Barbara Lewis
Reizenstein Middle School

Sharon Mihalich
Reizenstein Middle School

Marianne O'Connor
Frick International Studies Academy

Mark Sammartino
Reizenstein Middle School

Washington

Seattle

Chris Johnson
University Preparatory Academy

Rick Purn
University Preparatory Academy

Contents

Rational numbers are the heart of the middle-grades experiences with number concepts. From classroom experience, we know that the concepts of fractions, decimals, and percents can be difficult for students. From research on student learning, we know that part of the reason for students' confusion about rational numbers is a result of the rush to symbol manipulation with fractions and decimals.

In *Bits and Pieces I*, the first unit on rational numbers, the investigations asked students to make sense of the meaning of fractions, decimals, and percents in different contexts. In *Bits and Pieces II*, students will use these new numbers to help make sense of many different situations.

This unit does not teach specific algorithms for working with rational numbers. Instead, it helps the teacher create a classroom environment where students consider interesting problems in which ideas of fractions, decimals, and percents are embedded. Students bump into these important ideas as they struggle to make sense of problem situations. As they work individually, in groups, and as a whole class on the problems, they will find ways of thinking about and operating with rational numbers.

The teacher's role is to help students make explicit their growing ideas about the world of rational numbers and, when students are ready, to inject ideas and strategies into the conversation along with the ideas and strategies generated by the students. Simply giving students algorithms for moving symbols for rational numbers around on paper would be a mistake—and the temptation to do so is often great. All teachers want their students to succeed, and showing them how to do something—such as how to cross multiply to compare two fractions—gives the *impression* of immediate success. Students can do the algorithm by memorizing. However, evidence from student assessments shows that students do not understand algorithms that are given to them in this way and therefore cannot remember or figure out what to do in a given situation.

This unit provides a rich set of experiences that focus on developing *meaning* for computations with rational numbers. We expect students to finish this unit knowing algorithms for computation that they understand and can use with facility.

B*its and Pieces II* **was created to help students**

- Continue to build understanding of fractions, decimals, and percents and the relationships among these concepts and their representations

- Explore situations that involve operations with rational numbers

- Use strategies to quickly estimate sums and products

- Use 0, $\frac{1}{2}$, 1, $1\frac{1}{2}$, and 2 as benchmarks to make sense of how large a sum is

- Develop strategies for adding and subtracting fractions and decimals

- Understand when addition or subtraction is the appropriate operation

- Develop ways to model sums and differences

- Become facile at changing a fraction to a decimal and at estimating what fraction a given decimal is near

- Develop an understanding of the multiplication of fractions and of decimals

- Use an area model to represent the product of two fractions

- Explore the relationship between two numbers and their product to generalize the conditions under which the product is larger than both factors, between the factors, or smaller than both factors

- Understand how to use percent as an expression of frequency when a data set contains more than or fewer than 100 pieces of data

- Represent $1.00 as 100 pennies so that a special application of the hundredths grid can be used to visualize percents of a dollar

- Use percents to estimate or compute taxes, tips, and discounts

- Draw pictorial models to represent a situation; for example, showing that $\frac{1}{2}$ of $\frac{1}{2}$ is $\frac{1}{4}$ by drawing an area model

- Look for and generalize patterns

- Use estimation to help make decisions

- Use a problem's context to help reason about the problem

The overall goal of Connected Mathematics is to help students develop sound mathematical habits. Through their work in this and other number units, students learn important questions to ask themselves about any situation that is represented and modeled mathematically, such as: *In what kinds of situations is it appropriate to use percents? What kinds of graphs can be created from information in percent form? How are percents like fractions and decimals? How are they different? What kinds of models can be developed to show computation with fractions and decimals? What algorithms can be developed from these models? Will these algorithms apply to all fractional quantities? How does the concept of multiplication of whole numbers extend to multiplication of fractions? To multiplication of numbers in decimal form? Do results always match those found by using models? How can estimation skills and algorithm skills reinforce one another?"*

Summary of Investigations

Investigation 1: Using Percents

This investigation builds on the last investigation in *Bits and Pieces I*. The typical situations of discounts, taxes, and tips help students think about taking a percent of a number. The discount and tax situations help students to consider the amount left when a reduction is made and the total when taxes are added.

Investigation 2: More About Percents

In this investigation students are asked to think about percents in situations in which the number of objects is greater than or fewer than 100. Students use percents to help construct and make sense of circle graphs.

Investigation 3: Estimating with Fractions and Decimals

This investigation focuses on estimating sums of fractions and decimals. Students play two games in which they use benchmarks to help them estimate how big sums are.

Investigation 4: Adding and Subtracting Fractions

This investigation does not *give* students algorithms for computation. Instead, it prepares students to figure out how to add and subtract fractions by emphasizing flexibility in finding equivalent fractions and in changing between fractions and decimals. In the course of struggling with the problems, most students will *invent* ways of adding fractions that you and the class can help make more explicit and efficient. The last problem gives students an opportunity to summarize what they have developed by asking them to write efficient algorithms for adding and subtracting fractions.

Investigation 5: Finding Areas and Other Products

This investigation has the same goals as Investigation 4 except the operation explored is multiplication. The area model is introduced to help students make sense of multiplication of fractions. The first three problems focus on developing ways to model multiplying fractions, and the last problem focuses on developing algorithms for multiplying fractions.

Investigation 6: Computing with Decimals

Since students will have had some experience in computing with decimals, this investigation presents a game and real-world situations that use decimals. Addition, subtraction, and multiplication, with a little division, are developed. By looking for patterns, students focus on what happens to numbers when they are multiplied or divided by a power of 10. The problems challenge students to make sense of the decimal point and its role in addition and multiplication. The investigation closes with a problem-solving situation that requires students to apply their ideas about computation with decimals.

Investigation 7: Dividing Fractions

This investigation focuses on developing the meaning of division with fractions and the strategies and algorithms for dividing them. Everyday situations are used to help students make sense of when division is an appropriate operation. Other operations with fractions are reviewed and the relationship between division and multiplication is explored.

Connections to Other Units

The ideas in *Bits and Pieces II* build on and connect to several big ideas in other Connected Mathematics units.

Big Idea	Prior Work	Future Work
performing computations involving percents	defining, comparing, and applying percents (*Bits and Pieces I*); interpreting percents as probabilities (*How Likely Is It?*)	using percents to make comparisons (*Comparing and Scaling*); interpreting percents as probabilities (*What Do You Expect?*, *Samples and Populations*); applying percents to analyze data (*Data Around Us*)
performing mathematical operations with fractions	interpreting fractions as part/whole relationships; combining and comparing fractions; finding equivalent fractions (*Bits and Pieces I*); interpreting fractions as probabilities (*How Likely Is It?*)	interpreting fractions as scale factors, ratios, and proportions (*Stretching and Shrinking, Comparing and Scaling*); interpreting fractions as constants and variable coefficients in linear and nonlinear equations and relationships (*Variables and Patterns; Moving Straight Ahead; Thinking with Mathematical Models; Growing, Growing, Growing; Frogs, Fleas, and Painted Cubes; Say It With Symbols*); using fractions to help understand irrational numbers (*Looking for Pythagoras*); interpreting and applying fractions (*What Do You Expect?*, *Samples and Populations*)
performing mathematical operations with decimals	interpreting decimals as fractions; understanding place value of decimals; combining and comparing decimals (*Bits and Pieces I*); interpreting decimals as probabilities (*How Likely Is It?*)	interpreting decimals as ratios and proportions (*Comparing and Scaling*); exploring the relationship between repeating decimals and irrational numbers (*Looking for Pythagoras*); interpreting decimals as probabilities (*What Do You Expect?*, *Samples and Populations*); using decimals in scientific notation (*Data Around Us*); interpreting decimals as coefficients in linear and nonlinear equations (*Variables and Patterns; Moving Straight Ahead; Thinking with Mathematical Models; Growing, Growing, Growing; Frogs, Fleas, and Painted Cubes; Say It With Symbols*)
developing and applying algorithms for performing calculations with fractions, decimals, and percents	connecting fractions, decimals, and percents; estimating to check reasonableness of answers (*Bits and Pieces I*); developing algorithms for finding the area and perimeter of 2-D shapes (*Covering and Surrounding*)	applying decimals, fractions, and percents in studying probability (*What Do You Expect?*, *Samples and Populations*); applying ratios, proportions, and scale factors (*Stretching and Shrinking, Comparing and Scaling*)

Materials

For students

- Labsheets
- Calculators
- Getting Close cards (provided as blackline masters)
- Getting Close number squares (provided as a blackline master)
- Hundredths grids (provided as a blackline master)
- Hundredths strips (provided as a blackline master)
- Sheet of squares (provided as a blackline master)
- Grid paper (provided as a blackline master)
- Markers, tiles, or paper squares (about 12 per student)
- Rulers
- Angle rulers
- Large sheets of paper (optional)
- Blank transparency film (optional)
- Transparency markers (optional)
- Colored square tiles (optional)

For the teacher

- Transparencies and transparency markers (optional)

Pacing Chart

This pacing chart gives estimates of the class time required for each investigation and assessment piece. Shaded rows indicate opportunities for assessment.

Investigations and Assessments	Class Time
1 Using Percents	5 days
2 More About Percents	2 days
Check-Up 1	$\frac{1}{2}$ day
3 Estimating With Fractions and Decimals	2 days
4 Adding and Subtracting Fractions	5 days
Check-Up 2	$\frac{1}{2}$ day
5 Finding Areas and Other Products	4 days
6 Computing with Decimals	5 days
Check-Up 3	$\frac{1}{2}$ day
Self-Assessment	Take home
Unit Test	1 day
7 Division of Fractions	5 days

Technology

Connected Mathematics was developed with the belief that calculators should always be available and that students should decide when to use them. For this reason, we do not designate specific problems as "calculator problems." Fraction calculators are *not* required for this unit. However, if fraction calculators are available, your students can use them as an additional tool for exploring the ideas of this unit.

Vocabulary

The following words and concepts are used in *Bits and Pieces II*. Concepts in the left column are those that are essential for student understanding of this and future units. Only one new vocabulary word, *algorithm*, is introduced in this unit; all of the other words were introduced in *Bits and Pieces I*. This is an opportunity for students to further develop their understanding of these concepts. The Descriptive Glossary gives descriptions of many of these and other words used in *Bits and Pieces II*.

Essential	**Nonessential**
decimal	algorithm
denominator	base ten number system
equivalent fractions	benchmark
fraction	unit fraction
numerator	
percent	

Assessment Summary

Embedded Assessment

Opportunities for informal assessment of student progress are embedded throughout *Bits and Pieces II* in the problems, ACE questions, and Mathematical Reflections. Suggestions for observing as students explore and discover mathematical ideas, for probing to guide their progress in developing concepts and skills, and for questioning to determine their level of understanding can be found in the Launch, Explore, or Summarize sections of all investigation problems. Some examples:

- Investigation 5, Problem 5.2 *Launch* (page 63c) suggests two ways you can model $\frac{1}{3}$ of $\frac{1}{3}$ for your students so they might better understand multiplication of fractions.

- Investigation 6, Problem 6.1 *Explore* (page 76a) suggests questions you might ask students as they play the School Supply game.

- Investigation 2, Problem 2.4 *Summarize* (page 30d) suggests ways that you can extend your students' understanding of how circle graphs are constructed.

ACE Assignments

An ACE (Applications—Connections—Extensions) section appears at the end of each investigation. To help you assign ACE questions, a list of assignment choices is given in the margin next to the reduced student page for each problem. Each list indicates the ACE questions that students should be able to answer after they complete the problem.

Check-Ups

Three check-ups, which may be given after Investigations 2, 4, and 6, are provided for use as quick quizzes or warm-up activities. Check-ups are designed for students to complete individually. You will find the check-ups and their answer keys in the Assessment Resources section.

Question Bank

A Question Bank provides questions you can use for homework, reviews, or quizzes. You will find the Question Bank and its answer key in the Assessment Resources section.

Notebook/Journal

Students should have notebooks to record and organize their work. Their notebooks should include their journals along with sections for vocabulary, homework, and quizzes and check-ups. In their journals, students can take notes, solve investigation problems, and record their mathematical reflections. You should assess student journals for completeness rather than correctness; journals should be seen as "safe" places where students can try out their thinking. A Notebook Checklist and a Self-Assessment are provided in the Assessment Resources section. The Notebook Checklist helps students organize their notebooks. The Self-Assessment guides students as they review their notebooks to determine which ideas they have mastered and which ideas they still need to work on.

The Unit Test

The final assessment in *Bits and Pieces II* is a two-part experience. The first part is an individual, in-class unit test. The second part is a short individual assignment meant to be a take-home portion of the test. For this part, students are to find three different items in a catalog that they would be interested in buying. They fill out a catalog order form and determine tax and shipping. They are then asked some questions about how much the items would cost if certain discounts were applied.

Introducing Your Students to *Bits and Pieces II*

Discuss the questions posed on the opening page of the student edition, which are designed to start students thinking about the kinds of questions and mathematics in the unit. Don't look for "correct" answers at this time. Do, however, present an opportunity for the class to discuss the questions and to start to think about what is needed to answer them. You may want to revisit these questions as students learn the mathematical ideas and techniques necessary to find the answers.

If it has been some time since your students have finished *Bits and Pieces I,* the first rational numbers unit, you may want to discuss what *percent* means and the relationships among fractions, decimals, and percents. ACE question 20 from Investigation 6 of *Bits and Pieces I* could be helpful in encouraging students to think again about rational numbers and their relationships.

Bits and Pieces II

You and two friends are at a pizza parlor. The total cost for your drinks and a large pizza is $14.90 before tax. The tax rate is 5%. Your group wants to leave a 15% tip. If you want to share the bill equally, how much should each person pay?

If each person in North America throws away $3\frac{2}{3}$ pounds of garbage every day, how many pounds of garbage does each person throw away in a year?

During their Season's End clearance, a store offers an additional 25% discount on items that have already been reduced by 30%. After both discounts are applied, will the cost of an item be the same as if the original price were discounted 55%?

How many bows can you make from 5 meters of ribbon if making a bow takes $\frac{1}{4}$ of a meter of ribbon?

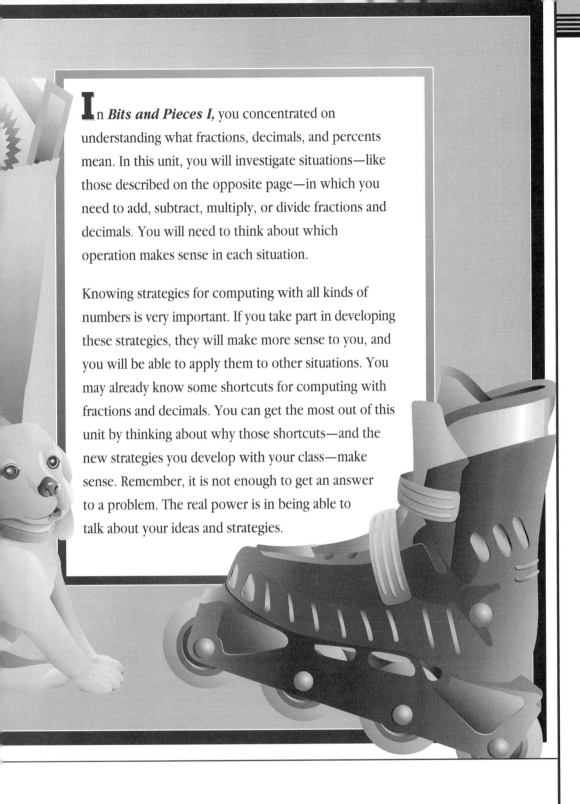

In *Bits and Pieces I,* you concentrated on understanding what fractions, decimals, and percents mean. In this unit, you will investigate situations—like those described on the opposite page—in which you need to add, subtract, multiply, or divide fractions and decimals. You will need to think about which operation makes sense in each situation.

Knowing strategies for computing with all kinds of numbers is very important. If you take part in developing these strategies, they will make more sense to you, and you will be able to apply them to other situations. You may already know some shortcuts for computing with fractions and decimals. You can get the most out of this unit by thinking about why those shortcuts—and the new strategies you develop with your class—make sense. Remember, it is not enough to get an answer to a problem. The real power is in being able to talk about your ideas and strategies.

Mathematical Highlights

The Mathematical Highlights page provides information to students and to parents and other family members. It gives students a preview of the activities and problems in *Bits and Pieces II*. As they work through the unit, students can refer back to the Mathematical Highlights page to review what they have learned and to preview what is still to come. This page also tells students' families what mathematical ideas and activities will be covered as the class works through *Bits and Pieces II*.

Mathematical Highlights

In *Bits and Pieces II* you will develop understanding of and algorithms for operations with fractions, decimals and percents. The unit should help you to

- Use benchmarks and other strategies to estimate sums, differences, products and quotients;

- Develop ways to model sums, differences, products and quotients, including strip models, number line models and area models;

- Understand when addition, subtraction, multiplication, or division is the appropriate operation to solve a problem;

- Develop strategies and algorithms for adding, subtracting, multiplying and dividing fractions and decimals;

- Become fluent at changing a fraction to a decimal and a percent and at estimating what fraction a given decimal is near;

- Use percents to estimate or compute taxes, tips, and discounts;

- Look for and generalize patterns in numbers; and

- Solve problems involving fractions, decimals, or percents.

As you work on the problems in this unit, make it a habit to ask questions about situations that involve fractions, decimals, or percents: *What models or diagrams might be helpful in understanding the situation and the relationships among the quantities in the problem? Will it be useful to express the quantities in the problem as fractions? As percents? As decimals? What models or diagrams might help decide which operation is useful in solving a problem? What is a reasonable estimate for the answer?*

The Investigations

The teaching materials for each investigation consist of three parts: an overview, student pages with teaching outlines, and detailed notes for teaching the investigation.

The overview of each investigation includes brief descriptions of the problems, the mathematical and problem-solving goals of the investigation, and a list of necessary materials.

Essential information for teaching the investigation is provided in the margins around the student pages. The "At a Glance" overviews are brief outlines of the Launch, Explore, and Summarize phases of each problem for reference as you work with the class. To help you assign homework, a list of "Assignment Choices" is provided next to each problem. Wherever space permits, answers to problems, follow-ups, ACE questions, and Mathematical Reflections appear next to the appropriate student pages.

The Teaching the Investigation section follows the student pages and is the heart of the Connected Mathematics curriculum. This section describes in detail the Launch, Explore, and Summarize phases for each problem. It includes all the information needed for teaching, along with suggestions for what you might say at key points in the teaching. Use this section to prepare lessons and as a guide for teaching an investigation.

Assessment Resources

The Assessment Resources section contains blackline masters and answer keys for check-ups, the unit test, and the Question Bank. Blackline masters for the Notebook Checklist and the Self-Assessment are given. These instruments support student self-evaluation, an important aspect of assessment in the Connected Mathematics curriculum.

Blackline Masters

The Blackline Masters section includes masters for all labsheets and transparencies. Blackline masters of grid paper, hundredths strips, hundredths grids, and Getting Close number squares and game cards are also provided.

Additional Practice

Practice pages for each investigation offer additional problems for students who need more practice with the basic concepts developed in the investigations as well as some continual review of earlier concepts.

Descriptive Glossary

The Descriptive Glossary provides descriptions and examples of the key concepts in *Bits and Pieces II*. These descriptions are not intended to be formal definitions, but are meant to give you an idea of how students might make sense of these important concepts.

Using Percents

In *Bits and Pieces I*, students were introduced to a visual model—the hundredths grid—for describing percents, and to the idea of "out of 100" as a way of conceptualizing percent. In this investigation, we return to these models as a means of thinking about finding the percent of a number. The more readily your students can move among representations of fractions, decimals, and percents, the greater their number sense will be. In this unit, we assume that students have some ideas about how to compute with decimals. The problems should help you determine what your students know about decimal computation.

This investigation presents settings that involve money. Students compute taxes, tips, and discounts. To help them conceptualize percents of $1.00, we encourage you to focus on both the visual model (a hundredths grid) *and* the idea of "out of 100." Students can think of a dollar as 100 pennies and let each square on a hundredths grid represent 1 cent.

In Problem 1.1, Taxing Tapes, students explore percents in the context of sales tax. In Problem 1.2, Computing Tips, they explore percents in the context of tipping in a restaurant. In Problem 1.3, Finding Bargains, they look at discounts and sales. The work culminates in Problem 1.4, Spending Money, in which students use all they have learned to examine one student's expenditures for an evening.

Mathematical and Problem-Solving Goals

- **To use the "out of 100" interpretation to develop an understanding of the concept of percent**

- **To think about representing $1.00 as 100 pennies and to relate this to the hundredths-grid model as a way to visualize the percent of a dollar**

- **To use percents in estimating or computing taxes, tips, and discounts**

Materials		
Problem	**For students**	**For the teacher**
All	Calculators	Transparencies 1.1 to 1.4 (optional)
1.1	Hundredths grids (provided as a blackline master)	Transparency of hundredths grid (optional; provided as a blackline master)
1.2	Labsheets 1.2A and 1.2B (1 each per group), transparencies of Labsheet 1.2B (optional; for sharing answers with the class), transparency markers	

Using Percents

In *Bits and Pieces I*, you discovered that percents are useful for reporting the results of surveys. Percents are also helpful in situations involving money. Discounts, taxes, and tips are all described with percents. Understanding what these percents mean and how they are used can make you a smarter consumer.

1.1 Taxing Tapes

Remember that a percent is a special way of representing a fraction with a denominator of 100. You can think of **percent** as meaning "out of 100."

Let's begin by looking at sales tax. A sales tax of 6% means that for every dollar an item costs, a person needs to pay an additional six hundredths of a dollar, or $0.06:

$1.00 + (6\% \text{ of } \$1.00) = \$1.00 + \$0.06 = \$1.06$

Or, since $1.00 is 100 pennies:

100 pennies + (6% of 100 pennies) = 100 pennies + 6 pennies = 106 pennies = $1.06

Answer to Problem 1.1

$7.95; Possible explanation: Since 6% means 6¢ for every dollar, and the price is 7.5 dollars, the tax is 6¢ × 7.5 = 45¢, bringing the total to $7.95.

Answers to Problem 1.1 Follow-Up

1. a. $2.12   b. $5.30   c. $0.53

    Explanations may vary. Possible explanation for part a: A sales tax of 6% means that, for every $1.00 an item costs, a person needs to pay an additional 6¢. Since the magazine costs $2.00, the sales tax adds an extra 12¢ to the cost. The total cost is therefore $2.12.

(Answers continued on next page.)

At a Glance

Grouping:
Pairs

Launch

■ Read the introduction and the problem with the class.

Explore

■ As pairs work, encourage them to look for more than one way to solve the problem.

■ Remind students that they must be able to explain their methods and ideas.

Summarize

■ Have pairs share their results and explanations.

■ Discuss the follow-up questions.

Assignment Choices

ACE questions 1, 5, 10, and 19–22

Problem 1.1

Jill wants to buy a cassette tape that is priced at $7.50. The sales tax is 6%. What will be the total cost of the tape? Try to find more than one way to solve this problem. Be prepared to explain the different methods you find.

■ Problem 1.1 Follow-Up

Developing shortcuts can help make estimating tax easier. To find a shortcut, you can begin by examining a way to mark hundredths grids to show percents. The grids below show what an item would cost if the price were $1.00 and the tax were 6%.

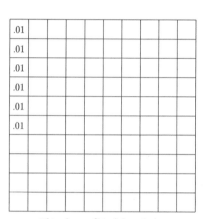

.01	.01	.01	.01	.01	.01	.01	.01	.01	.01
.01	.01	.01	.01	.01	.01	.01	.01	.01	.01
.01	.01	.01	.01	.01	.01	.01	.01	.01	.01
.01	.01	.01	.01	.01	.01	.01	.01	.01	.01
.01	.01	.01	.01	.01	.01	.01	.01	.01	.01
.01	.01	.01	.01	.01	.01	.01	.01	.01	.01
.01	.01	.01	.01	.01	.01	.01	.01	.01	.01
.01	.01	.01	.01	.01	.01	.01	.01	.01	.01
.01	.01	.01	.01	.01	.01	.01	.01	.01	.01
.01	.01	.01	.01	.01	.01	.01	.01	.01	.01

This shows 100% of the whole, which is $1.00.

This shows 6% of the whole, which is $0.06.

You would pay $1.06 for the item.

1. Use what you have discovered about percents to help you solve these problems. Explain your reasoning.
   a. What is the total price for a magazine that costs $2.00 plus 6% tax?
   b. What is the total price for a book on dogs that costs $5.00 plus 6% tax?
   c. What is the total price for a comic book that costs $0.50 plus 6% tax?

---

2. a. $1.05   b. $1.06
    c. $1.07   d. $1.08

Possible pattern: The percent tax on 1 dollar is just that many pennies, which we add to the dollar.

3. a. $5.15; Possible explanation: 3% sales tax adds 3¢ for every dollar. Because the item costs $5, the tax is 3¢ × 5 = 15¢.

    b. See page 17e.

4. See page 17e.

5. See page 17f.

2. Solve each problem. When you finish, describe any patterns you observe.

   a. What is the total price for a balloon that costs $1.00 plus 5% tax?

   b. What is the total price for a balloon that costs $1.00 plus 6% tax?

   c. What is the total price for a balloon that costs $1.00 plus 7% tax?

   d. What is the total price for a balloon that costs $1.00 plus 8% tax?

3. Use what you learned in questions 1 and 2 to help you answer these questions. Explain your reasoning.

   a. What is the total price of a pack of tennis balls that costs $5.00 plus 3% tax?

   b. What is the total price of a calculator that costs $19.50 plus 8% tax?

4. Kiah bought a portable cassette player. She does not remember the price, but she does know that the 6% sales tax was $4.80. What was the price of the portable cassette player? Explain your reasoning.

5. Frank bought a new video game. The 5% sales tax was $0.75. What was the price of the game? Explain your reasoning.

1.2 Computing Tips

At most restaurants, customers pay their server a tip for providing good service. A typical tip is 15% to 20% of the cost of the meal. Some people calculate the tip based on the cost of the meal *before* the tax is added, and others use the cost of the meal *after* the tax is added.

You have just finished lunch at Larry's Lunch Place. The food was delicious, and the service was excellent! The bill has just arrived.

Problem 1.2

Have each member of your group use the menu your teacher provides to make up a lunch order. Write all the items ordered by your group on the order check. Total the bill, and add your local sales tax.

A. What is your total bill for food and tax?

B. How much will you leave for the tip? (The tip must be between 15% and 20%.)

C. The members of your group decide to share the cost of the meal equally. About how much would each person need to contribute to pay the bill as well as the tip?

Try to find more than one way to solve parts A and B. Be prepared to explain the different methods you used.

Computing Tips

At a Glance

Grouping:
Small Groups

Launch

- Discuss tipping for service in restaurants.

- Talk about the difference between calculating a tip before tax is added and after tax is added.

Explore

- Encourage groups to explore a variety of ways to solve the problem.

Summarize

- As a class, share methods for solving the problem and determining how much each person would pay.

Answers to Problem 1.2

Answers will vary, depending on the groups' orders and the percent tip they leave.

Answers to Problem 1.2 Follow-Up

1. **a.** 10% is $2.00, 5% is $1.00. 5% is half as much as 10%.

   b. 10% is $2.45, and 20% is $4.90. 20% is twice as much as 10%.

   c. 10% rounds to $1.74. Since 15% is 10% plus 5%, and 5% is half of 10%, 15% of $17.35 is about $1.74 + $0.87 = $2.61. Since 20% is twice 10%, 20% of $17.35 is about $1.74 + $1.74 = $3.48.

(Answers continued on next page.)

Assignment Choices

ACE questions 2, 3, 18, 30–33, and unassigned choices from the previous problem

■ **Problem 1.2 Follow-Up**

1. Many people use benchmarks for determining tips. Jim explains his strategy for finding a tip: "I always figure out 10% of the bill, and then I use this information to calculate a 15% or 20% tip."

   a. Find 10% and 5% of $20.00. Explain how the two percents are related.

   b. Find 10% and 20% of $24.50. Explain how the two percents are related.

   c. Find 10% of $17.35. Use this to find 15% and 20% of $17.35. Explain your reasoning.

2. The sales tax in Kadisha's state is 5%. Kadisha says she computes a 15% tip by multiplying the tax shown on her bill by 3. For the bill shown here, Kadisha's tip would be $0.38 × 3 = $1.14.

Garden Cafe	
ITEM	AMOUNT
Food	$7.55
5% Tax	.38
TOTAL	$7.93

   a. Why does Kadisha's method work?

   b. Use a similar method to compute a 20% tip on Kadisha's bill. Explain your answer.

   c. Does Kadisha's method give 15% of the *entire bill* (including tax) or 15% of the cost *before* tax is added? Explain your thinking.

3. When people leave a 15% or 20% tip, they often round up to the nearest multiple of 5 or 10 cents. For example, in question 2, Kadisha might leave a tip of $1.15 rather than $1.14.

   a. If Kadisha always rounds up, what would she likely leave for a 20% tip on her bill?

   b. Omar always leaves a 20% tip based on the meal price before tax is added. Find a meal price for which Omar would leave a tip of $1.00 after rounding up to the nearest multiple of 5 or 10 cents.

   c. Marlene always leaves a 15% tip based on the meal price before tax is added. Find a meal price for which Marlene would leave a tip of $4.50 after rounding up to the nearest multiple of 5 or 10 cents.

   d. Customers left Jerome $2.50 as a tip for service. The tip was 20% of the bill for their food. How much was the bill?

---

2. a. Kadisha's method works because the tax is 5% of the price of the food, and 15% is 3 times 5%.

   b. $1.52; 20% is four times 5%, and $0.38 × 4 = $1.52.

   c. The cost before the tax is added, because she computed the tip from the sales tax, which was figured on the cost of the meal alone.

3. a. $1.55

   b. any price from $4.76 to $5.00

   c. any price from $29.67 to $30.00

   d. The bill was around $12.50.

1.3 Finding Bargains

At Loud Sounds Music Warehouse, CDs are regularly priced at $9.95 and tapes are regularly priced at $6.95. Every day this month, the store is offering a 10% discount on all CDs and tapes.

Launch

- Discuss store sales and discounts.

- Read the problem with the class, making sure they understand what they are to do.

Explore

- Encourage pairs to explore a variety of ways to solve the problem.

- Remind students that they will need to explain their strategies to the class.

Summarize

- Have a class discussion of the different ways students found their answers.

Problem 1.3

Joshua and Jeremy go to Loud Sounds to buy a tape and a CD. They do not have much money, so they have pooled their funds. When they get to the store, they find that there is another discount plan available just for that day—if they buy three or more items, they can save 20% (instead of 10%) on each item.

A. If they buy a CD and a tape, how much money will they spend after the store adds a 6% sales tax on the discounted prices?

B. Jeremy says he thinks they can buy three tapes for less money than the cost of a tape and a CD. Is he correct? Explain your reasoning.

Try to find more than one way to solve these problems. Be prepared to explain the different methods you discover.

▨ **Problem 1.3 Follow-Up**

1. Mr. Knapp wants to take advantage of the day's special to fill out his CD collection. There are 15 CDs he wants to buy.
  a. What is the total amount of the discount he will receive?
  b. What will the 15 CDs cost after a 6% sales tax has been added?

Answers to Problem 1.3

A. They will spend $16.12. The solution involves several steps:
  Step 1 Find the total cost before the discount: $9.95 + $6.95 = $16.90
  Step 2 Compute the 10% discount: 10% × $16.90 = $1.69
  Step 3 Calculate the discounted price: $16.90 − $1.69 = $15.21
  Step 4 Compute the tax: 6% × $15.21 = $0.9126, which rounds to $0.91
  Step 5 Compute the total cost including tax: $15.21 + $0.91 = $16.12

B. Three tapes cost 3 × $6.95 = $20.85 before the discount and $20.85 − 0.2 × $20.85 = $20.85 − $4.17 = $16.68 after the discount. The 6% tax on $16.68 is $1.00, so the total cost is $17.68. This is more than the $16.12 for a CD and a tape.

Spending Money

At a Glance

Grouping:
Pairs

Launch

■ Read through the problem with the class.

Explore

■ Have students work in pairs to organize the information and solve the problem.

Summarize

■ Ask students how much money Danny had at the beginning of the evening.

■ Have students explain how they found how much money Danny spent.

■ Ask students how much money Danny had when she returned home.

Assignment Choices

Unassigned choices from earlier problems

2. Look back at question 1.

    a. If the discount were only 1%, what total discount amount would Mr. Knapp receive on the 15 CDs?

    b. What is the relationship between 1% of the cost of 15 CDs and 20% of the cost of 15 CDs?

    c. If the discount were 10%, what total discount amount would Mr. Knapp receive for the 15 CDs?

    d. How is a 10% discount related to a 20% discount?

    e. How is a 10% discount related to a 1% discount?

    f. How could you use what you know about a 10% discount on the cost of the 15 CDs to find a 15% discount on the cost of the CDs?

    g. How could you use what you found out above to find a 16% discount on the cost of the 15 CDs? Can you find another way to compute 16% of the cost of the CDs? Explain your methods and how they are related.

3. You have been finding percents of numbers to compute taxes and tips. Explain how you can find *any* percent of a given number.

1.4 Spending Money

Do you ever keep track of what you spend for an evening out? Are you sometimes surprised to find that you have very little money left when you get home? Danny wanted to pay more attention to where her money goes, so she decided to keep track of what she spent for an evening.

Answers to Problem 1.3 Follow-Up

1. **a.** Before the discount, 15 CDs cost $15 \times \$9.95 = \$149.25$. A 20% discount on this amount is $\$149.25 \times 20\% = \$29.85$.

    b. The discounted cost before tax is $\$149.25 - \$29.85 = \$119.40$. The tax on this amount is $\$119.40 \times 6\% = \$7.164$, which rounds to $7.16. So, the total cost of the CDs is $\$119.40 + \$7.16 = \$126.56$.

2. **a.** $\$149.25 \times 1\% = \$1.4925$, which rounds to $1.49.

    b. 20% of the cost is 20 times more than 1% of the cost ($\$1.4925 \times 20 = \$29.85$).

    c. 10% of $149.25 is $14.925, which rounds to $14.93.

Problem 1.4

At the beginning of the evening, Danny had a twenty-dollar bill, five quarters, seven dimes, three nickels, and eight pennies.

A. Danny went to the Friday night school dance, which cost $2.50 to attend. How much money did she have left after paying for the dance?

B. After the dance, Danny and three friends bought a pizza for $6.99 and four soft drinks for 89¢ each. The bill for the pizza and drinks included a sales tax of 7%. How much was the bill? Show how you found your answer.

C. If Danny and her friends shared the cost of the pizza and drinks equally, how much was Danny's share of the bill?

D. On the way home, Danny stopped at a newsstand and bought a copy of *Stars and Planets* magazine for $2.50 plus 7% sales tax. How much had she spent for the evening?

E. How much money did Danny have left at the end of the evening?

■ **Problem 1.4 Follow-Up**

1. About what fraction of her money did Danny spend during the evening?
2. About what fraction of her money did Danny have left at the end of the evening?
3. About what percent of her money did Danny spend during the evening?
4. About what percent of her money did Danny have left?

d.   A 10% discount is half of a 20% discount.

e–g.   See page 17f.

3.   See page 17f.

Answers to Problem 1.4

See page 17f.

Answers to Problem 1.4 Follow-Up

1.   about $\frac{8}{22} = \frac{4}{11}$ 2.   about $\frac{14}{22} = \frac{7}{11}$ 3.   about 36%   4.   about 64%

Answers

Applications

1. Examples will vary; you may want to display and discuss them. Students should describe how percents are being used in each example.

2a. $0.69

2b. The bill will be $13.75 + 0.69 = $14.44. Since 10% of $14.40 is $1.44 and half of that is $0.72, the tip should be $1.44 + 0.72 = $2.16. They should leave about $2.15 or $2.20.

2c. The bill including tip will be about $14.44 + 2.20 = $16.64. Since $16.64 − $2.75 = $13.89 and half of $13.89 is about $6.95, Tat Ming should pay $6.95 and Faaiz should pay the rest, $9.69.

3a. $1.06

3b. Two sets of three balls would cost $1.00, while a set of six balls would cost $0.80. The savings is $0.20 out of $1.00, which is 20%.

4a. $\frac{35}{100} = \frac{7}{20}$

4b. $124.99 × 0.65 = $81.2435, which could be interpreted as $81.24 or $81.25.

4c. The tax is about $81.25 × 0.05 = $4.0625, which rounds to $4.06, so the cost would be about $81.25 + $4.06 = $85.31.

As you work on these ACE questions, use your calculator whenever you need it.

Applications

1. Find three examples of advertisements, news reports, or other information in which percents are used. Store windows, newspapers, magazines, radio, and television are good places to look. Write down each example, or cut it out and tape it to your paper. For each example, describe how percents are used and what they mean.

2. Faaiz and Tat Ming go to a restaurant for dinner. Their meals total $13.75.

   a. The local sales tax is 5%. How much tax will be added to the bill?

   b. They want to leave a 15% tip based on the bill and the tax combined. How much should they leave? Explain.

   c. If Faaiz decides he should pay $2.75 more than Tat Ming because he ordered the more expensive dinner, how much should each pay? Explain.

3. Jeremy and Jessica are at a carnival.

   a. At the food stand, hot dogs cost 99¢ each plus 7% tax. How much will Jeremy and Jessica be charged for one hot dog?

   b. They stop at a ball-toss game. The sign reads, "Get three balls for 50¢ or six balls for 80¢." What percent would they save by buying one set of six balls instead of two sets of three balls? Explain.

4. **a.** Roller blades are on sale for 35% off the regular price. What fraction off is this discount?

   b. If the original price of roller blades is $124.99, what is the sale price?

   c. If a tax of 5% is computed on the sale price, what will the roller blades cost?

5. a. Ted has done $\frac{3}{10}$ of his homework. What percent is this?

    b. What percent does he still have to do?

6. In a survey, 75% of 400 parents said yes, they give their children fruit as a snack. How many answered yes to the survey?

7. In a survey, 50% of 150 kindergarten teachers said yes, they give their students crackers as a snack. How many answered yes to the survey?

8. In a survey, 50% of 50 grandparents said yes, they give their grandchildren candy as a snack. How many answered yes to the survey?

9. In a survey, 5% of 100 children said yes, they get popcorn as a snack. How many answered yes to the survey?

10. Four friends ordered a square pizza. Maryann said she wasn't hungry and only wanted 10% of the pizza. Bill was very hungry and said he would eat 50% of the pizza. Jon said he would eat 35%, and Kwan thought she could eat 15%. Will this be possible? Explain your reasoning.

11. Science fiction books at the Book Bonanza are marked $\frac{1}{3}$ off. What percent is this?

12. A certain bean plant grows 15% of its height each day. Express this percent growth as a decimal.

13. The purchase of a new mountain bike at Ike's Bikes requires 25% of the cost as a down payment. What fraction of the cost is this percent?

14. A fifty-cent piece is $\frac{50}{100}$ of a dollar, or half of a dollar, or 50% of a dollar, or $0.50.

    a. Find three different ways to represent 30% of a dollar.

    b. Find three different ways to represent 120% of a dollar.

In 15–17, list the smallest number of coins needed to make each amount.

15. 4% of a dollar

16. 20% of a dollar

17. 137% of a dollar

Investigation 1: Using Percents   **13**

5a. 30%

5b. 70%

6. 300 parents

7. 75 teachers

8. 25 grandparents

9. 5 children

10. no; The total of these percents is 110%.

11. $33\frac{1}{3}$%

12. 0.15

13. $\frac{1}{4}$

14a. Possible answers: $0.30, 30¢, $\frac{30}{100}$ of a dollar, $\frac{3}{10}$ of a dollar, 3 dimes

14b. Possible answers: $1.20, 120¢, $\frac{120}{100}$ of a dollar, 1 and $\frac{2}{10}$ of a dollar, 12 dimes, 24 nickels

15. 4 coins (4 pennies)

16. 2 coins (2 dimes)

17. Possible answers: 6 coins (two 50-cent pieces, 1 quarter, 1 dime, 2 pennies); 5 coins (1 Susan B. Anthony dollar, 1 quarter, 1 dime, 2 pennies)

Connections

18. 16 prizes

19. $\frac{6}{9}$

20. $\frac{2}{6}$

21. $\frac{8}{12} = \frac{2}{3}$

Connections

18. Anna, Brenda, and Carma each sent an entry to the Spartan Running Shoe contest. The Spartan Company advertised that they would award prizes for 1% of the total number of entries. They reported that 1600 entries were received. How many prizes did they award?

In 19–22, ink has been spilled on the page, covering up part of the fraction strips. Use what is showing to reason about each set of strips, and to find fractions equivalent to those marked.

19.

20.

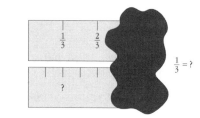

21.

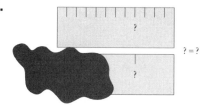

22.

$? = ?$

In 23–26, replace the question marks with numbers that will make the sentence true. There may be more than one solution. If so, show at least two solutions.

23. $\frac{4}{9} = \frac{?}{?}$

24. $\frac{?}{?} = \frac{3}{5}$

25. $\frac{?}{3} = \frac{8}{?}$

26. $\frac{5}{?} = \frac{?}{18}$

27. **a.** Write two fractions that are equivalent. Explain how you know that they are equivalent.

b. Look at the fractions you wrote in part a. Write two other fractions, one that is equivalent to your first fraction and one that is equivalent to your second fraction.

c. Are the four fractions you have written equivalent to each other? Why or why not?

28. **a.** Write two fractions that are not equivalent. Tell which is larger, and explain how you know.

b. Look at the fractions you wrote in part a. Write two other fractions, one that is *not* equivalent to your first fraction and one that is *not* equivalent to your second fraction. Show which fraction is larger in each pair.

c. Order the four fractions you have written from smallest to largest, and explain how you know the order is correct.

Extensions

29. Write a percent problem that involves discounts on food, cars, books, clothes, or other items. Solve your problem.

22. $\frac{3}{9} = \frac{6}{18}$

23. Possible answer: $\frac{8}{18}, \frac{12}{27}$

24. Possible answer: $\frac{6}{10}, \frac{12}{20}$

25. Possible answer: $\frac{2}{3} = \frac{8}{12}, \frac{4}{3} = \frac{8}{6}$

26. Possible answer: $\frac{5}{3} = \frac{30}{18}, \frac{5}{6} = \frac{15}{18}$

27a. Answers will vary. Possible explanations: I know they are equivalent, because equivalent fractions can be found by multiplying or dividing the numerator and denominator by the same number. I know they are equivalent, because I folded fraction strips and compared these amounts with the strips and they were equal.

27b. Answers will vary.

27c. yes; Possible explanation: See explanations from 27a.

28a. Answers will vary. Students might show which fraction is larger by finding common denominators and renaming the fractions.

28b. Answers will vary. Again, students may convert to fractions with common denominators to show which of two fractions is larger.

28c. Answers will vary. Students need to discuss how they compared their fractions to determine the order.

Extensions

29. See page 17g.

30. See below right.

31. See page 17g.

32. See page 17g.

33a. $\frac{1}{3} = \frac{3}{9} = \frac{2}{6}$

33b. $\frac{12}{18} = \frac{8}{12} = \frac{4}{6}$

33c. Possible answer:
$\frac{3}{4} = \frac{12}{16} = \frac{9}{12}$

33d. Possible answer:
$\frac{4}{3} = \frac{28}{21} = \frac{9\frac{1}{3}}{7}$

33e. c and d; Possible explanation: Because all of the numerators (in d) and all of the denominators (in c) are open, so you can choose any one of them and calculate the other fractions from that one. In a and b, the ratio of numerator to denominator is set.

In 30–32, copy the number line (including all the labeled marks), and mark it to show where 1 would be. Rewrite each fraction, including 1, as a decimal and a percent.

30.

31.

32.

33. In a–d, replace the question marks with numbers that will make the sentence true.

a. $\frac{1}{3} = \frac{?}{9} = \frac{?}{6}$ **b.** $\frac{?}{18} = \frac{8}{12} = \frac{4}{?}$

c. $\frac{3}{?} = \frac{12}{?} = \frac{9}{?}$ **d.** $\frac{?}{3} = \frac{?}{21} = \frac{?}{7}$

e. Which problems have more than one possible answer? Why do you think this is so?

30.

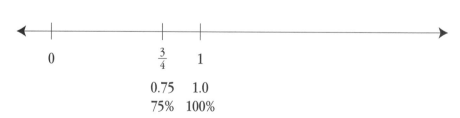

Mathematical Reflections

In this investigation, you solved problems that involved finding percents of numbers. You computed discounts, sale prices, tips, and sales taxes. These questions will help you summarize what you have learned:

1. If 1% of your bill for lunch at Pizza Muncho is 18¢, and you want to leave a 15% tip, how much money should you leave? How much money would you leave for a 20% tip? Explain how you got your answers and why your method works.

2. A sports outlet is having a 20% off sale on all merchandise. Describe a procedure you can use to find the sale price for any item in the store.

3. If you bought a calendar that was marked down by 30%, what percent of the original price did you pay? Explain your answer.

4. A store advertises an everyday discount of $\frac{1}{8}$ off the retail price of any item. Write an advertising slogan for the store that gives the everyday discount as a percent. Explain why the percent you have used in your slogan is equivalent to $\frac{1}{8}$.

Think about your answers to these questions, discuss your ideas with other students and your teacher, and then write a summary of your findings in your journal.

Tips for the Linguistically Diverse Classroom

Original Rebus The Original Rebus technique is described in detail in *Getting to Know Connected Mathematics*. Students make a copy of the text before it is discussed. During discussion, they generate their own rebuses for words they do not understand as the words are made comprehensible through pictures, objects, or demonstrations. Example: Question 2—key words for which students may make rebuses are *sports outlet* (a tennis racket and a football), *procedure* (+, −, ×, ÷), *sale price* ($), *store* (the outline of a building).

Possible Answers

1. For a 15% tip, I would leave 18¢ × 15 = $2.70. For a 20% tip, I would leave 18¢ × 20 = $3.60. This works because 15% is fifteen 1%'s and 20% is twenty 1%'s, so if I know 1% of the total, then 15% is 15 times that amount and 20% is 20 times that amount.

2. *Method 1:* Find 1% of the price by moving the decimal point two places to the left. Multiply the result by 20 (to get 20% of the price). Subtract your product from the original price.

Method 2: Find 1% of the price by moving the decimal point two places to the left. Multiply the result by 80 (since the sale is for 20% off, you must pay 80%).

Method 3: Multiply the price by 0.10 (to get 10% of the price). Double this answer to get 20% of the price. Subtract the result from the original price.

Method 4: Multiply the price by 0.10. Multiply the answer by 8 to get 80% of the original price (since you get 20% off, you pay 80%).

3. 70%; The original price is 100%. If the discount is 30%, you must pay 100% − 30% = 70%.

4. *$12\frac{1}{2}$% OFF THE RETAIL PRICE, EVERY DAY!* As a decimal, $\frac{1}{8}$ equals 0.125. This is equivalent to 12.5% or $12\frac{1}{2}$%.

TEACHING THE INVESTIGATION

1.1 • Taxing Tapes

This problem asks students to focus on the special role that "out of 100" plays in settings involving money. Students consider sales tax on purchases of goods. They visualize the tax by thinking of a dollar as 100 pennies and relating this to a hundredths grid.

Launch

Students may want to use hundredths grids to work on this problem, so be sure to have copies available. Read the introduction and the problem with your class. Ask about your local sales tax and how it compares to the 6% sales tax in the problem.

Explore

Have students work in pairs on the problem. As you observe them working, encourage them to look for more than one way to solve the problem. Remind them that they must be able to explain their methods and why their ideas make sense.

Summarize

In a class discussion, have several pairs share their results and explain how they solved the problem. The following exchange occurred in one classroom:

Teacher What is the total cost of the tape when you include the sales tax? How did you arrive at your answer? I'd like a pair of students to share their ideas.

Travis It would cost $7.95 with tax. We found that by thinking that Jill has to pay 6¢ for each dollar she spends. The tape costs $7.50, so we added 6¢ seven times for the seven dollars. Then we thought about the 50¢ part, and since that is half a dollar, she would need to pay half as much tax so that would be 3¢. When we added it all up we got $7.95.

Teacher So you had a total of $7.95—$7.50 for the tape and 45¢ for the tax. Comments or questions? Did anyone get something different or solve the problem a different way?

Brandy We sort of did what Travis and his partner did but differently. We thought that $7.50 is seven whole dollars and half of another dollar, and for each dollar we have to pay 6¢ tax. So, we just multiplied 7 times 6 and got 42¢ and then added on 3¢ for the half dollar. That gave 45¢ for tax and a total of $7.95 for the cost.

Teacher Comments or questions? Did anyone get something different or solve the problem a different way?

Victor We said that 6% means 6 out of 100 and rewrote it as the fraction $\frac{6}{100}$. Then we tried to write a fraction that would be equal to $\frac{6}{100}$ but have a denominator of 750. We got the new fraction $\frac{45}{750}$, and that means she paid 45¢ for the tax and $7.95 for the total bill.

The teacher continued the discussion until the students had presented all the methods they had used.

To finish the summary, you could discuss the follow-up questions as a class. Questions 1 and 2 will help students focus on patterns. Discuss the patterns that arise when the percent is held constant (question 1) and when the quantity is held constant (question 2) and how these patterns can help us think about finding the percent of any number.

1.2 • Computing Tips

In this problem, students consider the situation of determining tips for service in a restaurant. This multistep problem will be a challenge for many students. However, it presents an important real-world use of percents. Students will benefit in their everyday use of mathematics as adults if we can help them understand percents and develop a facility in estimating or quickly computing taxes and tips. The follow-up questions ask them to look at the relationships among 5%, 10%, 15%, and 20% of an amount.

Launch

Talk with your students about dining in restaurants in which servers take orders and bring food to the tables. Talk about the fact that it is customary in the United States to leave a 15% to 20% tip for service. You might want to make sure they understand the context.

> If your food bill is $10 and you want to leave a 15% tip, how much should the tip be? If you want to leave a 20% tip, how much should the tip be?
>
> If your bill is $12 and you want to leave a 15% tip, how much should the tip be? How did you find that amount? If you want to leave a 20% tip, how much should the tip be? How did you find that amount?

Be sure to ask your class whether it makes a difference if the tip is figured before or after sales tax is added and what difference it would make.

Read the problem with the class. Students should work in groups of three or four for this problem. Each group will need a copy of the menu (Labsheet 1.2A) and an order sheet (Labsheet 1.2B). You may want to make transparencies of the order sheets so groups can easily share their work with the class during the summary.

Explore

As the groups work, encourage them to explore a variety of ways to solve the problem. Each student should be able to explain his or her group's strategies to the class. Allow students to use a calculator to total the food bill and to compute the tax (as this is usually already computed when a food bill is presented). However, since most people don't bring along a calculator when they go to a restaurant, students need to develop efficient ways to find the amount of tip that should be left.

Remind students to show any computation they do to answer questions A through C.

Summarize

Have a class discussion about the ways groups approached the problem. You might have a couple of groups share their order and explain how they calculated the total bill (including tax), the tip, and the amount each person would pay.

This problem raises the issue of how to round off tax and tip to reasonable amounts. For example, if the bill for a meal is $19.45 and the sales tax is 5%, multiplying 19.45 by 0.05 gives 0.9725. How much money is $0.9725? Dealing with numbers like this is confusing for some students. The problems with decimal amounts that are not even dollars and cents may also come up when students have to share a bill. In many cases, a bill cannot be evenly divided by 4 (or 3, depending on how many are in a group). Talk with students about how to interpret the quotient and how to round in reasonable ways.

Keep asking questions about how a restaurant determines the amount of tax and how one can find the amount of tip that should be left. Use the follow-up questions to help with the summary of these two ideas. A discussion that includes the following relationships may help students:

- 10% of a number can be found by moving the decimal point one place to the left. For example, 10% of $3.00 is $0.30. Working with lots of examples and looking for patterns will help students develop this connection *with understanding*.

- 5% is half of 10%, so you can find 15% of a number by finding 10% and half of 10%, then adding the results. For example, suppose the bill for a meal, including tax, is $15.56. To compute a 15% tip, add 10% of $15.56, or about $1.56, and half of $1.56, or $0.78, which gives $2.34.

- 20% of a number can be found by doubling 10% of the number. Using the example above, 10% is $1.56. Doubling this gives $3.12.

1.3 • Finding Bargains

In this problem, students consider what a certain percent discount means. Dealing with sales tax is part of the problem setting.

Launch

Converse with your students about what it means when a store offers a sale or discount on items.

> What does it mean when a store has a sale in which everything is 25% off? If everything is 25% off, what percent of the price do you have to pay?
>
> If an item normally costs $10, how much would it cost during a 25% off sale? How much money would you save? If an item normally costs $50, how much would it cost during the sale? How much money would you save? How did you find those amounts?

Read the problem with the class, making sure they understand what they are to do.

Explore

Have students work in pairs. As they work, encourage them to explore a variety of ways to solve the problem. Remind them that they must be prepared to explain their strategies to the class.

Some pairs may struggle with this problem. Talk with these pairs and help them sort out the percents involved in each part of the problem. Return to these pairs frequently to check on their progress.

Summarize

As a class, discuss the strategies students employed to solve the problem.

After the discussion, have pairs work on follow-up question 1. Again, talk about how pairs solved the problem and why their strategies are reasonable. Then, have pairs consider question 2. Presenting the follow-up in this manner allows for in-class practice with these ideas in a supportive environment. The ideas in these problems are difficult for some students because several steps are required to arrive at a solution. Follow-up question 3 can serve as a summary of what has taken place in the unit so far.

1.4 • Spending Money

In this problem, students use their knowledge of rational numbers to keep track of several monetary transactions. This gives you an opportunity to observe what sense your students make of rational numbers when they must compute with them, and allows you to assess their understanding of decimal values.

Launch

Read through the problem with your class. It is rather straightforward, and the context is one most students get into easily.

Explore

Have students work in pairs. Ask them to record their work in an organized manner so that someone else could follow the transactions and understand their computations.

Ask pairs that finish early to move to the follow-up questions, which offer a review of fractions and percents.

Summarize

Begin the summary by establishing the starting point:

How much money did Danny have at the beginning of the evening?
(*$22.18*) How did you find that amount?

If students added with a calculator, ask exactly what they punched into their calculator, recording what they say on the board. This dialog occurred in one classroom:

Megan   I punched in 20 + 1.25 + .70 + .15 + .08.

Teacher   Where did the 1.25 come from, and what does it mean?

Megan   Danny had five quarters and that is $1.25.

Teacher   Where did the .70 come from, and what does it mean?

Megan   The .70 is seven dimes, which is 70¢.

Teacher   Why did you enter it as .70 and not just enter 70 without a decimal point like you did with the 20?

Megan   Because 20 is 20 dollars and 70 is 70 cents. I had to make the 70 less than the 20 because it is only part of a dollar, so I made it .70—which means 70 hundredths, and I need 100 hundredths to make a dollar.

Teacher   And why did you enter .08?

Megan   Because you write 8¢ as .08 for part of a dollar.

Teacher   You're saying I can't add 20 + 70 because they aren't the same value and that I can't add 7 and 8 because they aren't the same value. Place value is important when adding decimal numbers, just like it was in elementary school with adding whole numbers. How could I write an addition problem that would show what was added when you punched these numbers into your calculator?

The class developed the following representation of what took place:

$$
\begin{array}{r}
\$ \ 20.00 \\
\$ \ \ \ 1.25 \\
\$ \ \ \ \ .70 \\
.15 \\
.08 \\
\hline
\$ \ 22.18
\end{array}
$$

Ask pairs of students to explain their computations for each transaction. As you work through the problem, you may want to continue to ask them about which digits get added to and subtracted from which. The goal here is not to arrive at a rule for adding and subtracting decimals, but to help students *think about* what is happening when they use their calculator.

Additional Answers

Answers to Problem 1.1 Follow-Up

3. b. $21.06; Possible explanation: 8% sales tax adds 8¢ for every dollar. Because the item costs $19.50, the tax is 8¢ × 19 = 152¢, or $1.52, plus another 4¢ for the half dollar, making the total sales tax $1.56.

4. $80; Possible explanations: 6% means 6¢ for every dollar and $4.80 is 480¢. Since 6¢ × 80 is 480¢, the price of the CD player was $80. Or, for every dollar spent, the CD player cost 6¢ in tax. Dividing 480¢ (the amount of the tax) into groups of 6¢ makes 80 groups.

5. $15; Possible explanations: Since $5 \times 15 = 75$, the price of the video game was $15. Or, dividing 75¢ into groups of 5¢ makes 15 groups.

Answers to Problem 1.3 Follow-Up

2. e. A 10% discount is 10 times a 1% discount.

   f. Possible explanation: 15% is 10% + 5%, and 5% is half of 10%, so you can find 15% of a number by adding 10% of the number to half of 10% of the number. Since 10% of $149.25 is about $14.93 and half of $14.93 is about $7.47, a 15% discount would be about $14.93 + $7.47 = $22.40.

   g. Possible explanation: 16% is 10% + 5% + 1%. From the results in parts a–f, this is about $14.93 + $7.47 + $1.49 = $23.89. You could also think of 16% as 16¢ for every dollar. Since you have $149.25, or $149\frac{1}{4}$ dollars, you can find a 16% discount by multiplying 16¢ $\times$ 149 to get $23.84 and then adding $\frac{1}{4}$ of 16¢, or $0.04.

3. Several strategies are possible; here are two. *The meaning of percent:* Think about percent as "out of 100." For example, 5% means 5 out of every 100. To find a percent of a number that is not 100, think about how the number compares to 100. For example, 250 is two and a half groups of 100, so 5% of 250 is two and a half groups of 5, or $5 + 5 + 2\frac{1}{2} = 12\frac{1}{2}$. *The 1% method:* You can find 1% of any number by moving the decimal two places to the left, because 1% means 1 one-hundredth. Once you have found 1% of a number, you can find any other percent by multiplying. For example, to find 7% of 250, first find 1% of 250, which is 2.5, and then multiply by 7, which gives 17.5.

Answers to Problem 1.4

A. $22.18 − $2.50 = $19.68

B. $11.29; Several steps are involved in this solution:
   Step 1 Compute the cost of the drinks: $4 \times 89¢ = $3.56
   Step 2 Compute the cost of the meal before tax: $3.56 + 6.99 = $10.55
   Step 3 Compute the tax: $10.55 \times 7\% = $0.7385, which rounds to $0.74
   Step 4 Compute the total cost including tax: $10.55 + $0.74 = $11.29

For the Teacher: Computing Tax

Students may compute the tax on $10.55 by first multiplying 10 by 7 to get 70¢ and then figuring that since 55¢ is a little bit more than half of a dollar, another 4¢ should be added, for a total of 74¢. It is perfectly reasonable for students to compute tax this way.

C. Since $11.29 ÷ 4 = $2.8225, three people should pay $2.82 and one person should pay $2.83.

D. $8.01 ($7.99 and $8.00 are also reasonable); Possible explanation:
   Step 1 Compute the tax on the magazine: $2.50 \times 7\% = $0.175, which rounds to 18¢
   Step 2 Compute the cost of the magazine: $2.50 + $0.18 = $2.68
   Step 3 Add the costs of the dance, the food, and the magazine: $2.50 + $2.83 + $2.68 = $8.01

E. $22.18 − $8.01 = $14.17

ACE Answers

Extensions

29. Possible answer: Jeanine bought a new pair of jeans at a 25% off sale. The jeans were originally marked $30.00. What was the sale price? Answer: A 25% discount on $30.00 is $7.50, and $30.00 − $7.50 = $22.50.

31.

32.

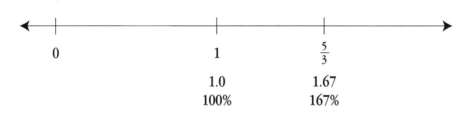

More About Percents

This investigation revisits the kinds of survey information presented in Investigation 6 of *Bits and Pieces I,* the first unit on fractions, decimals, and percents. Central to understanding surveys is the concept of percent, since answering interesting questions about survey data often requires finding a percent of a number as well as finding what percent a certain proportion of the survey represents. Remember that one of the useful properties of percents is that when we can express data as percents, we can compare different sets of data *even when the sample sizes are different.*

In Problem 2.1, Finding Percents, students investigate survey results. Students are given the number of people who responded in a certain way and the total number of people who were surveyed, and are asked to find methods for determining the percent of the people that responded in the given way. In Problem 2.2, Finding a General Strategy, students are asked to devise a general strategy for finding a percent when they are dealing with totals that are more than or less than 100. Problem 2.3, Clipping Coupons, offers students an opportunity to apply the strategies they listed in Problem 2.2 to determine the percent discount for a given coupon. In Problem 2.4, Making Circle Graphs, students are asked to apply their knowledge of percents and surveys to construct circle graphs. This builds on earlier work in this curriculum with statistics, circles, and measuring with an angle ruler.

Mathematical and Problem-Solving Goals

- **To use the "out of 100" interpretation to develop an understanding of the concept of percent**

- **To investigate the relationships among fractions, decimals, and percents**

- **To understand how to use percent as an expression of frequency in terms of "out of 100" when a set of data contains more than or less than 100 pieces of data**

	Materials	
Problem	**For students**	**For the teacher**
All	Calculators	Transparencies 2.1 to 2.4 (optional)
2.1	Hundredths grids (provided as a blackline master)	
2.2	Hundredths grids (provided as a blackline master), hundredths strips (provided as a blackline master)	
2.4	Angle rulers, large sheets of paper (optional)	

Student Pages 18–30   Teaching the Investigation 30a–30g

2.1

Finding Percents

At a Glance

Grouping:
Individuals or Pairs

Launch

- Depending on the class's understanding of percent, work through the problem as a class, allow students to explore the problem, or use the problem as a launch for Problem 2.2.

Explore

- Explore, or encourage students to explore, a variety of ways to solve the problem.

Summarize

- As a class, discuss the various strategies students or the class discovered.

- Talk about the follow-up questions. (_optional_)

More About Percents

In the last investigation, you found percents of numbers. For example, you started with the price of an item and the percent discount offered on the item, and you computed how much money you would save.

In this investigation, you will begin with two numbers and find a percent that describes how they are related. For example, suppose that 50 out of 100 sixth graders surveyed said they liked to play basketball. You could say that 50% of the sixth graders surveyed liked to play basketball.

2.1 Finding Percents

It was easy to determine that 50% of the sixth graders liked to play basketball because exactly 100 people were surveyed, and percent means "out of 100." Often, though, surveys involve more than or less than 100 people.

> **Problem 2.1**
>
> A survey asked cat owners, Does your cat have bad breath? Out of the 200 cat owners surveyed, 80 answered yes to this question. What _percent_ of the cat owners answered yes?
>
> Try to find more than one way to solve this problem. For example, you might begin by asking yourself what _fraction_ of the cat owners surveyed said their cats have bad breath. Be prepared to explain the different methods you use to solve the problem.

Assignment Choices

ACE questions 1–4, 11, 17–21, and unassigned choices from earlier problems

Answer to Problem 2.1

40%; See examples of strategies in the "Summarize" section on page 30a.

Answers to Problem 2.1 Follow-Up

1. 200; Possible explanation: 40% means 40 out of every 100, and 500 is five groups of 100, so 40% of 500 is $40 \times 5 = 200$.

2. 30; Possible explanation: You can think about the problem as $\frac{40}{100} = \frac{?}{75}$. Since $\frac{40}{100} = \frac{10}{25} = \frac{30}{75}$, the answer is 30.

Problem 2.1 Follow-Up

1. If you survey 500 cat owners, about how many would you expect to say their cats have bad breath? Explain your reasoning.

2. If you survey 75 cat owners, about how many would you expect to say their cats have bad breath? Explain your reasoning.

2.2 Finding a General Strategy

One of the powerful things about mathematics is that you can often find a way to solve one problem that will also work for solving similar problems.

> ### Problem 2.2
>
> Here are more questions that involve figuring out what percent of people have answered yes to a survey question. As you work on these questions, try to find a way to describe a general strategy you can use for solving these kinds of problems.
>
> **A.** If 80 out of 400 cat owners surveyed said their cats have bad breath, what percent of the cat owners is this? Is this percent greater than, equal to, or less than the percent represented by 80 out of 200 cat owners? Explain.
>
> **B.** If 120 out of 300 seventh graders surveyed said math is their favorite subject, what percent of these seventh graders is this?
>
> **C.** If 30 out of 50 adults surveyed said they enjoy their jobs, what percent of these adults is this?
>
> **D.** If 34 out of 125 sixth graders surveyed said they would like to try hang gliding, what percent of these sixth graders is this?
>
> **E.** If 5 out of 73 middle-school students said they look forward to fire drills, what percent of these middle-school students is this?
>
> **F.** Write an explanation for how to solve these kinds of problems.

Problem 2.2 Follow-Up

1. For each part of Problem 2.2, how would you find the *fraction* of people surveyed that answered in the given way? How does finding a fraction help you find a percent?

2. a. A pet store sells a new digestible mouthwash for cats. To promote the new product, the store is offering $0.50 off of the regular price of $2.00 for an 8-ounce bottle. Use the explanation you wrote in question 1 to find the percent of the discount.

   b. Change the dollar amounts in part a to numbers of pennies. Now find the percent discount on the mouthwash. How do your answers compare?

Launch

- Depending on students' understanding of percent, continue the summary conversation from Problem 2.1, or allow pairs to begin work on Problem 2.2.

Explore

- As you circulate, help students who are struggling with writing about their strategies.

- Make hundredths grids and hundredths strips available for students who want to use them.

Summarize

- As a class, record all the strategies students discovered.

- Have students copy the list of strategies into their journals.

Answers to Problem 2.2

A. 20%; This percent is less than the percent represented by 80 out of 200, which is 40%. Possible explanation: The "wholes" are not the same. To compare them, we need a common referent or whole: $\frac{80}{200} = \frac{40}{100}$, whereas $\frac{80}{400} = \frac{20}{100}$.

B. 40%

C. 60%

D–F. See page 30d.

Answers to Problem 2.2 Follow-Up

See page 30e.

Assignment Choices

ACE questions 12, 14–15, 26–30, and unassigned choices from earlier problems

Clipping Coupons

At a Glance

Grouping:
Pairs

Launch

■ Work through the example in the student edition about thinking in pennies to help with percent problems. (*optional*)

Explore

■ Have students work in pairs.

■ If pairs are having trouble, suggest they look at the list of strategies made in Problem 2.2.

Summarize

■ As a class, talk about the strategies students used to solve the problem.

■ Ask the class why $\frac{0.75}{3.00}$ and $\frac{75}{300}$ are equivalent.

Newspapers often have coupons for discounts on many different things. For example, the pet store mentioned in Problem 2.2 Follow-Up had a coupon for $1.50 off a 20-ounce bottle of mouthwash for cats. The regular price for the mouthwash is $5.00. Alicia wanted to figure out what percent discount this is. She thought about the problem this way:

"I need to find what percent $1.50 is of $5.00. I can think of these amounts in pennies. The fraction I want to represent as a percent is $\frac{150}{500}$, which is equivalent to $\frac{30}{100}$. As a decimal, this fraction is 0.3. This means that the discount is 30%!"

Coupons for cat mouthwash may not interest you, but you may be interested in coupons, like the one below, that give discounts for purchases of food at your favorite restaurant:

Problem 2.3

What percent discount do you get with the coupon above?

Try to find more than one way to solve this problem. Be prepared to explain the different methods you discover.

Assignment Choices

ACE questions 13, 23, 24, and unassigned choices from earlier problems

Answer to Problem 2.3

25%; See examples of strategies in the "Summarize" section on page 30c.

Answers to Problem 2.3 Follow-Up

1. Possible answers: About 10%, since 10% of $4.50 is $0.45. About 11%, since $\frac{50}{450}$ = 50 ÷ 450 = about 0.1111.

2. 40%; Possible explanations: This amount of reduction is about $12.00, and since 10% of $29.50 is about $3.00, and 4 × $3.00 = $12.00, the percent discount is about 4 × 10%. Or, $29.50 − $17.70 = $11.80, and $\frac{11.80}{29.50}$ = 0.4 = 40%.

(Answers continued on next page.)

Making Circle Graphs

Problem 2.3 Follow-Up

1. For the sale below, estimate the percent discount you get. Explain your reasoning.

2. For the sale below, estimate the percent discount you get. Explain your reasoning.

3. The discount on a skateboard is $24.75, which is 25% of the original cost. What was the original cost?

4. The regular price for the sneakers that Kelly wants is $68.98. The sneakers are on sale for 20% off. A sales tax of 6% will be computed on the sale price. How much will Kelly pay for the shoes?

2.4 Making Circle Graphs

Circle graphs, or *pie charts,* are special kinds of graphs used to show how a whole (100%) is divided into several categories. For example, dog and cat owners who said their pets had bad breath were asked, Which of these methods do you use most frequently to take care of your pet's bad breath? Here are the results of the survey:

	Dog owners	Cat owners
Toothpaste	54%	53%
Mouthwash	16%	14%
Dental floss	7%	24%
Other	23%	9%
Total	**100%**	**100%**

Notice that when you add the percents in each column, you get a total of 100%.

At a Glance

Grouping: Pairs or Small Groups

Launch

- Ask students how the circle graphs in the student edition were made.

- If students don't bring up angles and degrees at this time, leave the discussion for later.

Explore

- Have pairs or groups of three work on the problem.

- Have students work on large sheets of paper for display during the summary. (*optional*)

Summarize

- Display the students' work. (*optional*)

- Have groups describe the strategies they used to solve the problem.

---

3. $99.00; Possible explanation: 25% is the same as $\frac{1}{4}$, and if $\frac{1}{4}$ of the amount is $24.75, then the whole must be $24.75 × 4 = $99.00.

4. $58.49 or $58.50; The solution involves several steps:
Step 1 Find the discount: $68.98 × 20% = $13.796, which rounds to $13.80
Step 2 Find the sales price: $68.98 – 13.80 = $55.18
Step 3 Calculate the tax: $55.18 × 6% = $3.3108, which rounds to $3.31
Step 4 Find the total cost: $55.18 + $3.31 = $58.49

Assignment Choices

ACE questions 5–10, 16, 25, and unassigned choices from earlier problems

Assessment

It is appropriate to use Check-Up 1 after this problem.

This information is represented below in two circle graphs.

Methods Used by Dog Owners   **Methods Used by Cat Owners**

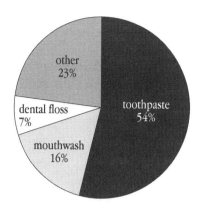

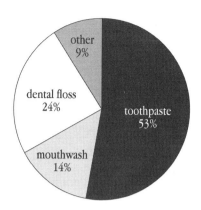

Problem 2.4

Study the circle graphs above. Use what you know about angle measures, circles, and percents to figure out how they were created. Then work on the problem below.

Cat and dog owners were asked, Do you let your pet lick your face? Here are the results of the survey:

	Cat owners	Dog owners
Yes	40%	75%
No	60%	25%
Total	**100%**	**100%**

Create two circle graphs to display this information.

Answers to Problem 2.4

Cat Owners Who Let Their   **Dog Owners Who Let Their**
Pets Lick Their Faces   **Pets Lick Their Faces**

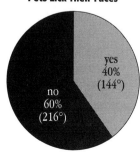

▮ Problem 2.4 Follow-Up

1. Cat and dog owners were asked, Does your pet sleep in the same room with you? The results are shown in the table. Make two circle graphs to display these results.

	Cat owners	Dog owners
Yes	73%	47%
No	27%	53%
Total	**100%**	**100%**

2. How do the answers of the cat owners and dog owners compare?

Answers to Problem 2.4 Follow-Up

1. See page 30e.

2. More cat owners let their pets sleep in the same room—about $\frac{3}{4}$ of the people surveyed. Less than half of the dog owners let their pets sleep in the same room.

Answers

Applications

1. 43%

2. 9%

3. 60%

4. 75%

5. 2; Possible explanation: 10% of 40 is 4, so 5% must be 2.

6. 60; 75% is $\frac{3}{4}$, and $\frac{3}{4}$ of 80 means three of four equal parts of 80. Each part is 20, so three parts is 60.

7. 48.4; 1% of 220 is 2.2, so 22% is $22 \times 1\% = 22 \times 2.2 = 48.4$.

8. 12.5%; 5 out of 40 is $\frac{5}{40} = \frac{1}{8} = 0.125$ or 12.5%.

9. 93.75%; 75 out of 80 is $\frac{75}{80} = \frac{15}{16} = 0.9375$ or 93.75%.

10. 10%; 22 out of 220 is $\frac{22}{220} = \frac{1}{10} = 0.1$ or 10%.

11. 15%

12. 5%

As you work on these ACE questions, use your calculator whenever you need it.

Applications

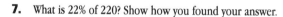

1. Suppose 43 out of 100 cat owners surveyed said their cats weigh under 10 pounds. What percent of cat owners surveyed is this?

2. Suppose 18 out of 200 race car owners surveyed said their cars are green. What percent of race car owners surveyed is this?

3. Suppose 15 out of 25 skydivers surveyed said they had never had a skydiving accident. What percent of skydivers surveyed is this?

4. Suppose 30 out of 40 private investigators surveyed said their jobs are exceedingly dull. What percent of private investigators surveyed is this?

5. What is 5% of 40? Show how you found your answer.

6. What is 75% of 80? Show how you found your answer.

7. What is 22% of 220? Show how you found your answer.

8. 5 is what percent of 40? Show how you found your answer.

9. 75 is what percent of 80? Show how you found your answer.

10. 22 is what percent of 220? Show how you found your answer.

11. In 1991, about 15 bike thefts were reported for every 100 people who owned bikes. What percent of the bike owners had their bikes stolen?

12. As part of a probability activity, Jack is counting the occurrence of different letters in a paragraph in his biology book. In the first 1000 letters in the paragraph, he found 50 b's. What percent of the letters were b's?

13. Estimate what percent discount Janey will receive if she buys the microscope kit advertised below. Explain.

MICROSCOPE KITS

Customers *usually* pay:	$7.95
Students *save* by paying only:	$6.76

14. The auto shop class conducted a survey to determine which math teacher's car was the most popular with the students. These were the results:

Ms. Grant's car	48 votes
Ms. Dole's car	35 votes
Mr. Manzine's car	12 votes
Ms. Block's car	75 votes

a. What percent of the votes did Mr. Manzine's car receive? Explain.

b. What percent of the votes did Ms. Dole's car receive? Explain.

c. One student said Ms. Grant's car received 48% of the votes. Is he correct? Explain.

15. Bob, Sally, and Chi belong to an after-school youth group. They joined the group at different times after the beginning of school. The chart shows their attendance so far at the various events, including meetings, held by the youth group.

Member	Events attended since joined	Total events held since joined
Bob	20	30
Sally	11	18
Chi	7	12

a. If the attendance pattern of all three students remains about the same for the next 30 events, who will have the highest percent of attendance at the 30 events? Explain your reasoning.

13. about 15%; The discount is $1.19 out of $7.95, or $\frac{119}{795}$, which gives 0.14969 on a calculator, or about 15%.

14a. about 7%; Of the 170 votes cast, 12 were for Mr. Manzine's car, and $\frac{12}{170}$ gives 0.070588 on a calculator, or about 7%.

14b. about 21%; Ms. Dole's car received 35 out of 170 votes, or $\frac{35}{170}$, which gives 0.20588 on a calculator, or about 21%.

14c. no; Ms. Grant's car received 48 votes, but this can't be 48% of the votes because the number of students who voted was not 100.

15a. Bob; Bob's percent of attendance is about 67%, Sally's is about 61%, and Chi's is about 58%.

15b. Bob: 0.67 × 120 ≈ 80; Sally: 0.61 × 120 ≈ 73; Chi: 0.58 × 120 ≈ 70

16a. See page 30f.

16b. Possible answer: More dog owners than cat owners have set feeding times for their pet.

Connections

17. 39 dog owners

18. 78 tarantula owners

19. 32 students

20. about 5 students

b. Out of the 120 events planned for the rest of the year, how many would you expect each of the students to attend if they kept the same percent of attendance? Explain your reasoning.

16. a. Dog and cat owners were asked, How often do you feed your pet? The results are shown in the table below. Make two circle graphs of the results.

	Cat owners	Dog owners
Night only	4%	2%
Morning only	6%	10%
Morning and night	42%	46%
Anytime	48%	42%
Total	**100%**	**100%**

b. Compare the feeding patterns of dog owners to cat owners.

Connections

17. In a survey of 100 dog owners about their pets' habits, 39% said that their dogs eat bugs. How many dog owners surveyed said this?

18. When 300 tarantula owners were surveyed, 26% said they let their spiders crawl on them. How many tarantula owners surveyed said this?

19. In a survey of 80 students, 40% said they had a savings account of their own. How many students surveyed said this?

20. During a survey of 80 student artists, about 6% said they had sold at least one of their works of art. About how many students surveyed said this?

21. a. Janelle said, "The median divides a set of data in half." What does she mean?

b. Randy added, "If the median divides a set of data in half, you always know what percent of the data is below the median and what percent of the data is above the median." Is Randy correct? Justify your answer.

22. In a–e, use the line plot to answer the question.

How Many Pets Does Your Family Have?

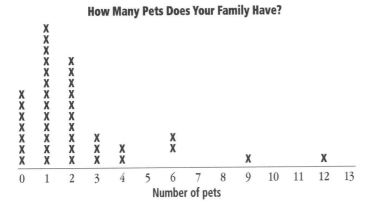

a. What percent of the 40 people surveyed have more than two pets? Explain how you found your answer.

b. What percent of the 40 people surveyed have fewer than three pets? Explain how you found your answer.

c. What is the median of the distribution?

d. What percent of the people surveyed are below the median?

e. What percent of the people surveyed are above the median?

21a. In an ordered set of data, the median is the middle value (or the mean of the two middle values if there are an even number of data values). There are equal numbers of data values above and below the median.

21b. Randy's statement is not correct. For example, the median of the data 1, 2, 3 is 2; $33\frac{1}{3}$% of the data are above the median and $33\frac{1}{3}$% of the data are below the median. For the data 1, 2, 3, 4, the median is 2.5; 50% of the data are above the median and 50% of the data are below the median.

22a. 25%; Ten respondents reported having more than two pets, which is $\frac{1}{4}$ of the total of 40 respondents, which is 0.25 or 25%.

22b. 75%; Since 25% have more than two pets, the rest must have fewer than three pets, and 100% − 25% = 75%.

22c. 1.5 pets; Half of the 40 pieces of data fall at 0 or 1, half fall at 2 or more, so halfway between 1 and 2 is the midpoint of the responses.

22d. 50%; 20 of the 40 data values are less than 1.5.

22e. 50%; 20 of the 40 data values are more than 1.5.

Extensions

23. 200; If 40% is 80, then 10% must be 20, and 100% must be 20 × 10 = 200.

24. 1100; If 20% is 220, then 10% must be 110, and 100% must be 110 × 10 = 1100.

25a. See page 30f.

25b. Possible answer: The majority of people responded that they have pets for love and companionship. The responses seem to indicate that cats are not as popular for security and protection as dogs are, but that dogs are not as good at catching rodents as are cats. Both dogs and cats appear to be entertaining.

Extensions

23. 80 is 40% of what number? Explain.

24. 220 is 20% of what number? Explain.

25. A circle graph is not always useful when you are working with percents. For example, when people are allowed to choose more than one answer to a survey question, the percents for the categories may add to *more than* 100%. For example, in one survey people were asked why they owned a pet. They were given several choices and were allowed to mark off more than one reason. Because multiple answers were allowed, the percents add to more than 100%.

	Dog owners	Cat owners
Love/companionship	88%	93%
Security	39%	0%
Protection	35%	0%
Entertainment	26%	33%
Catching rodents	0%	16%
Breeding (to make money)	16%	6%
Children grown/spouse died	4%	10%
Total	**208%**	**158%**

You can make a circle graph only when the percents add to 100%. When they add to more than 100%, you can make a bar graph to show the information.

a. Make bar graphs to display the data shown in the table. Before you make your bar graphs, think about these questions:

- What kind of data will you display in your graphs?
- What information will you show on the horizontal axis (the *x*-axis)?
- What information will you show on the vertical axis (the *y*-axis)?
- What scale will you use for the *y*-axis?

b. Write a paragraph comparing the responses of dog owners to cat owners in this survey.

In 26–30, replace the question marks with numbers that make the sentence true.

26. $\frac{6}{?} = \frac{18}{?} = \frac{?}{20}$

27. $\frac{12}{?} = \frac{?}{36} = \frac{?}{12}$

28. $\frac{2}{3} < \frac{?}{9}$

29. $\frac{2}{3} = \frac{?}{9}$

30. $\frac{2}{3} > \frac{?}{9}$

26. Possible answer:
$\frac{6}{40} = \frac{18}{120} = \frac{3}{20}$

27. Possible answer:
$\frac{12}{24} = \frac{18}{36} = \frac{6}{12}$

28. Possible answer:
$\frac{2}{3} < \frac{7}{9}$ (The question mark can be replaced with any number greater than 6.)

29. $\frac{2}{3} = \frac{6}{9}$

30. Possible answer:
$\frac{2}{3} > \frac{5}{9}$ (The question mark can be replaced with any number less than 6.)

Possible Answers

1. 30 out of 120 can be expressed as $\frac{30}{120} = \frac{1}{4} = \frac{25}{100}$, which is 25%. Alternatively, we can change the fraction $\frac{30}{120}$ to a decimal by dividing the numerator by the denominator, giving $30 \div 120 = 0.25$, which is the same as 25%.

2. We can think of 34 out of 135 as $\frac{34}{135}$ which is 0.2519 as a decimal, or about 25%.

3. Because there are 360° in a circle, I need to find 23% of 360°. I could do this by rewriting 23% as the fraction $\frac{23}{100}$ and then finding an equivalent fraction with a denominator of 360, $\frac{82.8}{360}$. I would need to mark off a section of the circle with a central angle measure of 82.8°.

Mathematical Reflections

In this investigation, you studied situations for which you needed to find the percent one number is of another number so that you could describe the situation or compare it to another situation. These questions will help you summarize what you have learned:

1 Describe at least two ways to find what percent 30 is of 120. Explain why each method works.

2 Describe how to find what percent 34 is of 135. Explain your method.

3 Explain how you would find what part of a circle graph should be shaded to show 23%.

Think about your answers to these questions, discuss your ideas with other students and your teacher, and then write a summary of your findings in your journal.

Tips for the Linguistically Diverse Classroom

Original Rebus The Original Rebus technique is described in detail in *Getting to Know Connected Mathematics*. Students make a copy of the text before it is discussed. During discussion, they generate their own rebuses for words they do not understand as the words are made comprehensible through pictures, objects, or demonstrations. Example: Question 3—key words for which students may make rebuses are *circle graph* (a circle graph), *shaded* (the same circle graph with a section shaded).

TEACHING THE INVESTIGATION

2.1 • Finding Percents

Much of the information we meet in our daily lives is in percent form and has been calculated from various kinds of statistical data, including opinion surveys. In this problem, students develop strategies for finding the percent of people surveyed who responded in a particular way.

Launch

Read Problem 2.1 with your class. If your class is struggling with basic ideas of percent, work through Problem 2.1 as a class. If they have a good grasp of the concept, let them work individually or in pairs as you informally assess where they are in their understanding. Or, you may choose to use this problem as a launch for Problem 2.2. In that case, discuss Problem 2.1 as a class, and then allow students to move on to Problem 2.2.

Explore

Encourage students to explore a variety of ways to solve this problem and the follow-up questions. As you circulate, remind them to think about and be prepared to explain their strategies for solving the problem.

Summarize

As a class, talk about the ways students found to solve the problem. Here are some strategies students have found:

- Joanna and Preben said that they thought about 80 out of 200 by visualizing two hundredths grids, showing the 80 evenly distributed across the two grids. Because 40 out of each 100 squares are shaded, and this is 40%, 80 out of 200 must also be 40%.

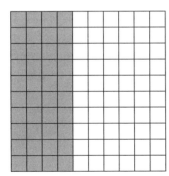 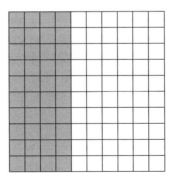

- Tomas and Julian said that they know they can write 80 out of 200 as the fraction $\frac{80}{200}$. Then they found an equivalent fraction, $\frac{40}{100}$, and immediately saw that this was 40%.

- Leah and Mickey used a calculator to handle $\frac{80}{200}$ as a division problem. The decimal 0.4 results, which is the same as 0.40, which is 40%.

Students may check their solutions by finding 40% of 200 using the strategies they found in Investigation 1. If no student suggests the strategies given above, you may want to present them to the class as ideas that were shared by other students (from another class or from a previous year). Sometimes when students are offering only weak ideas, it is necessary for you to bring forth additional information.

The summary could continue with a discussion of the follow-up questions.

> How could you write, in words and in symbols, how you solved these problems?

Asking students to think about ways to record their thinking helps them to make connections between what they are doing and symbolic notation.

2.2 • Finding a General Strategy

In this problem, students develop a general strategy for finding a percent when they are dealing with sample sizes that are more than or less than 100.

Launch

If you use Problem 2.1 as the launch to this problem, you could just assign Problem 2.2. If your students struggled with Problem 2.1, you might want to continue or review the summary conversation from that problem and try to clarify the strategies they are using.

Explore

Have students work in pairs. As you circulate, you may notice students struggling with writing about their strategies. Remind them that describing a strategy involves more than just giving an example.

> You might try writing in words the steps you took to solve part A and then determine whether the process you have described would work for part B.

Some students may want to use hundredths grids or hundredths strips in devising strategies, and you may want to suggest their use to pairs who are having difficulty.

Summarize

One way to summarize this problem that allows you to hear from each pair of students is to write the letters A through E across the top of the chalkboard and have pairs record their answers. You may want to ask pairs to initial their answers, as this will help you keep track of which groups have responded and identify who is struggling.

In a class discussion, have pairs explain how they found their answers, which will focus the conversation on strategies. Use question F to summarize this conversation. This will result in more efficient strategies being considered by everyone. As a class, record all the strategies on the board. You might ask students to copy this list of strategies in their journals, so you can refer back to this information throughout the unit.

Discuss the follow-up. Skip follow-up question 1 if your class has already discussed this idea when answering question F. Question 2 is a good lead-in to Problem 2.3.

2.3 • Clipping Coupons

The Follow-Up from the preceding problem was designed to give students ways of thinking that may assist them on this more challenging problem. In Problems 2.1 and 2.2, students found what percent one number is of another. The complexity in this problem is that they are dealing with money, which involves decimal computation.

Launch

Read through the problem with your class. The context should be familiar to them. The introduction to the problem in the student edition gives an example that shows how thinking in pennies can be used as a way to handle decimals. You may want to skip this example and allow students to work on the coupon problem first, then share the strategy in the example.

Explore

Have students work in pairs. As you observe them working, encourage them to explore a variety of ways to solve the problem. If pairs are struggling, suggest they look back at the list of strategies that was generated in Problem 2.2 and the example given in the introduction to the problem. Remind students that they will need to be able to explain their thinking to the rest of the class.

Summarize

As a class, talk about all the ways pairs found to solve the problem. You may want to ask students which strategies they used from the list made by the class in Problem 2.2. Here are some strategies students have suggested:

- Scott and Tandra realized that they could figure out how much they get off for each dollar, which would give them the part per hundred that is the percent. They said that since 300 pennies, or 3 dollars, is the whole, they could think of it as three groups of 100 pennies or 1 dollar. For a discount of 75¢, 25¢ applies to each $1.00, or 25 pennies to each 100 pennies. Thus the discount is the same as a 25% reduction.

- Val and Lauren knew they could write 75 out of 300 as the fraction $\frac{75}{300}$. Then, they named an equivalent fraction, $\frac{25}{100}$, which is 25%.

- Using a calculator, Raj and Terry handled $\frac{75}{300}$ as a division problem, getting the decimal 0.25, which they knew could be represented as 25%.

2.4 • Making Circle Graphs

The mathematical connection in this problem is that, to find the sector needed to represent a given percent of a circle, students must find the given percent of 360°. Students must then measure with an angle ruler to construct a sector of a circle with that number of degrees. Calculators and angle rulers should be available.

Launch

Read through the introduction on circle graphs with your students. Ask them to think about how the person who made the first graph figured out what 54% of the circle was, what 16% of the circle was, and so on. It's fine if students don't bring up angles and degrees at this time; the problem will present these ideas. We suggest you allow students to make sense of the suggestion and observe how information about percents and angle measures was used.

Explore

Have students work in pairs or groups of three. You may want to have them do their work on large sheets of paper that can be displayed during the summary for comparisons.

Summarize

Have groups discuss how they approached the problem. Some may have simply estimated the areas; talk about the strengths and weaknesses of that strategy. Groups will probably suggest making the circle graph for dog owners by dividing a circle into four equal sections; one of those sections would represent 25%, and the other three would represent 75%. By now, many students know the relationship between 25% and $\frac{1}{4}$ and 75% and $\frac{3}{4}$. If this strategy is suggested, ask:

> How could you use that same strategy to create the circle graph for the cat data of 40% and 60%?

This should lead to a discussion on how it is more difficult to divide a circle into 10 equal sections than into 4 equal sections.

From here, you may ask whether anyone used angle measures to help them make the circle graphs. If yes, ask the students to explain. If not, ask how they could use angle measures to draw the different sections.

After the class has discussed the use of angle measures for constructing circle graphs, have students try the techniques on follow-up question 1. Discuss question 2 after the graphs are constructed.

Additional Answers

Answers to Problem 2.2

D.   27.2%

E.   about 6.8%

F.   Possible explanation: You can write each situation as a fraction and then find an equivalent fraction with a denominator of 100. This strategy works well for part B ($\frac{120}{300} = \frac{40}{100}$) and part C ($\frac{30}{50} = \frac{60}{100}$). Or, you can use division to change the fraction to a decimal and then the decimal to a percent. This strategy is helpful when you have fractions that cannot easily be changed into equivalent fractions with denominators of 100, as in part D ($\frac{34}{125} = 34 \div 125 = 0.272 = 27.2\%$) and part E ($\frac{5}{73} = 5 \div 73 = 0.0684931507 = $ about 6.8% or 7%).

Answers to Problem 2.2 Follow-Up

1. Possible answer: The total number of people surveyed represents the *whole* (the denominator of the fraction). The number of people who answer yes to a particular question is the *part* (the numerator of the fraction). Once you write a fraction, you can find an equivalent fraction with a denominator of 100, which can easily be written as a percent.

2. a. The whole in this case is $2.00 and the part is $0.50. Thus, the fraction representing the discount is $\frac{0.50}{2.00}$. This fraction is equivalent to $\frac{50}{200} = \frac{25}{100}$, which can be written as 25%.

   b. You can form the fraction $\frac{50}{200}$, which is $\frac{1}{4}$ or 0.25 or 25%. The two answers are the same.

Answers to Problem 2.4 Follow-Up

1.

Cat sleeps in Same Room

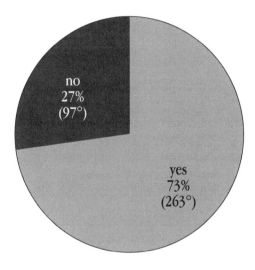

no
27%
(97°)

yes
73%
(263°)

Dog Sleeps in Same Room

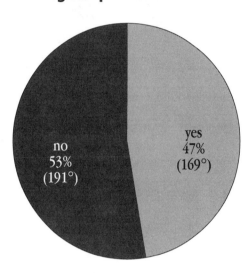

no
53%
(191°)

yes
47%
(169°)

ACE Answers

Applications

16a.

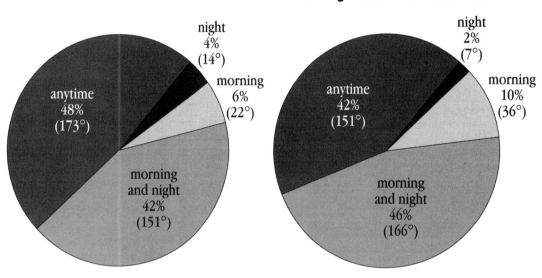

When Cat Owners Feed Their Pets

night
4%
(14°)

morning
6%
(22°)

anytime
48%
(173°)

morning
and night
42%
(151°)

When Dog Owners Feed Their Pets

night
2%
(7°)

morning
10%
(36°)

anytime
42%
(151°)

morning
and night
46%
(166°)

Extensions

25a.

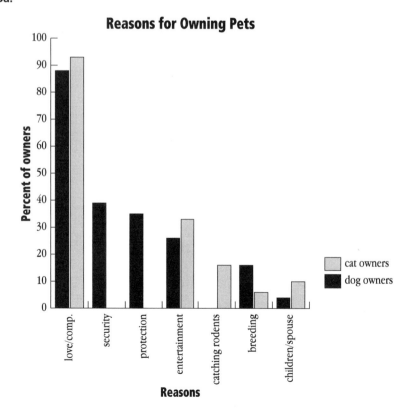

Reasons for Owning Pets

Percent of owners

Reasons

love/comp.
security
protection
entertainment
catching rodents
breeding
children/spouse

cat owners
dog owners

Estimating with Fractions and Decimals

The first two investigations of this unit focused on computations with percents. Investigations 3 through 6 focus on computations with fractions and decimals. The focus of this investigation is estimation. Encourage students to talk often about their thinking and to share and refine their strategies. At this point in this curriculum, students have had quite a bit of practice finding equivalent fractions and decimals and changing among fraction, decimal, and percent representations.

In Problem 3.1, Getting Close, and Problem 3.2, Getting Even Closer, students play a game that involves estimating sums of fractions and decimals. In Problem 3.1, they estimate which of three benchmarks—0, 1, or 2—each sum is nearest. In Problem 3.2, they must determine which of six benchmarks—0, 0.5, 1, 1.5, 2, or 2.5—a sum is nearest, which requires them to estimate sums with greater precision.

Mathematical and Problem-Solving Goals

- *To develop strategies for estimating sums of fractions and decimals*

- *To make sense of whether a situation requires an overestimate or an underestimate.*

- *To use 0, $\frac{1}{2}$, 1, $1\frac{1}{2}$, and 2 as benchmarks to make sense of the size of a sum*

- *To use estimation strategies to quickly approximate a particular sum*

Materials		
Problem	**For students**	**For the teacher**
All	Calculators, Getting Close cards (1 set per group; provided as blackline masters), Getting Close number squares (1 set per student; provided as a blackline master), hundredths grids (provided as a blackline master), hundredths strips (provided as a blackline master)	Transparencies 3.1 and 3.2 (optional)

Student Pages 31–42   Teaching the Investigation 42a–42c

Estimating with Fractions and Decimals

Sometimes when you need to find an amount of something, you will not need or will not be able to get an exact answer. In these situations, you can estimate an answer. This investigation will give you practice in making estimates with fractions and decimals.

3.1 Getting Close

Getting Close is a game that will sharpen your skills at estimating with fractions and decimals. In *Bits and Pieces I,* we developed a set of *benchmarks* for estimating fractions and decimals. You learned to find which benchmark a number is nearest. Look at this set of benchmarks:

$$0 \quad \frac{1}{4} \quad \frac{1}{2} \quad \frac{3}{4} \quad 1 \quad 1\frac{1}{4} \quad 1\frac{1}{2} \quad 1\frac{3}{4} \quad 2$$

Which benchmark is $\frac{5}{8}$ nearest? Five eighths is larger than $\frac{1}{2}$, because it is larger than $\frac{4}{8}$. Five eighths is smaller than $\frac{3}{4}$, because it is smaller than $\frac{6}{8}$. In fact, $\frac{5}{8}$ is exactly halfway between $\frac{1}{2}$ and $\frac{3}{4}$.

> ### Think about this!
>
> **H**ow could you use benchmarks to help you quickly estimate the sum of two fractions? For example, think about this sum:
>
> $$\frac{1}{8} + 1\frac{5}{7}$$
>
> Is this sum larger or smaller than 2? Now, look at this sum:
>
> $$\frac{1}{2} + \frac{5}{8}$$
>
> Is this sum closest to 0, to 1, or to 2?

Getting Close

At a Glance

Grouping:
Small Groups

Launch

- Explain to the class that they will play a game that involves estimating sums of fractions and decimals.

- Make sure students understand how to play the game.

Explore

- After students have played at least one full game, ask them to write about the strategies they are using.

Summarize

- As a class, discuss the Getting Close game.

- Ask students to share their estimation strategies.

Assignment Choices

ACE questions 1–10, 35–36, 38–43, and unassigned choices from earlier problems

When you play Getting Close, you will use benchmarks and other methods to estimate the sum of two numbers.

Getting Close Rules

Getting Close is played by two to four players.

Materials
- A set of Getting Close game cards
- A set of three number squares—0, 1, and 2 (1 set per player)

Playing
- All players hold their 0, 1, and 2 number squares in their hands, hidden from view of the other players.

- The game cards are placed face down in a pile in the center of the table.

- For a *round of play,* one player turns over two game cards from the pile. Each player mentally estimates the sum of the numbers on the two game cards, and puts the number square (0, 1, or 2) he or she thinks is closest to the sum face down in the center of the table.

- After each player has played a number square, find the actual sum by using a calculator or some other method.

- The first player who put the correct number square in the center of the table collects the two game cards. If there is a tie, all players who tied get one game card. Players who have tied may take game cards from the deck if necessary.

- Each player who chose the wrong number square must return one game card (if he or she has one) to the bottom of the pile.

- The player who wins the round turns over the next two game cards.

- When all of the game cards have been used, the player with the most game cards wins.

Answer to Problem 3.1 Follow-Up

Answers will vary.

Problem 3.1

Play Getting Close once or twice. Keep a record of the estimation strategies you find useful. You may find benchmarks, fraction strips, number lines, hundredths grids, or changing a fraction to a decimal or a decimal to a fraction helpful in making estimates. You may discover other ways of thinking that help. As you play the game, your group may use a calculator to check whether a player is correct—but not to estimate the sums!

■ **Problem 3.1 Follow-Up**

Describe or illustrate one estimation strategy that you found useful in the game.

3.2 Getting Even Closer

Now you will play the game Getting Even Closer, which requires you to estimate sums to the nearest 0.5. The rules are the same as for Getting Close, and the same game cards are used. However, each player will now have six number squares: 0, 0.5, 1, 1.5, 2, and 2.5.

Problem 3.2

Play Getting Even Closer once or twice. Keep a record of your strategies for estimating the sums. As before, your group may use a calculator to check whether a player is correct, but not to estimate the sums.

After a round of play, the player who won should explain the strategy he or she used to estimate the sum.

■ **Problem 3.2 Follow-Up**

1. **a.** The following fractions occur so often that it is useful to be able to recall their decimal and percent equivalents quickly:

$$\frac{1}{2} \quad \frac{1}{3} \quad \frac{1}{4} \quad \frac{2}{3} \quad \frac{3}{4} \quad \frac{1}{6} \quad \frac{1}{5}$$

For each of these important fractions, give the decimal and percent equivalents.
   b. Draw a number line. On your number line, label the point corresponding to each fraction listed in part a.

At a Glance

***Grouping:
Small Groups***

Launch

■ Explain that in this game, students will estimate sums to the nearest 0.5.

■ Assign students to new groups. (*optional*)

Explore

■ As students play, remind them to share their estimation strategies after each round.

Summarize

■ As a class, discuss how students revised their estimation strategies.

■ Ask students to write about how they can quickly estimate $\frac{1}{3} + 0.75$ as close to 0, 0.5, 1, 1.5, 2, or 2.5. (*optional*)

Answers to Problem 3.2 Follow-Up

1. **a.** $\frac{1}{2}$: 0.5 or 50%; $\frac{1}{3}$: about 0.333 or $33\frac{1}{3}$%; $\frac{1}{4}$: 0.25 or 25%; $\frac{2}{3}$: about 0.667 or $66\frac{2}{3}$%; $\frac{3}{4}$: 0.75 or 75%; $\frac{1}{6}$: about 0.1667 or $16\frac{2}{3}$%; $\frac{1}{5}$: 0.2 or 20%

   b.

2. **a.** $1.08 = \frac{3}{4} + 0.33$.   **b.** $0.45 = \frac{1}{5} + 0.25$.

3. **a.** slightly less than 1.75 (or 1.74999999. . .)

   b. slightly more than 1.25 (Some students will argue for 1.25, if the convention of rounding up is used.)

Assignment Choices

ACE questions 11–34, 37, and unassigned choices from earlier problems

2. Suppose you played Getting Close with only these game cards:

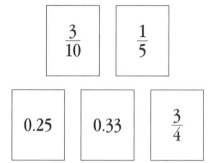

a. What is the largest sum possible?

b. What is the smallest sum possible?

3. a. If you add two numbers and the sum is closest to 1.5 (using the set of benchmarks 0, 0.5, 1, 1.5, 2, and 2.5), what is the largest the sum could actually be?

b. If you add two numbers and the sum is closest to 1.5 (using the set of benchmarks 0, 0.5, 1, 1.5, 2, and 2.5), what is the smallest the sum could actually be?

Applications • Connections • Extensions

As you work on these ACE questions, use your calculator whenever you need it.

Applications

1. Ask an adult to describe some situations in which a very close estimate is needed and some situations in which an estimate can just be "in the ballpark."

2. Ask an adult to describe some situations in which an overestimate is needed.

3. Ask an adult to describe some situations in which an underestimate is needed.

4. Many sewing patterns have a $\frac{5}{8}$-inch allowance for sewing the seam. Is this allowance closer to 0, $\frac{1}{2}$, or 1 inch? Explain your reasoning.

In 5–10, tell whether the fraction is closest to 0, $\frac{1}{2}$, or 1. Explain your reasoning.

5. $\frac{4}{9}$ 6. $\frac{9}{16}$

7. $\frac{4}{7}$ 8. $\frac{500}{1000}$

9. $\frac{5}{6}$ 10. $\frac{48}{100}$

In 11–19, find two fractions with a sum that is between the two given numbers.

11. 0 and 1   12. 0 and $\frac{1}{2}$ 13. $\frac{1}{2}$ and 1

14. 1 and 2   15. 1 and $1\frac{1}{2}$ 16. $1\frac{1}{2}$ and 2

17. 2 and 3   18. 2 and $2\frac{1}{2}$ 19. $2\frac{1}{2}$ and 3

In 20–23, the sum is a student's solution to the problem: "Find two fractions with a sum greater than $\frac{3}{4}$." Tell whether the solution is correct and explain your reasoning.

20. $\frac{1}{8} + \frac{2}{4}$ 21. $\frac{3}{6} + \frac{2}{4}$

22. $\frac{5}{12} + \frac{5}{6}$ 23. $\frac{5}{10} + \frac{3}{8}$

Answers

Applications

1. Possible answer: A very close estimate is needed when cutting expensive fabric to make clothing. A ballpark estimate is needed when determining travel time for a long trip.

2. Possible answer: An overestimate may be useful when determining how much money to bring to the store to buy groceries.

3. Possible answer: An underestimate is adequate when figuring out how much food to buy for a party, because not everyone you invite will come and not everyone you invite will eat.

4. $\frac{1}{2}$ inch; Students might reason by drawing a picture or by changing the fractions into decimals to make comparisons easier.

5. $\frac{1}{2}$; Explanations will vary. Students might draw pictures or convert fractions to decimals.

6. $\frac{1}{2}$; Explanations will vary.

7. $\frac{1}{2}$; Explanations will vary.

8. $\frac{1}{2}$; Explanations will vary.

9. 1; Explanations will vary.

10. $\frac{1}{2}$; Explanations will vary.

11. Possible answer: $\frac{1}{4} + \frac{5}{8}$

12. Possible answer: $\frac{1}{4} + \frac{1}{8}$

13–23. See page 42c.

24. 0.5; Explanations will vary.

25. 1; Explanations will vary.

26. 0; Explanations will vary.

27. 1; Explanations will vary.

28. 0.5; Explanations will vary.

29. 1.5; Explanations will vary.

30. Possible answer: Janine should buy a half gallon of orange juice and a quart of grapefruit juice. This way, each student could have between 1 and $1\frac{1}{2}$ pints of juice, and Janine would save money by not buying individual pints.

31. $0.21 + 0.31 \approx 0.5$

32. $0.13 + 0.12 = 0.25$

33. $0.33 + 0.33 \approx 0.75$

34. $0.21 + 0.21 \approx 0.4$

Connections

35. 30% is 0.3, so you sleep $24 \times 0.3 = 7.2$ hours each day. There are about 365 days in a year, so you sleep about $365 \times 7.2 = 2628$ hours per year. In 12 years, you sleep about $2628 \times 12 = 31,536$ hours. (Anything between 25,000 and 35,000 hours is reasonable.)

36. 5.96, 5.693, 5.67, 5.639, 5.599

In 24–29, tell whether the number is closest to 0, 0.5, 1, or 1.5, and explain your reasoning.

24. 0.67   **25.** 1.15   **26.** 0.000999

27. 0.78   **28.** 0.26   **29.** 1.90

30. Janine is having seven friends over for breakfast. Of the eight people who will be eating breakfast, six like orange juice best, and two prefer grapefruit juice. Both kinds of juice cost $2.89 for a half gallon, $2.09 for a quart ($\frac{1}{4}$ of a gallon), and $1.29 for a pint ($\frac{1}{8}$ of a gallon). How many of each size container of each type of juice should Janine buy? Use estimation to help you decide. Explain your reasoning.

In 31–34, fill in each blank with 1, 2, or 3 to form decimal numbers so that each sum is as close as possible to the given number. You may use the same digit twice in one number. For example, you may write 0.33. The symbol $\approx$ means "is approximately equal to."

31. $0.\_\_\,\_\_ + 0.\_\_\,\_\_ \approx 0.5$

32. $0.\_\_\,\_\_ + 0.\_\_\,\_\_ \approx 0.25$

33. $0.\_\_\,\_\_ + 0.\_\_\,\_\_ \approx 0.75$

34. $0.\_\_\,\_\_ + 0.\_\_\,\_\_ \approx 0.4$

Connections

35. If you sleep about 30% of each day, estimate how many hours you have slept by the time you are 12 years old. Explain your reasoning.

36. Order these decimals from largest to smallest.

    5.693   5.639   5.96   5.67   5.599

37. Julio is at the grocery store near his apartment. He has $10.00, but no calculator or paper and pencil. At right is a list of the items he would like to buy.

Use mental computation and estimation to answer questions a–c.

Item	Price
Milk	$2.47
Eggs	$1.09
Cheese	$1.95
Bread	$0.68
Honey	$1.19
Cereal	$3.25
Avocado	$0.50

a. Can Julio buy all the items with the money he has? Explain your reasoning.

b. If Julio had only $5.00, what could he buy? Give two possibilities.

c. What different items could Julio buy to come as close as possible to spending $5.00?

In 38–40, copy the figure onto your paper and shade about $\frac{1}{3}$ of the figure.

38.

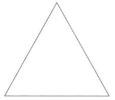

39.

40.

In 41–43, copy the figure onto your paper and shade about $\frac{1}{4}$ of the figure.

41.

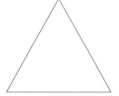

42.

43.

37a. no; Julio does not have enough money to buy everything. Estimate: $2 + $1 + $2 + $1 + $1 + $3 = $11; Julio needs about $11.

37b. Possible answer: cereal, eggs, and an avocado ($4.84); milk, honey, bread, and an avocado ($4.84)

37c. cereal, honey, and an avocado ($4.94)

38. Possible answer:

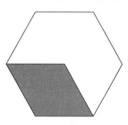

39. Possible answer:

40. Possible answer:

41–43. See left.

41. Possible answer:

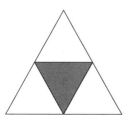

42. Possible answer:

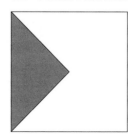

43. Possible answer:

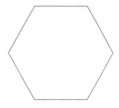

44a. Since $\frac{7}{8} > \frac{1}{2}$ and $\frac{3}{4} > \frac{1}{2}$, the sum of $\frac{7}{8}$ and $\frac{3}{4}$ will be more than 1. Hence, Seth's trip will be more than a mile.

44b. To get to the cave, Seth will have gone about $\frac{7}{8} + \frac{3}{4}$ = about $1\frac{3}{4}$ inches on the map. He will travel another $\frac{3}{4} + \frac{3}{4} = 1\frac{1}{2}$ inches for his side trip to the rock formation. This gives a total of $1\frac{3}{4} + 1\frac{1}{2}$ = about 3 inches, or a little over 3 miles.

44c. Seth has already walked a little over 3 miles to the cave, and he has now walked just over another mile, so he has walked about $4\frac{1}{2}$ miles altogether.

44d. Seth will have walked just over 1 mile from the swimming hole to the cave, and about $1\frac{3}{4}$ miles from the cave to his starting point. If we add this to the $4\frac{1}{2}$ miles he walked on the way there, he has walked about 7 miles altogether.

Extensions

44. Here is a map of the area where Seth is hiking.

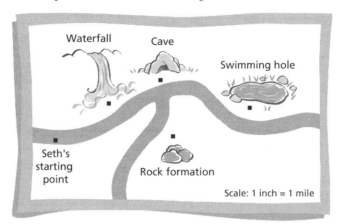

a. The distance from where Seth starts to the waterfall is $\frac{7}{8}$ of an inch. The distance from the waterfall to the mouth of the cave is $\frac{3}{4}$ of an inch. Will Seth's trip to the waterfall and then the cave be shorter or longer than a mile? Explain.

b. When Seth gets to the cave, he decides to take a side trip to see the rock formation. On the map, the rock formation is about 75% of an inch from the cave. After visiting the rock formation, Seth retraces his steps to return to the main trail. When he gets back to the main trail, about how many miles has he hiked since he started his travels?

c. After the side trip, Seth heads for the swimming hole. On the map, this is about $1\frac{1}{4}$ inches from the cave. When he arrives at the swimming hole, about how many miles has he walked altogether?

Tips for the Linguistically Diverse Classroom

Enactment The Enactment technique is described in detail in *Getting to Know Connected Mathematics*. Students act out mini-scenes, using props, to make information comprehensible. Example: Place pictures of a waterfall, a cave, a rock formation, and a swimming hole at various spots in the room. Have a student act out Seth's hike as you read the text aloud.

d. Seth's buddy, who lives on the other side of the swimming hole, meets him for a swim. Late in the day, they retrace Seth's steps to where Seth started. They do not make the side trip to the rock formation. About how many miles has Seth now walked altogether?

In 45–48, tell what percent of the whole rectangle each numbered section represents.

45.

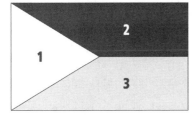

46.

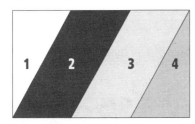

47.

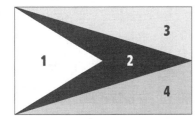

45. Answers will vary but should be close to these: section 1: $16\frac{2}{3}$%; section 2: $33\frac{1}{3}$%; section 3: $33\frac{1}{3}$%; section 4: $16\frac{2}{3}$%.

46. Answers will vary but should be close to these: section 1: 25%; section 2: 25%; section 3: 25%; section 4: 25%.

47. Answers will vary but should be close to these: section 1: 25%; section 2: 37.5%; section 3: 37.5%.

48. Answers will vary but should be close to these: section 1: 25%; section 2: 12.5%; section 3: 37.5%; section 4: 25%.

49a. oxygen, silicon, aluminum, iron, calcium, sodium, potassium, magnesium

49b. Students should use the data for oxygen, silicon, and aluminum to find an answer. Answers will vary depending on how students estimate. Estimates should fall between 0.80 and 0.90. (The exact amount is 0.8245.)

49c. about 82%. Estimates will vary depending on how students estimate.

49d. sodium + potassium + magnesium = 0.0283 + 0.0259 + 0.0209. This is roughly 0.08 (the exact answer is 0.0751), or about 8%.

48.

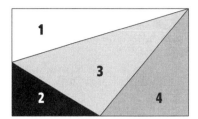

49. The table below lists the abundance of the eight most common elements in the earth's crust.

Element	Portion of earth's crust
Oxygen	0.4660
Iron	0.0500
Silicon	0.2772
Aluminum	0.0813
Sodium	0.0283
Calcium	0.0363
Potassium	0.0259
Magnesium	0.0209

a. Order the elements in the earth's crust from most abundant to least abundant.

b. Estimate how much of the earth's crust is made up of the *three* most abundant elements.

c. About what percent of the crust is made up of these three elements?

d. About what percent of the crust is made up of the three least abundant elements listed in the table?

In 50–54, find a decimal number in the given interval.

50. between $\frac{1}{2}$ and 1

51. between $\frac{1}{3}$ and $\frac{1}{2}$

52. between $\frac{1}{4}$ and $\frac{1}{3}$

53. between $\frac{1}{5}$ and $\frac{1}{4}$

54. between $\frac{1}{6}$ and $\frac{1}{5}$

55. In 50–54, can you find another decimal in each interval? Why or why not?

In 56 and 57, ink has been spilled on the page, concealing part of the fraction strips. Use what is showing to reason about each pair of strips, and find the equivalent fractions indicated by the question marks.

56.

57.

50. Possible answers: 0.75, 0.83, 0.9

51. Possible answers: 0.45, 0.40, 0.43

52. Possible answers: 0.26, 0.28, 0.30

53. Possible answers: 0.205, 0.21, 0.245

54. Possible answers: 0.167, 0.17, 0.185

55. See page 42c.

56. $\frac{12}{20} = \frac{3}{5}$

57. $\frac{2}{4} = \frac{10}{20}$

Possible Answers

1. You can use benchmarks to help estimate sums. You first need to decide which benchmark each number is closest to, then add the two benchmarks to get an estimate of the sum.

2. The smallest possible sum is $\frac{71}{63}$, which is the sum of the two smallest cards in the game between 0.5 and 0.75 (the cards are $\frac{5}{9}$ and $\frac{4}{7}$). The largest possible sum is 1.37, which is the sum of the two largest cards in the game between 0.5 and 0.75 (the cards are $\frac{7}{10}$ and 0.67).

3. $1\frac{3}{4}$, because it is the sum of $\frac{1}{4}$ and $1\frac{1}{2}$.

Mathematical Reflections

In this investigation, you played two games that helped you develop strategies for estimating the sum of two fractions or decimals. These questions will help you summarize what you have learned:

(1) Describe one strategy that you found helpful in estimating sums. Explain why it was helpful to you.

(2) If the two game cards turned up are both between 0.5 and 0.75, what is the smallest the sum could be? What is the largest the sum could be? Explain your reasoning.

(3) If you are estimating the sum of two numbers and one is nearest the benchmark $\frac{1}{4}$ and the other is nearest the benchmark $1\frac{1}{2}$, what estimate would you give? Why?

Think about your answers to these questions, discuss your ideas with other students and your teacher, and then write a summary of your findings in your journal.

TEACHING THE INVESTIGATION

3.1 • Getting Close

In this problem, students play a game based on estimating sums of fractions and decimals. While playing the game, they practice making estimates and explore estimation strategies. The primary objective is for them to use benchmarks for making sense of fractions and decimals as quantities. Decimal and fraction cards are mixed to help students build flexibility in moving between representations.

Launch

Explain to your class that they are going to play a game that involves fractions and decimals, and the use of estimation, addition, and benchmarks. Read the introduction with the class, and discuss the questions in the "Think about this!" box.

> How would you determine whether the first sum is larger or smaller than 2? How would you determine whether the second sum is closest to 0, 1, or 2?

Once students determine that the second sum, $\frac{1}{2} + \frac{5}{8}$, is greater than 1, ask whether it is closer to 1 or $1\frac{1}{2}$. Students may use their understanding of benchmarks to support their answers.

Read through the rules for playing the Getting Close game, and make sure students understand how to play. You might have two students play a couple of rounds to demonstrate. Distribute a set of three number squares (0, 1, and 2) to each student and a set of Getting Close cards to each group. This game works well as a two- to four-person game.

Explore

Have your students play a couple of games. After they have played at least one full game, encourage them to write about the strategies they are using to estimate the sums.

Summarize

Before discussing the strategies students found for estimating sums, you might want to ask questions about other elements of the game.

> Is there an advantage to being the card turner? Is there a disadvantage?

> What kinds of sums were easy to estimate? Did you find it easier if the cards were either both decimals or both fractions? What did you do when one card was a fraction and the other was a decimal?

Conclude the discussion by asking students to share their strategies for estimating sums of fractions and decimals. Here are some strategies students have used:

- Mia rounded the numbers being added to get "nice" numbers she could manipulate mentally. For example, to estimate $\frac{9}{10} + 0.875$, she rounded both numbers to 1 and then estimated the sum as 2. To estimate $0.67 + \frac{4}{7}$, she rounded both numbers to $\frac{1}{2}$ and estimated the sum as 1.

- Katie said that if the numbers are in different forms, she renames one of them so they are both fractions or both decimals. For example, to compute $\frac{1}{4}$ + 1.1, she converted $\frac{1}{4}$ to 0.25 and added the two decimals in her head.

- Robbie says he uses benchmarks. For example, $\frac{1}{10}$ is close to 0, and 1.125 is close to 1, so $\frac{1}{10}$ + 1.125 is close to 0 + 1, or 1.

3.2 • Getting Even Closer

In Getting Even Closer, students must make more precise estimates than they made in the last problem. Again, the objective is for students to develop benchmarks for making sense of fractions and decimals as quantities, and to refine their strategies for estimating sums. In this game, the same set of game cards is used, but now each player needs a set of six number squares: 0, 0.5, 1, 1.5, 2, and 2.5.

Launch

Because this game is so similar to Getting Close, understanding the game should not be a problem. You will want to point out that three number squares have been added and that students will have to make closer estimates. You will probably want to change groups to allow students to listen to and make sense of others' thinking and to further refine their own ideas.

Explore

Allow students to play the new game a couple of times. Tell them that they are to share their strategies after each round. If you hear groups discussing and using new strategies, make a note of them to make sure they are shared in the summary.

Summarize

Ask students to share how they revised their strategies to play this new game.

How is this game easier than the first game? How is it more difficult?

The follow-up questions could be discussed as part of the summary. You might want to ask the following as a final check on your students' understanding of the game:

Suppose a friend from another school drops by to play the Getting Even Closer game. Two cards are turned up. (*Write the following numbers on the board.*)

$\frac{1}{3}$ 0.75

Write an explanation for your friend about how you can quickly estimate whether the sum of the two numbers is closest to 0, 0.5, 1, 1.5, 2, or 2.5.

Additional Answers

ACE Answers

Applications

13. Possible answer: $\frac{3}{4} + \frac{1}{8}$

14. Possible answer: $\frac{3}{4} + \frac{7}{8}$

15. Possible answer: $\frac{3}{4} + \frac{3}{8}$

16. Possible answer: $\frac{5}{4} + \frac{5}{8}$

17. Possible answer: $\frac{5}{4} + \frac{11}{8}$

18. Possible answer: $\frac{5}{4} + \frac{9}{8}$

19. Possible answer: $\frac{7}{4} + \frac{9}{8}$

20. The solution is incorrect. The sum is $\frac{5}{8}$, which is less than $\frac{3}{4}$.

21. The solution is correct. Both fractions equal $\frac{1}{2}$, so their sum is 1, which is greater than $\frac{3}{4}$.

22. The solution is correct. The sum is greater than $\frac{3}{4}$ because $\frac{5}{6}$ is greater than $\frac{3}{4}$.

23. The solution is correct. The sum is $\frac{7}{8}$, which is greater than $\frac{3}{4}$.

Connections

55. yes; Possible explanation: Because there are lots and lots of numbers in each of the intervals.

For the Teacher: The Density Property

There are an infinite number of decimals in each of the intervals. This problem illustrates the *density property* of rational numbers: between any two distinct rational numbers, no matter how close, lies another rational number.

Adding and Subtracting Fractions

The contexts in this investigation help students make sense of how and why addition and subtraction of fractions work. The student edition does not give algorithms for adding and subtracting fractions. Instead, strategies are developed during the class discussions after students have worked on the problems.

In this investigation, it is important to ask questions that encourage your students to develop methods for adding and subtracting. Giving algorithms to students who do not understand the concepts or who have not wrestled with combining or removing quantities is unlikely to have a positive result: students may memorize the rules but have no idea why they work or when they should be applied. Letting students struggle to make sense of situations takes more time than showing them the algorithms, but the payoff in the long run is that they learn to reason about mathematical situations. Students' invented algorithms are often very efficient and, with a teacher's help, can become powerful tools.

In Problem 4.1, Dividing Land, students use the area model of fractions. Students continue their work with fractions in Problem 4.2, Redrawing the Map. Problem 4.3, Pirating Pizza, raises not only the need to add, multiply, and subtract fractions, but lends itself to many ways of modeling computations with fractions. In Problem 4.4, Designing Algorithms, students are asked to reflect and record their strategies for adding and subtracting fractions.

Mathematical and Problem-Solving Goals

- **To develop strategies for adding and subtracting fractions**

- **To understand when addition or subtraction is the appropriate operation**

- **To develop ways of modeling sums and differences**

- **To continue to develop ways to estimate the results of adding or subtracting fractions**

- **To reinforce understanding of equivalence of fractions**

- **To employ pictorial models (for example, showing that $\frac{1}{2}$ of $\frac{1}{2}$ is $\frac{1}{4}$ by drawing an area model)**

- **To search for and to generalize patterns**

- **To use estimation to help make decisions**

	Materials	
Problem	**For students**	**For the teacher**
All	Calculators	Transparencies 4.1 to 4.4 (optional)
4.1	Labsheet 4.1 (1 per student plus extras; you may want to photocopy the blackline master on both sides of each sheet of paper), rulers	Transparency of Labsheet 4.1 (optional)
4.2	Labsheet 4.1 (1 per student), grid paper (provided as a blackline master), colored square tiles (optional)	
4.4	Large sheets of paper or blank transparency film (optional)	

INVESTIGATION 4

Adding and Subtracting Fractions

Knowing how to combine and remove quantities is a skill that is helpful for understanding the world around you. The mathematical names for combining and removing are adding and subtracting. For example, if you owned two lots of land and you bought another half a lot, you could combine the two lots and the half lot to determine that you owned $2 + \frac{1}{2}$, or $2\frac{1}{2}$, lots of land.

The problems in this investigation require you to add and subtract fractions. As you work on these problems, use what you have learned in earlier investigations about finding equivalent fractions and rewriting fractions as decimals.

4.1 Dividing Land

When Tupelo township was founded, the land was divided into sections that could be farmed. Each *section* is a square that is 1 mile long on each edge—that is, each section is 1 square mile of land. There are 640 acres of land in a 1-square-mile section.

The diagram on the next page shows two *adjacent* sections of land, sections 18 and 19. Each section is divided among several owners. The diagram shows the part of the land each person owns.

Problem 4.1

Determine what fraction of a section each person owns. Explain your reasoning.

▓ Problem 4.1 Follow-Up

Determine how many acres of land each person owns. Explain your reasoning.

Answer to Problem 4.1

See page 53g.

Answer to Problem 4.1 Follow-Up

See page 53h.

Grouping:
Pairs

Launch

- Read the story of Tupelo township.

- Lead a discussion about naming fractional parts of a whole. (*optional*)

Explore

- Have students work in pairs to name the fractional amounts each person owns.

- Ask groups that finish early to copy their solutions onto transparencies. (*optional*)

Summarize

- As a class, discuss how groups found the fractions.

- Ask a few groups to demonstrate their strategies at the overhead projector. (*optional*)

Assignment Choices

ACE questions 10–26 and unassigned choices from earlier problems

Redrawing the Map

Grouping:
Small Groups

Launch

- Read through the problem with your class, making sure they understand that their solution must satisfy all the clues.

Explore

- As groups work, remind them to keep track of their work and to organize their results.

- Build a physical model of the situation using square tiles. (*optional*)

Summarize

- As a class, talk about strategies for keeping track of the clues and for adding and subtracting fractions.

Assignment Choices

ACE questions 1, 3, and unassigned choices from earlier problems

Section 18　　　　　　　**Section 19**

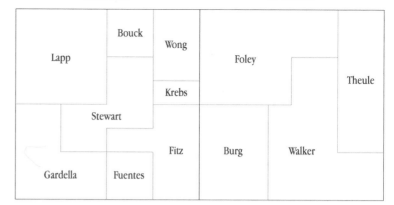

4.2 Redrawing the Map

As time goes by, some people in sections 18 and 19 want to sell their farms, and other people want to buy more land to expand their farms. In the real world, transactions to buy and sell land occur every day.

Problem 4.2

Some of the owners of land in sections 18 and 19 sold their land to other people who already owned land in these sections. The clues below describe the results of several transactions.

Clue 1 When all the sales are completed, four people—Theule, Fuentes, Wong, and Gardella—own all of the land in the two sections.

Clue 2 Theule bought from one person and now owns land equivalent to $\frac{1}{2}$ of one section.

Clue 3 Fuentes bought from three people and now owns the equivalent of $\frac{13}{32}$ of one section.

Clue 4 Gardella now owns the equivalent of $\frac{1}{2}$ of a section.

Clue 5 Wong now owns all of the rest of the land in the two sections.

Clue 6 Each of the four owners can walk around all of their land without having to cross onto another person's land.

A. Use the clues to determine what transactions took place. Determine exactly which pieces of land Theule, Fuentes, Wong, and Gardella bought, and explain how you know you are correct.

B. Draw a new map of the two sections, outlining the land belonging to each of the four owners. Tell how many acres each person now owns.

■ Problem 4.2 Follow-Up

After a few years, Fuentes wants to acquire more land to put in new pastures for his livestock. Gardella sells $\frac{1}{2}$ of a section to Fuentes, Theule sells $\frac{1}{8}$ of a section to Fuentes, and Wong sells $\frac{1}{16}$ of a section to Fuentes. What fraction of a section does each person now own?

Answers to Problem 4.2

See page 53h.

Answer to Problem 4.2 Follow-Up

Gardella owns no land, Theule owns $\frac{3}{8}$ of a section, Wong owns $\frac{17}{32}$ of a section, and Fuentes owns $1\frac{3}{32}$ of a section.

Pirating Pizza

At a Glance

Grouping:
Small Groups

Launch

- Tell the story of the Pizza Pirate.

- Make sure students understand that the Pizza Pirate is eating half of what remained of the pizza each day.

Explore

- As groups of three or four work, remind them to organize the information they discover for each day.

Summarize

- Discuss the solutions groups found and the patterns in their tables and charts.

- Create a model to physically demonstrate the pizza-eating process. (*optional*)

4.3 Pirating Pizza

In this problem, you can use what you have discovered about adding and subtracting fractions to make sense of the havoc that the infamous Pizza Pirate is causing! As you work on the problem, look for patterns that can help you to solve it.

Problem 4.3

Courtney's class made a gigantic square pizza for a class party to be held the day after the final exam. They made it a week before the party so they would have time to study. To keep the pizza fresh, they stored it in the cafeteria freezer.

Unfortunately, the notorious Pizza Pirate was lurking in the area. That night, the Pizza Pirate disguised himself as a janitor, tiptoed into the cafeteria, and gobbled down half of the pizza! On the second night, he ate half of what was left of the pizza. Each night after that, he crept in and ate half of the pizza that remained.

After the final exam, Courtney's class went to get their pizza to start their celebration—and were stunned by what they found!

What fraction of the pizza was left for the party?

To help you answer this question, make a table or chart showing

- the fraction of the pizza the Pizza Pirate ate each day

- the fraction of the pizza he had eaten so far at the end of each day

- the fraction of the pizza that remained at the end of each day

Write a summary of how your group solved this problem. Draw any diagrams that will help you to show your thinking.

Assignment Choices

ACE questions 2, 4, and unassigned choices from earlier problems

Tips for the Linguistically Diverse Classroom

Rebus Scenario The Rebus Scenario technique is described in detail in *Getting to Know Connected Mathematics*. This technique involves sketching rebuses on the chalkboard that correspond to key words in the story or information you present orally. Example: some key words and phrases for which you may need to draw rebuses while discussing the material on this page: *gigantic square pizza* (a square pizza), *Pizza Pirate* (a sketch of the pirate that appears on this page), *night* (the moon with the number 1 written next to it), *janitor* (the same pirate, but with custodian clothes), *second night* (the moon with the number 2 written next to it), *each night after that* (the moon with the numbers 3–7 written next to it), *Courtney's class* (a group of stick figures).

■ **Problem 4.3 Follow-Up**

1. a. Make a graph of the total amount eaten so far by the Pizza Pirate for each of the seven days.

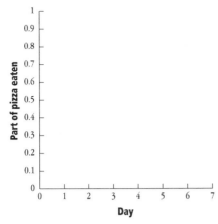

b. Make a graph of how much pizza remains at the end of the day for each of the seven days.

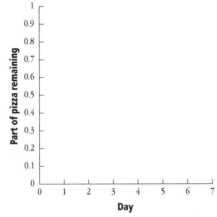

c. How are the graphs you made in parts a and b related?

2. If the students canceled the party and left the pizza in the freezer for a long time, would the Pizza Pirate ever eat all of the pizza?

Investigation 4: Adding and Subtracting Fractions **47**

Answers to Problem 4.3

$\frac{1}{128}$; See the table in the "Summarize" section on page 53e.

Answers to Problem 4.3 Follow-Up

1. a–b. See page 53i.

   c. The graphs of the amount eaten and the amount remaining are reflections of each other.

2. No; The piece of pizza remaining would theoretically get smaller and smaller forever, eventually becoming microscopically small. Realistically, though, the pieces would soon become too small to matter.

Designing Algorithms

Launch

- Discuss the meaning of the word *algorithm*.

- As a class, develop an algorithm for a simple mathematical procedure, such as adding whole numbers.

Explore

- Have students write algorithms individually and then share and revise them in their groups.

- Make large sheets of paper or blank transparency film available for students to share their final versions. (*optional*)

Summarize

- As a class, share and discuss algorithms.

- Talk about whether each algorithm proposed is helpful and how it compares to the other algorithms.

- Develop a master list of all the algorithms presented. (*optional*)

4.4 Designing Algorithms

To become skillful at handling situations that call for the addition and subtraction of fractions, you need a good plan for carrying out your computations. In mathematics, a plan—or a series of steps—for doing a computation is called an **algorithm.** For an algorithm to be useful, each step should be clear and precise so that other people will be able to carry out the steps and get correct answers.

In this problem, you will work with your group to develop algorithms for adding and subtracting fractions. Your group may develop more than one algorithm for each computation. What is important is that each member of your group understands and feels comfortable with at least one algorithm for adding fractions and at least one algorithm for subtracting fractions.

Problem 4.4

Work with your group to develop at least one algorithm for adding fractions and at least one algorithm for subtracting fractions. You might want to look back over the first three problems in this investigation and discuss how each person in your group thought about them. Look for ideas that you think will help you develop algorithms for adding and subtracting fractions that will always work, even with mixed numbers.

Test your algorithms on a few problems, such as these:

$$\frac{5}{8} + \frac{7}{8} \qquad \frac{3}{5} + \frac{5}{3} \qquad 3\frac{3}{4} + 7\frac{2}{9}$$

$$\frac{3}{4} - \frac{1}{8} \qquad 5\frac{4}{6} - 2\frac{1}{3} \qquad \frac{5}{6} - \frac{1}{4}$$

If necessary, make adjustments to your algorithms until you think they will work all the time. Write up a final version of each algorithm. Make sure they are neat and precise so others can follow them.

Problem 4.4 Follow-Up

1. Exchange your addition algorithm with that of another group. Test the other group's plan. Write a paragraph explaining how your algorithm and the other group's algorithm are alike and how they are different.

2. Exchange your subtraction algorithm with that of another group (a different group from the group you exchanged with in part 1). Test the other group's plan. Write a paragraph explaining how your algorithm and the other group's algorithm are alike and how they are different.

Assignment Choices

ACE questions 5–9, 27, and unassigned choices from earlier problems

Assessment

It is appropriate to use Check-Up 2 after this problem.

Answers to Problem 4.4

See page 53i.

Answers to Problem 4.4 Follow-Up

Answers will vary.

As you work on these ACE questions, use your calculator whenever you need it.

Applications

1. A local magazine sells advertising space. It charges advertisers according to the fraction of a page their ad will fill.

a. For page 20 in the magazine, advertisers have purchased $\frac{1}{8}$ of the page and $\frac{1}{16}$ of the page. What fraction of the page will be used for ads? What fraction of the page will remain for other uses? Explain your reasoning.

b. The Cool Sub Shop is having its grand opening and has purchased several ads. They buy three $\frac{1}{4}$-page ads, four $\frac{1}{8}$-page ads, and ten $\frac{1}{16}$-page ads. What is the total amount of space that they have bought? Explain your reasoning.

c. The magazine wants to make $160 for each page of advertising sold. What might the magazine charge for each size ad if ads can be any of the following sizes: $\frac{1}{32}, \frac{1}{16}, \frac{1}{8}, \frac{1}{4}, \frac{1}{2}$, or a whole page? Explain your reasoning.

d. Using the pricing scheme you developed in part c, what would the bill for the Cool Sub Shop be for the ads they purchased in part b? Explain your reasoning.

e. For an upcoming issue, a local promoter has purchased a total of $2\frac{3}{4}$ pages of ads to promote two concerts. Now, one of the concerts must be canceled because the lead guitarist broke her finger. The promoter calls to cancel $1\frac{5}{8}$ pages of ads for that concert. How much advertising space does the promoter want to keep? Explain your reasoning.

f. The senior class is having a fund-raiser to help raise money for their senior trip. They have $80 dollars to spend on advertising. Geraldo says they can purchase two $\frac{1}{8}$-page ads and four $\frac{1}{16}$-page ads for their money. According to your answer to part c, is he correct? Explain your reasoning.

g. Give four different sets of ad sizes that the senior class could purchase with their $80 (using your pricing scheme from part c). Show why your answers work.

Answers

Applications

1a. $\frac{1}{8} + \frac{1}{16} = \frac{3}{16}$ of the page will be used for ads. $1 - \frac{3}{16} = \frac{13}{16}$ of the page will remain.

1b. $3 \times \frac{1}{4} + 4 \times \frac{1}{8} + 10 \times \frac{1}{16} = \frac{3}{4} + \frac{1}{2} + \frac{5}{8} = \frac{15}{8} = 1\frac{7}{8}$ pages

1c. The magazine could charge $160 \times \frac{1}{32} = \$5$ for $\frac{1}{32}$ of a page, $160 \times \frac{1}{16} = \$10$ for $\frac{1}{16}$ of a page, $160 \times \frac{1}{8} = \$20$ for $\frac{1}{8}$ of a page, $160 \times \frac{1}{4} = \$40$ for $\frac{1}{4}$ of a page, $160 \times \frac{1}{2} = \$80$ for $\frac{1}{2}$ of a page, and $160 for a whole page.

1d. $3 \times \$40 + 4 \times \$20 + 10 \times \$10 = \$300$

1e. $2\frac{3}{4} - 1\frac{5}{8} = 1\frac{1}{8}$ pages

1f. yes; $2 \times \$20 + 4 \times \$10 = \$80$

1g. Possible answers: two $\frac{1}{4}$-page ads ($2 \times \$40 = \$80$); four $\frac{1}{8}$-page ads ($4 \times \$20 = \$80$); eight $\frac{1}{16}$-page ads ($8 \times \$10 = \$80$); sixteen $\frac{1}{32}$-page ads ($16 \times \$5 = \$80$); one $\frac{1}{4}$-page ad and two $\frac{1}{8}$-page ads ($1 \times \$40 + 2 \times \$20 = \$80$); two $\frac{1}{8}$-page ads and four $\frac{1}{16}$-page ads ($2 \times \$20 + 4 \times \$10 = \$80$)

2. $1 - \frac{1}{16} - \frac{1}{32} = \frac{29}{32}$ of the cake

3. $\frac{3}{4} + \frac{1}{8} = \frac{7}{8}$ of a pizza

4. $27\frac{3}{4} - 26\frac{1}{8} = 1\frac{5}{8}$

5. On Tuesday, the stock went up $2\frac{1}{8} - 1\frac{15}{16} = \frac{3}{16}$. On Wednesday, it went up $2\frac{3}{8} - 2\frac{1}{8} = \frac{1}{4}$. On Thursday, it dropped $2\frac{3}{8} - 2\frac{3}{16} = \frac{3}{16}$. On Friday, it went up $2\frac{1}{4} - 2\frac{3}{16} = \frac{1}{16}$.

6. $\frac{2}{3} + \frac{5}{6} = \frac{4}{6} + \frac{5}{6} = \frac{9}{6} = 1\frac{1}{2}$ $= 1\frac{10}{20}$ and $\frac{3}{4} + \frac{4}{5} = \frac{15}{20} + \frac{16}{20} = 1\frac{11}{20}$. $\frac{3}{4} + \frac{4}{5}$ is larger.

7. $\frac{7}{6} - \frac{2}{3} = \frac{7}{6} - \frac{4}{6} = \frac{1}{2} = \frac{5}{10}$ and $\frac{3}{5} - \frac{5}{10} = \frac{6}{10} - \frac{5}{10} = \frac{1}{10}$. $\frac{7}{6} - \frac{2}{3}$ is larger.

8. $\frac{1}{4} + \frac{5}{6} = \frac{3}{12} + \frac{10}{12} = 1\frac{1}{12} = 1\frac{10}{120}$ and $\frac{1}{5} + \frac{7}{8} = \frac{8}{40} + \frac{35}{40} = 1\frac{3}{40} = 1\frac{9}{120}$. $\frac{1}{4} + \frac{5}{6}$ is larger.

9. $\frac{1}{16} + \frac{1}{12} = \frac{3}{48} + \frac{4}{48} = \frac{7}{48} = \frac{35}{240}$ and $\frac{5}{4} - \frac{4}{5} = \frac{25}{20} - \frac{16}{20} = \frac{9}{20} = \frac{108}{240}$. $\frac{5}{4} - \frac{4}{5}$ is larger.

Connections

10. $\frac{3}{12} = \frac{2}{8}$

11. $\frac{3}{4} = \frac{6}{8}$

12. $\frac{1}{2} = \frac{6}{12}$

13. $\frac{8}{12} = \frac{2}{3}$

14. $\frac{7}{8} = \frac{14}{16}$

15. $\frac{5}{12} = \frac{10}{24}$

---

2. The Pizza Pirate and a friend broke into the school cafeteria and ate part of the huge sheet cake that was being stored for a party. The Pizza Pirate ate $\frac{1}{16}$ of the cake, and the accomplice ate $\frac{1}{32}$ of the cake. How much cake was left?

3. If you eat $\frac{3}{4}$ of a pizza and then eat $\frac{1}{8}$ of another pizza of the same size, how much of a whole pizza have you eaten altogether?

4. On the stock market report yesterday, the price of a stock that Ms. Jennings is watching was $27\frac{3}{4}$ dollars. Today the stock is reported at $26\frac{1}{8}$ dollars. How much did the stock price decline?

5. Ms. Jennings is watching another stock. These are the prices reported for a week in March: $1\frac{15}{16}$ on Monday, $2\frac{1}{8}$ on Tuesday, $2\frac{3}{8}$ on Wednesday, $2\frac{3}{16}$ on Thursday, and $2\frac{1}{4}$ on Friday. For each day of the week, beginning with Tuesday, how much did the stock go up or down?

In 6–9, tell which sum or difference is larger. Show your work.

6. $\frac{2}{3} + \frac{5}{6}$ or $\frac{3}{4} + \frac{4}{5}$

7. $\frac{7}{6} - \frac{2}{3}$ or $\frac{3}{5} - \frac{5}{10}$

8. $\frac{1}{4} + \frac{5}{6}$ or $\frac{1}{5} + \frac{7}{8}$

9. $\frac{1}{16} + \frac{1}{12}$ or $\frac{5}{4} - \frac{4}{5}$

Connections

In 10–15, replace the question mark with a number that will make the sentence true.

10. $\frac{3}{12} = \frac{?}{8}$

11. $\frac{?}{4} = \frac{6}{8}$

12. $\frac{1}{2} = \frac{?}{12}$

13. $\frac{?}{12} = \frac{2}{3}$

14. $\frac{?}{8} = \frac{14}{16}$

15. $\frac{5}{12} = \frac{10}{?}$

In 16–18, ink has spilled on the page, obscuring part of the fraction strips. Use what is showing to reason about each set of strips and to find the equivalent fractions indicated by the question marks.

16.

17.

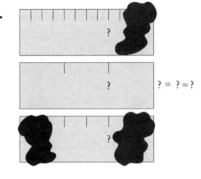

18.

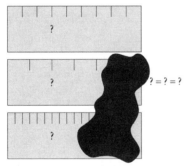

16. $\frac{2}{6} = \frac{4}{12}$

17. $\frac{8}{12} = \frac{2}{3} = \frac{4}{6}$

18. $\frac{3}{9} = \frac{2}{6} = \frac{6}{18}$

19. $18.156 < 18.17$

20. $3.184 < 31.84$

21. $5.78329 > 5.78239$

22. $4.0074 > 4.0008$

23. 0.6

24. 1.5

25. 0.625

26. 0.9375

Extensions

27a. Possible answer:
$\frac{1}{2} - \frac{1}{3} = \frac{1}{6}$

27b. Possible answer:
$\frac{1}{4} - \frac{1}{5} = \frac{1}{20}$. (**Teaching Tip:** To follow up on 27b, you can point out that for any whole number x the following is true:

$$\frac{1}{x} - \frac{1}{x+1} = \frac{1}{x(x+1)}$$

This can be seen by finding a common denominator and subtracting on the left side. So, $\frac{1}{2} - \frac{1}{3} = \frac{1}{6}$, $\frac{1}{3} - \frac{1}{4} = \frac{1}{12}$, and so on. Each of these can be made into an additional statement: $\frac{1}{6} + \frac{1}{3} = \frac{1}{2}$, and so on.)

In 19–22, insert $<$, $=$, or $>$ to make a true statement.

19. 18.156 _____ 18.17 **20.** 3.184 _____ 31.84

21. 5.78329 _____ 5.78239 **22.** 4.0074 _____ 4.0008

In 23–26, express the fraction as a decimal.

23. $\frac{3}{5}$ **24.** $\frac{18}{12}$

25. $\frac{5}{8}$ **26.** $\frac{15}{16}$

Extensions

27. **a.** Find three numbers for the denominators to make the sentence true.

$$\frac{1}{?} - \frac{1}{?} = \frac{1}{?}$$

b. Can you find another set of numbers that works?

Mathematical Reflections

In this investigation, you explored ways to add and subtract fractions. These questions will help you summarize what you have learned:

1 Describe how you can add or subtract two fractions that have the same denominator. Explain why your method makes sense.

2 Describe and illustrate with an example your algorithm for adding two fractions that have different denominators. Do the same for your algorithm for subtracting two fractions with different denominators.

3 Describe how you can use what you know about adding and subtracting fractions to add or subtract mixed numbers.

Think about your answers to these questions, discuss your ideas with other students and your teacher, and then write a summary of your findings in your journal.

Possible Answers

1. To add two fractions with the same denominator, add the numerators; the denominator remains the same. The denominator tells the number of pieces the same size that make up the whole. So, if the denominators of two fractions are the same, the pieces are the same size. So, if you are adding you add only the numerators because the numerator tells you the number of pieces you have.

To subtract two fractions with the same denominator, subtract the numerators and keep the same denominator. Because the pieces are the same size (the denominators are the same), you only have to subtract the numerators, which tell the number of pieces you have.

2. To add two fractions with unlike denominators, first rename them so they have the same denominator. To do this, find a common multiple of the two denominators, and then change each fraction into an equivalent fraction with this common multiple as the denominator. Then, just add the numerators. For example: $\frac{5}{8} + \frac{2}{3} = \frac{15}{24} + \frac{16}{24} = \frac{31}{24}$.

To subtract two fractions with unlike denominators, rename them so they have the same denominator, and then just subtract the numerators. For example: $\frac{1}{2} - \frac{1}{3} = \frac{3}{6} - \frac{2}{6} = \frac{1}{6}$.

3. See page 53i.

TEACHING THE INVESTIGATION

4.1 • Dividing Land

In this problem, students write fractions to represent portions of a section of land.

Launch

To launch the problem, either read the problem with your students and then allow them to begin work, or have a discussion about naming fractional parts of a whole. If you choose to have a discussion, start by posing a few questions:

> How many sections of land are being discussed in this problem? Does anyone own a whole section?
>
> Who owns the largest piece of a section?
>
> About how much land does Foley own?
>
> What makes it hard to think about naming the part of a section that each person owns? What might we do to make naming the parts easier?

This should generate a conversation that leads to dividing a section into equal-size pieces so that the fraction each person owns can be easily named. If no one suggests this, find a way to propose the idea while students are working.

Explore

Have students work in pairs. Each student will need a copy of Labsheet 4.1. Students may want to use a ruler to divide the sections into equal parts. (Have extra copies of Labsheet 4.1 on hand for students who go too far in the wrong direction. You may want to plan for this by copying the map on both sides of the paper.)

If some groups finish early, you might have them copy their solution onto a transparency of Labsheet 4.1 to share with the class during the summary.

Summarize

Start the summary by asking students to discuss how they found the fractional parts for each person's land. Groups that transferred their work onto a transparency could show their work and discuss their strategy.

The most common strategy is to divide each section into 64ths:

Section 18   **Section 19**

When asked how she decided to divide each section into 64ths, one student said the following:

I didn't know it had to be 64ths when I started. I took the property lines and extended them until they reached the section borders. I did this for each property line. Then, I looked to see where else I needed to add lines to make each piece in the section the same size. When I was done, the pieces were all the same size, and then I could just count how many of the pieces each person had out of the 64 pieces that made a whole section.

The student explained that she drew in the new lines with a different color so she could clearly see the original property lines.

To conclude the summary, you could discuss the follow-up question as a class.

4.2 • Redrawing the Map

The setting of this problem is the buying and selling of land. Students work with a list of clues to deduce which plots of land were sold to whom; each clue reduces the number of possibilities. Students employ mathematical reasoning skills as they solve the mystery of who owns what.

Launch

Each student will need another copy of Labsheet 4.1. Because this is a continuation of Problem 4.1, the summary of that problem could serve to launch this one. Read through Problem 4.2 with your class, making sure they understand that their final solution must take into account the information in each clue. For example, clue 2 says that Theule bought from one person and now owns land equivalent to $\frac{1}{2}$ of one section. If we consider this clue in isolation, we could reason that Theule bought from either Foley or Walker. As we work with the remaining clues, however, we find that one of these solutions is eliminated.

If your class is having trouble getting started, you may want to discuss the possible solutions for Theule based on the second clue, and have students explain why they know Foley and Walker are both possible at this point. This will allow for some discussion about adding fractions. Students may suggest using their segmented maps from Problem 4.1 and counting the small, equal-size pieces to get $\frac{32}{64}$. Don't go too far with the discussion, however; you don't want to take away the problem-solving experience this problem offers.

Explore

Groups of three or four work well for this problem. Remind groups to keep track of their work along the way, as they will be asked to explain to the class how they arrived at their solution. Encourage them to find sensible ways to organize their results.

If students are struggling, you might use colored square tiles to construct a physical representation of the beginning configuration of land, using a different color for each owner. Use the fractions from Problem 4.1 to build the model.

Summarize

The reasoning this problem requires is as important as the computations. The summary should include an exploration of the strategies students used to keep track of the set of possibilities and to add and subtract fractions. The class discussion gives you another chance to help students focus on the power of equivalent representations of fractions and on the area model for fractions. The following exchange took place in one classroom:

Teacher I need one group to start the conversation about Problem 4.2 by explaining what transactions they think took place and why they think they are correct.

Anne We had more than one possible answer for some of the transactions until we read all the clues, and then we ended up with this answer:

(Other members of Anne's group displayed their work on a large sheet of paper at the front of the classroom.)

> Theule bought Walker's land: $\frac{3}{16} + \frac{5}{16} = \frac{8}{16} = \frac{1}{2}$
>
> Fuentes bought Stewart's, Krebs', and Fitz's land: $\frac{2}{32} + \frac{5}{32} + \frac{1}{32} + \frac{5}{32} = \frac{13}{32}$
>
> Gardella bought Lapp's and Bouck's land: $\frac{3}{16} + \frac{4}{16} + \frac{1}{16} = \frac{8}{16} = \frac{1}{2}$
>
> Wong bought Foley's and Burg's land: $\frac{3}{32} + \frac{10}{32} + \frac{6}{32} = \frac{19}{32}$

We think we are right because we have accounted for all the land. We have shown that each person has the amount they are supposed to have, which for Theule and Gardella was $\frac{1}{2}$ a section each and for Fuentes was $\frac{13}{32}$ of a section. We checked our work by thinking about how Theule and Gardella each own $\frac{1}{2}$ a section, and $\frac{1}{2} + \frac{1}{2}$ is a whole section. And if you add Fuentes' and Wong's land, you have $\frac{13}{32} + \frac{19}{32}$ and that equals $\frac{32}{32}$, which is a whole section. So, our group has accounted for all the land in the two sections.

Here is our map that shows how the land is now owned. You can see that each owner can walk around all the land they own and not cross onto another person's property.

Teacher Where did you get the fractions that you wrote for each person's land purchases?

Anne We got those from our answers to Problem 4.1. On our sheets we had that Theule owns $\frac{12}{64}$ of a section, which is the same as $\frac{3}{16}$. And Walker owned $\frac{20}{64}$, which is $\frac{5}{16}$.

Teacher How do you know that $\frac{12}{64}$ equals $\frac{3}{16}$ and that $\frac{20}{64}$ equals $\frac{5}{16}$?

Anne Because we know that if you multiply or divide the numerator and denominator by the same number you get an equivalent fraction. For these fractions, we divided the numerators and denominators by 4 to get the equivalent fractions.

Teacher Why did you rename the fractions as 16ths and not leave them as 64ths?

Anne We had done it on our map and thought it was easier to work with fractions with denominators of 16ths.

Teacher How do you know that $\frac{3}{16}$ and $\frac{5}{16}$ gives you $\frac{8}{16}$, which you say is $\frac{1}{2}$?

Anne Well, the denominators tell us the size of the pieces, and because the denominators are the same we know that for these two fractions the size of the pieces are the same. But we have different amounts of pieces—because the numerators are different, and it is the numerators that tell us how many pieces we have. So, we thought that if we had 3 pieces that were each a 16th and 5 pieces that were each a 16th, we would have a total of 8 pieces—each of which is a 16th—and $\frac{8}{16}$ is the same as $\frac{1}{2}$.

Teacher When I look at the other purchases, I see that you have given fractional names for each person's property and that those names always have the same denominators. Why did you do that?

Anne So we could add the amounts. Like before, we need the pieces to be the same size so that we can tell how many there are altogether.

After a group has presented its strategy, ask the class these questions:

What do others think about this group's strategy? Does it seem reasonable? Did anyone else use this strategy?

Did anyone have a different answer or use a different strategy?

You can conclude the summary by discussing the follow-up question.

4.3 • Pirating Pizza

This is a fanciful problem that is rich in mathematical ideas. The engaging context will give students a better chance of persevering in a fairly demanding mathematical situation. Meeting the infinite process is a bonus for students' growing maturity in mathematical thinking.

Launch

To engage students in this problem, tell the story of the Pizza Pirate. Make sure they understand that the Pizza Pirate is eating half of the pizza that remains each day and that they need to develop a table or chart to show what is happening each day.

Explore

This problem works well for groups of three or four. In preparing the written summary, groups should include all the strategies that members of the group used to make sense of the computations needed to solve the problem.

As groups are working, you may need to suggest that they create diagrams to guide their thinking. It is important that the model they use makes sense to them. You may need to remind them to organize their information as they find the amount eaten for each day, the total amount eaten so far, and how much pizza remains at the end of each day. Discovering patterns in the amounts found for the first several days can show them a way to compute solutions for large numbers of days and, ideally, to generalize the solution to any number of days.

Summarize

This problem is so abundant in mathematical possibilities that you will want to take sufficient time to discuss the solutions students find, as well as the patterns that can be seen in their tables and charts.

A group's work might be organized as shown here.

Day	Amount eaten	Total amount eaten	Amount remaining
1	$\frac{1}{2}$ of $1 = \frac{1}{2}$	$\frac{1}{2}$	$1 - \frac{1}{2} = \frac{1}{2}$
2	$\frac{1}{2}$ of $\frac{1}{2} = \frac{1}{4}$	$\frac{3}{4}$	$\frac{1}{2} - \frac{1}{4} = \frac{1}{4}$
3	$\frac{1}{2}$ of $\frac{1}{4} = \frac{1}{8}$	$\frac{7}{8}$	$\frac{1}{4} - \frac{1}{8} = \frac{1}{8}$
4	$\frac{1}{2}$ of $\frac{1}{8} = \frac{1}{16}$	$\frac{15}{16}$	$\frac{1}{8} - \frac{1}{16} = \frac{1}{16}$
5	$\frac{1}{2}$ of $\frac{1}{16} = \frac{1}{32}$	$\frac{31}{32}$	$\frac{1}{16} - \frac{1}{32} = \frac{1}{32}$
6	$\frac{1}{2}$ of $\frac{1}{32} = \frac{1}{64}$	$\frac{63}{64}$	$\frac{1}{32} - \frac{1}{64} = \frac{1}{64}$
7	$\frac{1}{2}$ of $\frac{1}{64} = \frac{1}{128}$	$\frac{127}{128}$	$\frac{1}{64} - \frac{1}{128} = \frac{1}{128}$

Groups will likely be able to calculate the solutions for the first several days. The patterns in the table will be helpful in predicting what the amounts will be for large numbers of days. Students might notice that the amount eaten each day is a sequence of unit fractions with each denominator twice as large as the one before.

Can anyone offer an explanation of why this pattern makes sense?

This is an opportunity to focus attention once again on what the denominator means: the number of equal-size pieces into which the whole (or the unit) has been separated. When the Pizza Pirate takes half of what is left, he is really dividing the remaining piece into two equal parts. If the original pizza had been divided into parts of this size, there would be twice as many parts as before, and the new pieces would be half as large.

A pattern in the "Total Amount Eaten" column is that each fraction has a denominator 1 greater than the numerator. In addition, the denominators are powers of 2. This makes sense, because the Pizza Pirate always leaves one piece of the new-size pieces on the plate—meaning the amount eaten so far is all but one of the new-size pieces.

There are several ways to physically represent this problem. One fun and meaningful way is to model the pizza with a square of paper. Fold the paper in half, and cut it to show what is left and what has been eaten. The piece representing what remains can then be folded and cut in half to show the next night's pizza. Now we have two pieces in the "eaten" pile and one smaller piece left. As you continue with the demonstration, make sure the relationship between the pieces in the model and the mathematical symbols is clear. The pieces in the "eaten" pile can be reassembled at each stage to model the amount of the pizza eaten so far.

For the Teacher: Zeno's Paradox

Follow-up question 2, which raises an example of Zeno's paradox, is an opportunity for students to think about an infinite process in an informal way. It is not expected that students will understand the idea of the limit of an infinite sequence, but the discussion of a process that gets as close as you wish to the goal without ever reaching the goal is mathematically helpful and interesting for students.

Another way to model Zeno's paradox is to draw a diagram to show each stage. Using a number-line model, the problem can be posed as a bunny on a number line, hopping from 0 to 1. The bunny hops half the distance that remains each day. In this version, we would ask whether the bunny ever reaches 1.

4.4 • Designing Algorithms

In this problem, students write algorithms for adding and subtracting fractions. Students who are familiar with computers may know the word *algorithm*. Computers in many businesses work the same kind of problem over and over—as in computing the monthly electric bills for a city. The numbers in each situation may be different, but the process, or algorithm, is the same.

Launch

Talk with your class about what an *algorithm* is in mathematics.

> Can someone state the algorithm they use for adding and subtracting whole numbers? Can someone state the algorithm they use for changing fractions to decimals and decimals to fractions?

Recording what students say and revising the written algorithm until the class agrees that what is written makes sense will help students to understand what is necessary for a complete description.

Read the problem with your class, and make sure everyone understands what their group is to do.

Explore

This problem works well with groups of two to four. You may want to ask students to first talk about their strategies in their group and then work individually to write their algorithms. They can then share their drafts, and group members may make suggestions as to how each algorithm can be improved. All students should write at least two drafts of their algorithm; having only one person in the group write will not help the other students develop their mathematical reasoning and communication skills. You may want to have large sheets of paper or sheets of blank transparency film available for groups to share the final written versions of their algorithms.

Summarize

Each student is expected to have developed at least one algorithm for adding fractions and one algorithm for subtracting fractions. Many students will describe the traditional algorithm of writing the fractions with common denominators and then adding (or subtracting) the numerators. Some students may have strategies that are not the traditional algorithm but are also effective. Make sure all students have an opportunity to present their ideas for discussion and that their ideas are given the same consideration that any other algorithm is given.

If groups have put their final work on large sheets of paper or transparencies, these can be shared for discussion with the class. You may want to develop a master list of the algorithms that are presented. Evaluating whether each algorithm is usable and helpful, and how it compares with other algorithms will further students' understanding of adding and subtracting fractions.

After the class discussion, you might ask students to take their algorithms home to show their families to see whether they can understand what the student has written and why the strategy makes sense.

Additional Answers

Answer to Problem 4.1

For section 18: Lapp: $\frac{16}{64} = \frac{1}{4}$; Bouck: $\frac{4}{64} = \frac{1}{16}$; Wong: $\frac{6}{64} = \frac{3}{32}$; Stewart: $\frac{10}{64} = \frac{5}{32}$; Krebs: $\frac{2}{64} = \frac{1}{32}$; Fitz: $\frac{10}{64} = \frac{5}{32}$; Gardella: $\frac{12}{64} = \frac{3}{16}$; Fuentes: $\frac{4}{64} = \frac{1}{16}$; Possible explanation: Section 18 can be divided into four quarters so that Lapp has one quarter, so Lapp has $\frac{1}{4}$ of a section. Extending each of the dotted lines for Lapp's land shows that Gardella has one of the four quarters minus a fourth of the quarter (which is $\frac{1}{16}$ of the section), so Gardella has $\frac{1}{4} - \frac{1}{16} = \frac{3}{16}$ of a section. Fuentes' land and Bouck's land are both the same size as the piece Gardella is missing, so Fuentes and Bouck have $\frac{1}{16}$ of a section. Krebs' land is half the size of Bouck's, so Krebs has $\frac{1}{32}$ of a section. Wong's land is the size of Bouck's and Krebs' combined, so Wong has $\frac{3}{32}$ of a section. Fitz's land is the size of Wong's plus two of Krebs', so Fitz has $\frac{5}{32}$ of a section. Stewart's land is the size of two of Bouck's plus one of Kreb's, or $\frac{5}{32}$ of a section.

For section 19: Foley: $\frac{20}{64} = \frac{5}{16}$; Theule: $\frac{12}{64} = \frac{3}{16}$; Burg: $\frac{12}{64} = \frac{3}{16}$; Walker: $\frac{20}{64} = \frac{5}{16}$; Possible explanation: The dotted lines can be extended until they touch the borders of the section. Theule's land is the size of three of Bouck's, so Theule has $\frac{3}{16}$ of a section. Foley's land is the size of Lapp's and Bouck's together, so Foley has $\frac{5}{16}$ of a section. Burg's land is the size of six of Krebs', so Burg has $\frac{3}{16}$ of a section. Walker has the same area as Burg plus two of Bouck's, so Walker has $\frac{5}{16}$ of a section.

Answer to Problem 4.1 Follow-Up

Lapp: 160 acres; Bouck: 40 acres; Wong: 60 acres; Stewart: 100 acres; Krebs: 20 acres; Fitz: 100 acres; Gardella: 120 acres; Fuentes: 40 acres; Foley: 200 acres; Theule: 120 acres; Burg: 120 acres; Walker: 200 acres

---

For the Teacher: Calculating Problem 4.1 Follow-Up

Most students will not use the traditional multiplication algorithm for the follow-up. Instead, if they write all the land segments as fractions with denominators of 64, they can take $640 \div 64 = 10$ and multiply the numerator (which is how many 64ths that piece of land is) by 10 to obtain the number of acres.

Answers to Problem 4.2

A. Theule bought Walker's land: $\frac{3}{16} + \frac{5}{16} = \frac{8}{16} = \frac{1}{2}$
Fuentes bought Stewart's, Krebs', and Fitz's land: $\frac{2}{32} + \frac{5}{32} + \frac{1}{32} + \frac{5}{32} = \frac{13}{32}$
Gardella bought Lapp's and Bouck's land: $\frac{3}{16} + \frac{4}{16} + \frac{1}{16} = \frac{8}{16} = \frac{1}{2}$
Wong bought Foley's and Burg's land: $\frac{3}{32} + \frac{10}{32} + \frac{6}{32} = \frac{19}{32}$

Possible explanation: Clue 2 indicates that Theule bought $\frac{5}{16}$ to add to her $\frac{3}{16}$. She could have bought Foley's or Walker's land. Fuentes originally owned $\frac{2}{32}$ of a section. Clue 3 indicates that he now owns $\frac{13}{32}$, so he could have bought from Lapp, Bouck, and Krebs ($\frac{8}{32} + \frac{2}{32} + \frac{1}{32} = \frac{11}{32}$) or Stewart, Fitz, and Krebs ($\frac{5}{32} + \frac{5}{32} + \frac{1}{32} = \frac{11}{32}$). Clue 6 lets us rule out the first possibility, so Fuentes must have bought from Stewart, Fitz, and Krebs. Gardella started with $\frac{3}{16}$ of a section. According to clue 4, he now owns $\frac{1}{2}$ a section, so he bought $\frac{5}{16}$ of a section. He must have bought $\frac{4}{16}$ from Lapp and $\frac{1}{16}$ from Bouck (the other possibility—$\frac{5}{32}$ from Stewart and $\frac{5}{32}$ from Fitz—can be eliminated because Fuentes already bought this land). Clue 5 tells us that Wong bought the remaining land. This would be Burg's land and either Foley's or Walker's land. Clue 6 eliminates Walker's land, so Wong bought land from Foley and Burg. Returning to Clue 2, we now know that Theule must have bought Walker's land.

B.

$\frac{3}{16} + \frac{1}{4} + \frac{3}{16} = \frac{1}{2}$	$\frac{3}{32} + \frac{5}{16} + \frac{3}{16} = \frac{19}{32}$	
Gardella	Wong	
	$\frac{1}{16} + \frac{5}{32} + \frac{1}{32} + \frac{5}{32} = \frac{13}{32}$	$\frac{3}{16} + \frac{5}{16} = \frac{1}{2}$
	Fuentes	Theule
320 acres *260 acres*	*380 acres*	*320 acres*

Answers to Problem 4.3 Follow-Up

1.   Parts a and b are shown on the graph below.

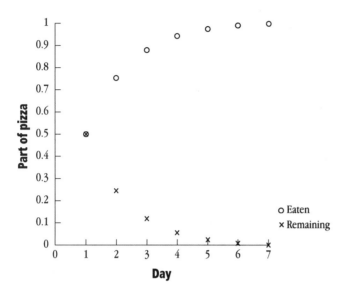

Answers to Problem 4.4

Possible answer (from a student's work):

For adding fractions: If the fractions have the same denominator, add their numerators and keep the same denominator. For example: $\frac{1}{6} + \frac{4}{6} = \frac{5}{6}$. If the fractions have different denominators, find a common multiple of the two denominators, then find an equivalent fraction for each fraction with a denominator that is the common multiple. Once you have equivalent fractions with like denominators, use the algorithm that helps you add two fractions with the same denominator. For example: $\frac{4}{5} + \frac{3}{7} = \frac{28}{35} + \frac{15}{35} = \frac{43}{35} = 1\frac{8}{35}$.

For subtracting fractions: If the fractions have the same denominator, subtract their numerators and keep the same denominator. For example: $\frac{4}{6} - \frac{1}{6} = \frac{3}{6}$. If the fractions have different denominators, find a common multiple of the two denominators, then find an equivalent fraction for each fraction with a denominator that is the common multiple. Once you have equivalent fractions with like denominators, use the algorithm that helps you subtract two fractions with the same denominator. For example: $\frac{4}{5} - \frac{3}{7} = \frac{28}{35} - \frac{15}{35} = \frac{13}{35}$.

Mathematical Reflections

Possible answer (from a student's work):

3. To add or subtract mixed numbers, add or subtract the whole numbers and then add or subtract the fractions. If the fractions have the same denominator, just add or subtract the numerators. If the fractions have different denominators, first rename the fractions to equivalent fractions with the same denominator. Mixed numbers can be more complicated, though, because if you are adding and the sum of the fractions is an improper fraction, you really should rename the mixed number so that it is a whole number and a proper fraction and not a whole number and an improper fraction. If you are subtracting mixed numbers and the fraction you are subtracting is larger than the fraction you are subtracting from, you will need to borrow from the whole number.

Finding Areas and Other Products

This investigation poses problems that require multiplying fractions and decimals. Your students may not yet have developed ways of making sense of multiplication of fractions. This investigation will introduce them to the area model as a way to represent finding a fraction of a fraction. Square baking pans offer a natural context for introducing students to an area model for fraction multiplication. The goal at the beginning of the investigation is not proficiency with algorithms for computation; it is for students to develop ways to estimate and to model computation with understanding. Some students will observe that one simply has to multiply numerators and denominators to obtain the product of two fractions. Encourage these students to try to develop an explanation for why this technique works. Using area models to represent the problems should help them figure out why this works.

In Problem 5.1, Selling Brownies, students find fractional parts of fractions of pans of brownies, and then calculate the cost of part of a pan based on the cost of a whole pan. In Problem 5.2, Discounting Brownies, students deal with mixed numbers and with a reduced price. In Problem 5.3, Buying the Biggest Lot, students must multiply fractions to find which of two rectangular plots has the largest area. In Problem 5.4, Designing a Multiplication Algorithm, students draw from their experiences in this investigation to develop an algorithm for multiplying fractions.

Mathematical and Problem-Solving Goals

- **To develop an understanding of multiplication of fractions**

- **To use an area model to represent the product of two fractions**

- **To find a fraction of a whole number**

- **To explore the relationship between two numbers and their product**

- **To use estimation as a way to make sense of products**

- **To draw pictures to represent problem situations**

- **To search for and to generalize patterns**

- **To use a problem's context to help reason about the answer**

	Materials	
Problem	**For students**	**For the teacher**
All	Calculators, large sheets of paper or sheets of blank transparency film (optional)	Transparencies 5.1 to 5.4 (optional)
5.1	Sheets of squares (provided as a blackline master)	
5.2	Sheets of squares (provided as a blackline master)	

5.1

Selling Brownies

At a Glance

Grouping:
Small Groups

Launch

- Pose the question of what it means to find a fraction of a fraction.

- Read the problem to the class.

Explore

- Have students, in groups of two or three, investigate the brownie problems.

- As you circulate, continue to question students about what finding a fraction of a fraction means.

Summarize

- As a class, discuss solutions and strategies.

- Make sure students understand the area model presented in the follow-up.

Assignment Choices

ACE questions 11–17 and unassigned choices from earlier problems

Finding Areas and Other Products

Sometimes rather than adding or subtracting fractions, you need to multiply them. For example, suppose you are taking inventory at the sporting goods store where you work. There are $13\frac{1}{2}$ boxes of footballs in the stock room, and there are 12 footballs in a full box. How can you find the total number of footballs without opening all the boxes? Or, suppose $\frac{1}{4}$ of a pizza was left over and you ate $\frac{1}{2}$ of this amount. What number shows the amount of pizza you ate?

In this investigation, you will see how you can relate what you already know about multiplication to situations involving fractions. Remember, to make sense of a situation, you can draw a model or change a fraction to an equivalent fraction or an equivalent form.

5.1 Selling Brownies

Paulo and Paula are tending the brownie booth at the school fair. All evening long they have run into interesting situations in which they have to find fractional parts of other fractions.

Think about this!

What operation is called for when you find a fractional part of another fraction: $+$, $-$, $\times$, or $\div$? For example, how much is $\frac{1}{2}$ of $\frac{1}{4}$? How could you write this problem using a mathematics operation sign?

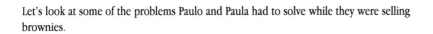

Let's look at some of the problems Paulo and Paula had to solve while they were selling brownies.

Problem 5.1

The brownies are baked in square pans, and they are sold as fractional parts of a pan. A whole pan of brownies costs $24 dollars. The cost of any fractional part of a pan is that fraction of $24.

A. One pan of brownies was $\frac{2}{3}$ full. Mr. Sims bought $\frac{1}{2}$ of what was in the pan. What fraction of a full pan did Mr. Sims buy? How much did he pay?

B. Paulo's aunt Serena asked to buy $\frac{3}{4}$ of what was left in another pan. The pan was half full. How much of a whole pan did Aunt Serena buy? How much did she pay?

Problem 5.1 Follow-Up

For A and B above, draw a picture to show what each brownie pan looked like before Mr. Sims and Aunt Serena bought part of what remained. Then draw a picture that shows how much of each pan the customer got and how much was left. Mark your drawings so that someone else can easily see what fraction of the pan each customer bought.

Model of a Brownie Pan

Use the drawings to check your computations in A and B for the fraction of the brownie pan and the price each customer paid.

Investigation 5: Finding Areas and Other Products **55**

Answers to Problem 5.1

A. $\frac{2}{3} \times \frac{1}{2} = \frac{2}{6} = \frac{1}{3}$ of a pan; $24 \times \frac{1}{3} = \$8$

B. $\frac{3}{4} \times \frac{1}{2} = \frac{3}{8}$ of a pan; $24 \times \frac{3}{8} = \$9$

Answers to Problem 5.1 Follow-Up

See page 63g.

Discounting Brownies

Grouping:
Small Groups

Launch

- Talk about the introduction to the problem and why $\frac{1}{3}$ of $\frac{1}{3}$ is $\frac{1}{9}$.

- Ask students to compare Problem 5.2 to Problem 5.1. (*optional*)

Explore

- Have students work in groups of two or three.

- As you visit the groups, suggest that they draw pictures to help them understand the problem.

Summarize

- Have groups share their solutions and strategies, including their drawings.

- Help students connect finding a fraction of a mixed number to multiplication.

- Have students work on and then discuss the follow-up questions.

Assignment Choices

ACE questions 1–5 and unassigned choices from earlier problems

---

5.2 **Discounting Brownies**

There are many occasions in which you will want to find a fraction times a fraction or a fraction times a whole number. When you solve problems involving multiplication with fractions, it helps to remember that finding a fraction *times* a number is the same as finding a fraction *of* a number. It is also helpful to draw models to show fractions and fraction operations.

At the brownie booth, a customer wanted to buy $\frac{1}{3}$ of a pan that was $\frac{1}{3}$ full. Paula said that they had to find $\frac{1}{3}$ of $\frac{1}{3}$. Paulo said that this is the same as $\frac{1}{3} \times \frac{1}{3}$. They decided to make a drawing to figure out how much the customer would get.

First, they made a drawing to show how much was in the pan:

Then, they showed how much the customer wanted, which was $\frac{1}{3}$ of $\frac{1}{3}$ of a pan:

They extended the horizontal lines to form nine equal parts. They then figured out that the customer would buy $\frac{1}{9}$ of a pan:

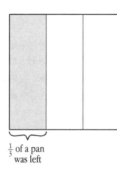
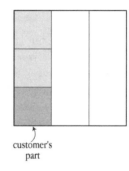
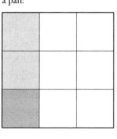

$\frac{1}{3}$ of a pan was left

customer's part

From inspecting their drawing, Paula and Paulo figured out that they should charge the customer $\frac{1}{9}$ of $24, or $2.67.

> **Think about this!**
>
> **W**hy does it make sense that $\frac{1}{3}$ of $\frac{1}{3}$, or $\frac{1}{3} \times \frac{1}{3}$, is $\frac{1}{9}$?

Problem 5.2

The school fair was almost over. Paulo and Paula wanted to sell all the remaining brownies in a hurry, so they decided to offer a discount of 20% on all sales. They had $2\frac{1}{4}$ pans of brownies left. Remember, they originally sold a pan of brownies for $24.

Mr. Vargas offered to buy half of all that they had left.

A. How much will Mr. Vargas purchase?

B. How much should Paulo and Paula charge Mr. Vargas?

■ Problem 5.2 Follow-Up

When Mr. Vargas got his bill, he realized he had only $20 in his wallet, so he said, "I guess I'll only buy $\frac{1}{3}$ of what you have left."

1. Now how much will Mr. Vargas buy?

2. Can he afford this much? Explain your reasoning.

Answers to Problem 5.2

A. See page 63h.

B. Before the discount, the brownies would cost $24 + ($\frac{1}{8}$ of $24) = $27; 20% off $27 (or 80% of $27) is $21.60.

Answers to Problem 5.2 Follow-Up

1. See page 63h.

2. yes; The regular price of $\frac{3}{4}$ of a pan of brownies is $\frac{3}{4}$ of $24, or $18. With a 20% discount, Mr. Vargas would pay only $0.8 \times $18 = $14.40.

5.3

Buying the Biggest Lot

At a Glance

**Grouping:
Small Groups**

Launch

■ Tell the story of Miguel's mother.

■ Review finding the area of rectangles.

Explore

■ As students work in small groups on the problem, encourage them to use pictorial models and mathematical symbols.

■ Look for particularly good drawings to share with the class later.

Summarize

■ Have groups share solutions and strategies.

■ Have groups work on and discuss the follow-up.

Assignment Choices

ACE questions 6, 19, and unassigned choices from earlier problems

---

In the area where Miguel lives, land is expensive because many people want to live there. The lots for houses are small compared to the lots needed for farmland.

Miguel's mother builds and sells houses. She wants to buy a piece of land in their area on which to build several houses. There are two large lots for sale. One is a rectangular plot that is $\frac{3}{8}$ of a mile by $\frac{2}{3}$ of a mile. The other is a square plot that is $\frac{2}{5}$ of a mile by $\frac{2}{5}$ of a mile.

Problem 5.3

A. Which lot should Miguel's mother buy if she wants the biggest lot? Explain your reasoning.

B. If land in this area sells for $750,000 a square mile, about how much should Miguel's mother expect to pay?

■ Problem 5.3 Follow-Up

Miguel's mother has an idea for a beautiful trailer park. The trailer park would have lots of open areas for children to play in and a set of shops. She finds a farm for sale that is $1\frac{1}{4}$ miles $\times$ $2\frac{1}{5}$ miles. The farm has a pretty lake and lots of trees. She thinks it would be perfect for her trailer park.

1. How many square miles does the farm cover?

2. If land costs $750,000 a square mile, how much should she expect to pay?

3. If Miguel's mother receives a 7% discount because she is buying a large lot, how much will she have to pay?

Answers to Problem 5.3

A. See page 63i.

B. Miguel's mother would pay $\frac{1}{4}$ of $750,000, or $187,500.

Answers to Problem 5.3 Follow-Up

1. $1\frac{1}{4} \times 2\frac{1}{5} = \frac{5}{4} \times \frac{11}{5} = \frac{11}{4} = 2\frac{3}{4}$ square miles

2. $750,000 \times \frac{11}{4} = $2,062,500

3. If she receives a 7% discount, she will pay 93% of the price, and 93% $\times$ $2,062,500 = $1,918,125.

5.4 **Designing a Multiplication Algorithm**

In Investigation 4, you wrote algorithms for adding and subtracting fractions. Recall that an *algorithm* is a plan, or a series of steps, for doing a computation. In this problem, you will work with your group to develop an algorithm for multiplying fractions.

Your group may develop more than one algorithm. What is important is that each member of your group understands and feels comfortable with at least one algorithm for multiplying fractions. Remember, for an algorithm to be useful, each step should be clear and precise so that other people will be able to carry out the steps and get correct answers.

Problem 5.4

Work with your group to develop at least one algorithm for multiplying fractions. You might want to look back over the first three problems in this investigation and discuss how each person in your group thought about them. Look for ideas that you think will help you develop an algorithm for multiplying fractions that will always work, even with mixed numbers.

Test your algorithm on a few problems, such as these:

$$\frac{1}{5} \times 25 \qquad 24 \times \frac{2}{3} \qquad \frac{5}{8} \times 12$$

$$\frac{3}{8} \times \frac{3}{4} \qquad \frac{1}{2} \times 2\frac{2}{3} \qquad 3\frac{1}{3} \times 2\frac{4}{5}$$

If necessary, make adjustments to your algorithm until you think it will work all the time. Write up a final version of the algorithm. Make sure it is neat and precise so others can follow it.

■ **Problem 5.4 Follow-Up**

Exchange your algorithm with that of another group. Test the other group's plan. Write a paragraph explaining how your algorithm and the other group's algorithm are alike and how they are different.

- - - - - - - - -
At a Glance

Grouping:
Small Groups

Launch

- Read the introduction to the problem to the class.

- Review how to write a clear and concise algorithm. (*optional*)

Explore

- Have students write algorithms individually and then share and revise them in their groups.

- Have groups exchange their algorithms.

Summarize

- As a class, share and discuss algorithms.

- Develop a master list of all the algorithms presented. (*optional*)

Answer to Problem 5.4

Possible answer: If the fractions are simple fractions, multiply the numerators together, and that will be the numerator in the answer. Then multiply the denominators together, and that will be the denominator in the answer. For example: $\frac{3}{5} \times \frac{4}{7} = \frac{12}{35}$. If one of the fractions is a mixed number, change the whole number to a fraction with the same denominator as the fraction part, and add that fraction to the fraction part. Then you can multiply this improper fraction and the other fraction by multiplying the numerators and the denominators. For example: $\frac{3}{4} \times 2\frac{1}{3} = \frac{3}{4} \times \frac{7}{3} = \frac{21}{12} = 1\frac{3}{4}$.

Answer to Problem 5.4 Follow-Up

Answers will vary.

Assignment Choices

ACE questions 7–10, 18, 20, and unassigned choices from earlier problems

Answers

Applications

1. $\frac{2}{3} \times \frac{4}{5} = \frac{8}{15}$ of a section

2a. $\frac{1}{2} \times \frac{7}{8} = \frac{7}{16}$ of a yard

2b. $\frac{7}{16} \times \$2.00 = 0.875$ or about $0.88

3. $\frac{1}{2} \times 3\frac{1}{4} = \frac{13}{8} = 1\frac{5}{8}$ of a cup

4a. See below right.

4b. The vacuum, microwave oven, television, and one CD would cost, with tax, $470 + 0.05 × $470 = $493.50.

As you work on these ACE questions, use your calculator whenever you need it.

Applications

1. Ms. Guerdin owns $\frac{4}{5}$ of a section of land in Tupelo township. She wants to sell $\frac{2}{3}$ of her land to her neighbor. What fraction of a section does she want to sell?

2. **a.** Sarah uses balsa wood to build airplane models. After completing a model, she had a strip of balsa wood measuring $\frac{7}{8}$ of a yard left over. Shawn wants to buy half of the strip from Sarah. What fraction of a yard does Shawn want to buy?

   b. If Sarah paid $2.00 for each yard, how much should she charge Shawn for the strip he buys?

3. A recipe for a large batch of cookies calls for $3\frac{1}{4}$ cups of flour. Amos wants to make half of a batch of cookies. How much flour should he use?

4. Murphy's department store is having a two-week sale during which all prices are reduced by $\frac{1}{3}$. Ophelia wants to buy the following items for her new apartment:

Item	Regular price
Vacuum cleaner	$120
Microwave oven	$240
Television	$330
4 CDs	$15 each
2 Speakers	$75 each

   a. Ophelia has $500 saved for the purchases. Can she buy everything on her list?

   b. There is a 5% sales tax. What is the most Ophelia could spend and on which items?

4a.

Item	Sale price	Total
Vacuum cleaner	$80	$80
Microwave oven	$160	$160
Television	$220	$220
4 CDs	$10 each	$40
2 Speakers	$50 each	$100

The total for all the items is $80 + $160 + $220 + $40 + $100 = $600. Ophelia cannot buy all the items with only $500.

5. Rubin and Lea went to the amusement park on Saturday. Lea spent $\frac{1}{2}$ of her money, and Rubin spent $\frac{1}{4}$ of his money. Is it possible for Rubin to have spent more money than Lea? Explain your reasoning.

6. Mr. Jones' garden has an area of 21 square meters. He wants to increase its size by $\frac{1}{2}$. Draw a picture to show what his new garden might look like. Be sure to give the new area and dimensions, and show your reasoning.

7. Find a fraction and a whole number with a product that is a whole number.

8. Find a fraction and a whole number with a product less than $\frac{1}{2}$.

9. Find a fraction and a whole number with a product between $\frac{1}{2}$ and 1.

10. Find a fraction and a whole number with a product greater than 1.

Connections

11. Write a fraction between $\frac{1}{2}$ and $\frac{2}{3}$. Explain how you know your fraction is between $\frac{1}{2}$ and $\frac{2}{3}$.

12. The following table shows the number of people surveyed that intend to vote for each of the candidates for president. Make a circle graph for this data.

Candidate	Expected votes
Murningham	31
Graves	58
McKane	91

13. Inflation has caused a store owner to decide that she must increase all prices by 8%. What should she charge for the following items?

Item	Current price
basketball	$30
skateboard	$50
roller blades	$110
tennis racket	$75

12.

Expected Percent of Votes

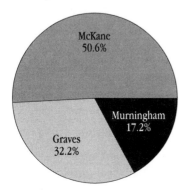

---

5. yes; Possible explanation: If Rubin started with $20, but Lea only had $5, Rubin would have spent $5, while Lea would have only spent $2.50.

6. The garden's new size will be 21 + 10.5 = 31.5 square meters. Possible solutions:

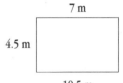

7. Possible answer: $\frac{2}{3} \times 6 = 4$

8. Possible answer: $\frac{1}{8} \times 3 = \frac{3}{8}$

9. Possible answer: $\frac{1}{4} \times 3 = \frac{3}{4}$

10. Possible answer: $\frac{4}{5} \times 2 = 1\frac{3}{5}$

Connections

11. $\frac{7}{12}$; I know this is between $\frac{1}{2}$ and $\frac{2}{3}$, because $\frac{1}{2} = \frac{6}{12}$ and $\frac{2}{3} = \frac{8}{12}$, and $\frac{7}{12}$ is between $\frac{6}{12}$ and $\frac{8}{12}$.

12. See below left.

13. basketball: $30 + 0.08 \times 30 = $32.40

skateboard: $50 + 0.08 \times 50 = $54.00

roller blades: $110 + 0.08 \times 110 = $118.80

tennis racket: $75 + 0.08 \times 75 = $81.00

14. $\frac{3}{5} < \frac{7}{8}$

15. $\frac{12}{15} > \frac{3}{4}$

16. $\frac{5}{8} = \frac{10}{16}$

17. 0.4, 0.32, 0.302, 0.167, 0.1, 0.099

Extensions

18. The Pizza Pirate ate $\frac{1}{2} + \frac{1}{3} + \frac{1}{4} + \frac{1}{6} = \frac{6}{12} + \frac{4}{12} + \frac{3}{12} + \frac{2}{12} = 1\frac{3}{12} = 1\frac{1}{4}$ pizzas, so there is $2 - 1\frac{1}{4} = \frac{3}{4}$ of a pizza left.

19a. $\frac{1}{5}$ of an inch represents 1 mile.

19b. $\frac{5}{12} \times 5 = \frac{25}{12} = 2\frac{1}{12}$ miles

20. Since $108 \div 6.5 = 16.61$, it will take about 17 tiles to cover the length of the room, and the same for the width. The entire room will take about $17 \times 17 =$ about 289 tiles.

In 14–16, insert <, >, or = to make the statement true.

14. $\frac{3}{5}$ _____ $\frac{7}{8}$

15. $\frac{12}{15}$ _____ $\frac{3}{4}$

16. $\frac{5}{8}$ _____ $\frac{10}{16}$

17. Order these decimals from greatest to least.

0.302   0.1   0.099   0.167   0.32   0.4

Extensions

18. The Pizza Pirate has been up to new tricks. The archery club put two pizzas in the freezer for a party. Of the two pizzas, the Pizza Pirate ate $\frac{1}{2}$ of a pizza, then $\frac{1}{3}$ of a pizza, then $\frac{1}{4}$ of a pizza, and then $\frac{1}{6}$ of a pizza. How much pizza is left?

19. On a map of the city of Detroit, the library is $\frac{5}{12}$ of an inch from the post office. On the map, 1 inch represents 5 miles.

a. What fraction of an inch represents 1 mile?

b. How far apart are the post office and the library?

20. While traveling in Mexico, Samantha found some beautiful ceramic tiles. The tiles are square, $6\frac{1}{2}$ inches on each side. Samantha wants to buy enough tiles to cover the floor of her sun room. The sun room is also square, 108 inches on each side. How many tiles does Samantha need?

Mathematical Reflections

In this investigation, you explored situations in which you need to find a fraction of another fraction or a fraction of a whole number. You discovered that $\frac{2}{3}$ *of* $\frac{1}{2}$ is the same as $\frac{2}{3} \times \frac{1}{2}$. These questions will help you summarize what you have learned:

1 You can model the product of whole numbers by thinking of multiplication as finding area. For example, you can think of 6×7 as the area of a rectangle with dimensions of 6 and 7. Describe and show how you can mark a square to show $\frac{2}{3} \times \frac{1}{2}$.

2 Look back over all of the examples of multiplying fractions—or finding a fractional part of another fraction—that you worked with in this investigation. What patterns do you see that helped you develop an algorithm for multiplying fractions?

3 When you multiply two whole numbers, the product is larger than the factors. Is the product of two fractions larger than the fractions? Explain your reasoning.

Think about your answers to these questions, discuss your ideas with other students and your teacher, and then write a summary of your findings in your journal.

Possible Answers

1. $\frac{2}{3} \times \frac{1}{2}$ can be modeled by dividing a square into halves and then dividing each of the two equal parts into three equal parts so that you have actually divided the whole into six equal parts. The portion of the whole that results is $\frac{2}{6}$.

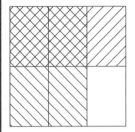

2. In finding a fractional part of another fraction, the resulting fraction's numerator is the product of the numerators of the original fractions, and its denominator is the product of the denominators of the original fractions. If the original fractions are mixed numbers, you must convert the mixed numbers to improper fractions before you can multiply the numerators and denominators.

3. If the fractions are less than 1, you are taking a part of something that is *part* of a whole, so the product could not be bigger than either of the two fractions being multiplied together.

5.1 • **Selling Brownies**

In *Bits and Pieces I* students were introduced to the area model for fractions by dividing square pans of brownies into equal-size pieces. In this problem, students return to this context. Here, they model multiplication of fractions by finding fractional parts of fractions of whole pans of brownies.

Launch

Read through the introduction to the problem. Talk about the question posed in the "Think about this!" box, which asks about which operation works for finding fractions of fractions.

> What does it mean to find $\frac{1}{2}$ of $\frac{1}{4}$? Does this mean that we should add $\frac{1}{2}$ and $\frac{1}{4}$?

Students should be able to eliminate addition as the operation, because it is not reasonable that $\frac{1}{2}$ *of* $\frac{1}{4}$ is the sum of $\frac{1}{2}$ and $\frac{1}{4}$, which is $\frac{3}{4}$. This is far enough to take this concept at this time.

Read through the problem with your class.

> As you work on this problem, think about what you already know about fractions. And remember, drawing models might be a helpful way to make sense of the problem.

Explore

As students work in groups of two or three, have copies of the Sheet of Squares (provided as a blackline master) available for students who want to draw models of the brownie pans. As you circulate, ask students what it means to find a fraction—such as $\frac{1}{2}$ or $\frac{3}{4}$—of something.

As groups finish, ask whether their answers seem reasonable and how they could express what they did using a mathematics operation sign. You may want to have large sheets of paper or sheets of blank transparency film available for groups to share their drawings.

Summarize

Have groups share their solutions and strategies. If they drew pictures, have them show their drawings or reproduce them at the board. The follow-up suggests a strategy for drawing pictures for the problem. If none of your students have created drawings as suggested in the follow-up, go through this strategy with them, helping them to connect the drawing to what is happening in the problem. Ask them to notice how the drawing shows the solution.

Some students will solve part A by starting with $\frac{2}{3}$ and dividing by 2.

> Why is it reasonable that taking half of something is the same as dividing by 2?

Students often have trouble using a similar division strategy with problems like part B; some students may divide by 4 (to divide the half pan into four parts) and then multiply by 3 (to take three of the four parts).

What operation do you think is being used in these problems?

It is easy to verify that subtraction is incorrect, since $\frac{2}{3} - \frac{1}{2}$ is not $\frac{1}{3}$, which is the solution to part A, nor is $\frac{3}{4} - \frac{1}{2}$ equal to $\frac{3}{8}$, which is the solution to part B. Students are now left with two possibilities—multiplication or division. Discuss what the operations of multiplication and division mean.

Can you describe some situations that call for multiplication? Can you describe some situations that call for division?

Discuss the relationship between multiplication and division. Students should understand that multiplication and division are opposite (inverse) operations—if you multiply two numbers to get a product, you can divide the product by one of the numbers to get the other number. Again ask what operation could be used to solve Problem 5.1. You want students to begin to see a relationship between multiplication and division. This idea is revisited in the upcoming problems to help students better understand.

Once everyone seems to understand how to find the fractions of fractions that were purchased, talk about the cost of the brownies, asking students to explain how they arrived at their answers.

For the Teacher: Modeling Fraction Multiplication

For numbers with large denominators, area models can get complicated. A modeling strategy that keeps things manageable is to represent one fraction by dividing a square (or any rectangle) with, say, horizontal lines, and the second fraction by dividing the square with vertical lines.

For example, to show $\frac{2}{3} \times \frac{3}{4}$ with an area model, first represent the $\frac{3}{4}$ by dividing a square into fourths and shading three of the fourths.

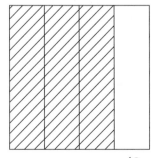

(Continued on the next page.)

To represent taking $\frac{2}{3}$ of the $\frac{3}{4}$, divide the whole into thirds by cutting the square the opposite way, then shade two of the three sections. The part where the shaded sections overlap represents the product, $\frac{6}{12}$.

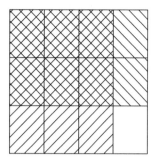

If students instead divide a square with both horizontal and vertical lines for the first fraction, they often get confused; for example, if they represent $\frac{3}{4}$ like this:

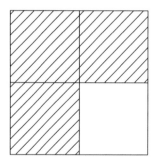

5.2 • Discounting Brownies

This problem is a continuation of Problem 5.1. In this problem, students find fractions of mixed numbers. The problem also requires them to compute a 20% discount.

Launch

Read and discuss the introduction to the problem and the question posed in the "Think about this!" box.

When you find $\frac{1}{3}$ of $\frac{1}{3}$, should you get something larger or smaller than $\frac{1}{3}$? (*Since $\frac{1}{3}$ of $\frac{1}{3}$ is a part of a part, you end up with something smaller.*)

Before you discuss the area model for finding $\frac{1}{3}$ of $\frac{1}{3}$, you might model $\frac{1}{3}$ of $\frac{1}{3}$ by finding $\frac{1}{3}$ of $\frac{1}{3}$ of a whole number:

Let's look at some ways of modeling $\frac{1}{3}$ of $\frac{1}{3}$. Suppose some students in a class of 27 students will be selected to go on a trip. The students are selected in two stages. In the first stage, $\frac{1}{3}$ of the class will be selected based on their math projects. How many students will be selected at this stage? ($\frac{1}{3}$ *of 27, which is 9.*)

In the second stage, the 9 students that were selected based on their projects do oral presentations. Of this group, $\frac{1}{3}$ are selected to go on the trip. How many students get to go on the trip? ($\frac{1}{3}$ *of 9, which is 3.*)

Let's look at what we have done. We found $\frac{1}{3}$ of 27 and then found $\frac{1}{3}$ of that result. This gave us $\frac{1}{3}$ of $\frac{1}{3}$ of 27, which is 3. What fraction of 27 is 3? ($\frac{3}{27}$ *or* $\frac{1}{9}$)

So, we found that $\frac{1}{3}$ of $\frac{1}{3}$ of a group is the same as $\frac{1}{9}$ of the group.

Continue the discussion by referring students to page 56 of the student edition and discussing the area model Paula and Paulo used to represent $\frac{1}{3}$ of $\frac{1}{3}$.

Let's look at another way to model $\frac{1}{3}$ of $\frac{1}{3}$. In the brownie booth at the school fair, Paula and Paulo had to find $\frac{1}{3}$ of $\frac{1}{3}$ of a whole pan of brownies. Look at page 56 in your book to see how they did this.

Paula and Paulo drew a diagram to find $\frac{1}{3}$ of $\frac{1}{3}$. The square represents a pan of brownies.

The pan started out $\frac{1}{3}$ full. How did they represent this in their diagram? (*They divided the square into 3 equal parts and shaded 1 of the parts to represent the brownies.*)

A customer wanted to buy $\frac{1}{3}$ of what was left. How did Paula and Paulo represent this? (*They divided the $\frac{1}{3}$ strip representing the brownies into 3 equal parts and shading one of the parts darkly.*)

How did they name the part of a whole pan this represented? (*They extended the horizontal lines. The square was then divided into 9 equal parts, and one part was shaded darkly, so the customer wanted to buy $\frac{1}{9}$ of a pan.*)

So Paula and Paulo's diagram shows that $\frac{1}{3}$ of $\frac{1}{3}$ is $\frac{1}{9}$. This is the same as saying that $\frac{1}{3}$ times $\frac{1}{3}$ equals $\frac{1}{9}$.

Read Problem 5.2 with your students. If they are struggling to understand what to do, help them get started by asking how the problem differs from Problem 5.1 and how it is the same. As in Problem 5.1, they are being asked to find part of an amount. This time, however, they begin with a mixed number rather than a fraction.

Explore

Have students work in groups of two or three. Encourage them to draw pictures to determine how much Mr. Vargas will get, showing the brownies that remain then finding $\frac{1}{2}$ of that amount.

Calculating how much to charge Mr. Vargas involves multiple steps, which might be difficult for some students. If they are having difficulty, suggest that they first find what they would charge him if there were no discount. Only offer this scaffolding question if groups are stuck and no longer making progress.

Summarize

Have groups share their solutions and strategies. If they drew pictures, ask them to share or reproduce their drawings on the overhead projector or the board. For part A, students could reason that getting half of something is the same as dividing by 2. Help them to connect this observation with multiplication.

> How might you write a multiplication problem to find the amount of brownies Mr. Vargas would get? What would you do to the numerators and denominators of the fractions to find the solution?

(If students have written $\frac{1}{2} \times 2\frac{1}{4}$, you may need to suggest that they write both numbers as fractions.) Some students will see the pattern that the product of fractions is the product of the numerators over the product of the denominators. If so, ask them why this technique works.

When you think your students have some grasp of this, ask them to try the follow-up questions. Make sure they give a visual solution as well as a multiplication sentence with symbols. Help students see that the solutions in the two representations are the same.

5.3 • Buying the Biggest Lot

This problem involves determining which of two rectangular plots with side lengths expressed in fractions has the greater area. Since students worked earlier on a problem that involved buying land, referring to land as a fraction of a whole will be familiar. In that problem, students *added* and *subtracted* the areas of property—which were fractional amounts—to compute the areas that resulted from sales of the land. In this problem, they *multiply* fractions to find the amount of land—the area—for each of two plots, then use the price per square mile to calculate the price for each plot.

Launch

Launch the problem by telling the story of Miguel's mother. To solve the problem, students will need to find the areas of the two rectangular pieces of property. In *Covering and Surrounding*, students learned that the area of a rectangle is length times width. Review this idea with them before they begin the problem.

Explore

When you feel students understand the problem and have some thoughts about how to solve it, let them explore it in small groups.

As you visit the groups, remind them that they must be able to justify their answers and show their reasoning. Encourage them to represent what they have done both by drawing pictures and by using mathematical symbols and operations. Look for particularly good drawings that should be shared during the summary.

Summarize

Have groups share their solutions and strategies. Make sure students can represent what they have done with both pictures and mathematical symbols.

Once groups have made sense of this problem and have found correct solutions, have them work on the follow-up. The follow-up involves finding the area and cost of a section of land, but this time the dimensions of the property are mixed numbers. It provides practice with multiplying fractions and mixed numbers and helps students to sort out these ideas. Again, ask groups to share their solutions and strategies.

5.4 • Designing a Multiplication Algorithm

You may need to review the word *algorithm*—which was introduced in Problem 4.4—and review what students learned about writing complete and clear algorithms.

Launch

Read the introduction and the problem with your students.

Explore

This problem works well with groups of two to four. You may want to ask students to first talk about their strategies in their group and then work individually to write their algorithms. They can then share their drafts, and group members may make suggestions as to how each algorithm can be improved. All students should write at least two drafts of their algorithm. You may want to have large sheets of paper or sheets of blank transparency film available for groups to share the final written versions of their algorithms.

As groups finish, have them work on the follow-up, which asks them to exchange their algorithm with another group's algorithm.

Summarize

Each student is expected to have developed at least one algorithm for multiplying fractions. Several students may offer the traditional algorithm of multiplying numerators together and denominators together; discuss why that method works. Some students may have developed different rules for different types of fractions. For example, they may have an algorithm for multiplying unit fractions times whole numbers, which states that you just divide the whole number by the denominator of the unit fraction. Again, ask students to discuss why this makes sense.

If groups have put their final work on large sheets of paper or transparencies, these can be shared with the class. You may want to develop a master list of the algorithms that are presented. Evaluating whether each algorithm is usable and helpful, and how it compares with other algorithms will further students' understanding of multiplication of fractions, mixed numbers, and whole numbers.

After the class discussion, you might ask students to take their algorithms home and ask family members to try to follow them.

Additional Answers

Answers to Problem 5.1 Follow-Up

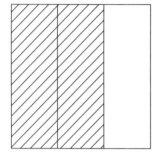

The pan was $\frac{2}{3}$ full.

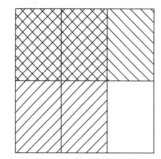

Mr. Sims bought $\frac{1}{2}$ of the $\frac{2}{3}$, which is $\frac{2}{6}$ of a whole pan.

The pan was $\frac{1}{2}$ full.

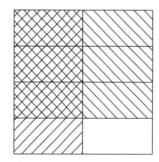

Aunt Serena bought $\frac{3}{4}$ of the $\frac{1}{2}$, which is $\frac{3}{8}$ of a whole pan.

Answers to Problem 5.2

A. Students may reason by multiplying or by drawing a diagram. Mr. Vargas wants $\frac{1}{2} \times 2\frac{1}{4} = \frac{1}{2} \times \frac{9}{4} = \frac{9}{8} = 1\frac{1}{8}$ pans of brownies.

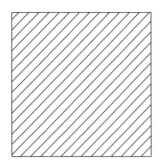  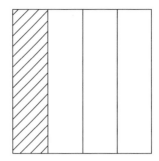

There are $2\frac{1}{4}$ pans of brownies left.

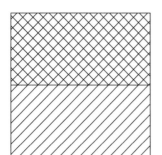 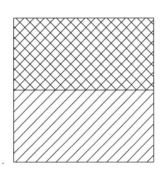 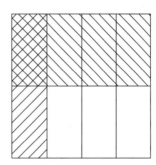

Mr. Vargas wants $\frac{1}{2}$ of the $2\frac{1}{4}$ pans, which is $\frac{1}{2} + \frac{1}{2} + \frac{1}{8} = 1\frac{1}{8}$ of a pan.

Answers to Problem 5.2 Follow-Up

1. Students may reason by multiplying or by drawing a diagram. Mr. Vargas will buy $\frac{1}{3} \times 2\frac{1}{4} = \frac{1}{3} \times \frac{9}{4} = \frac{9}{12} = \frac{3}{4}$ of a pan of brownies.

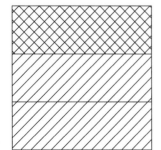 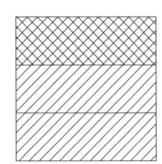 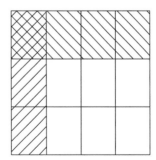

Mr. Vargas will buy $\frac{1}{3}$ of the $2\frac{1}{4}$ pans, which is $\frac{1}{3} + \frac{1}{3} + \frac{1}{12} = \frac{9}{12} = \frac{3}{4}$ of a pan.

Answers to Problem 5.3

A. She should buy the $\frac{3}{8}$ mile $\times \frac{2}{3}$ mile plot, because this plot, which has an area of $\frac{6}{24} = \frac{1}{4}$ of a square mile is larger than the $\frac{2}{5}$ mile $\times \frac{2}{5}$ mile plot, which has an area of $\frac{4}{25}$ of a square mile. Here are diagrams of 1-square-mile sections of land with portions shaded to represent the plots.

$\frac{3}{8}$

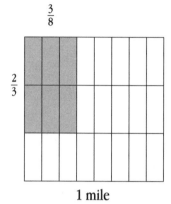

$\frac{2}{3}$

1 mile

1 mile

The area of the plot is $\frac{6}{24} = \frac{1}{4}$ square mile.

$\frac{2}{5}$

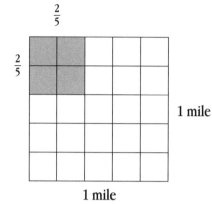

$\frac{2}{5}$

1 mile

1 mile

The area of the plot is $\frac{4}{25}$ square mile.

Computing with Decimals

This investigation engages students in adding, subtracting, multiplying, and possibly dividing decimals in contexts that help them make sense of the process. We are assuming that students have some experience with decimal computation but are not yet proficient. In this investigation, students focus on what the operations mean and how to handle the decimal point. With decimal multiplication, the problem is the size of the number we expect for an answer—how many decimal places will it have?

Problem 6.1, Buying School Supplies, employs students' familiarity with the decimal notation for money in a game designed to help them practice estimating sums and differences of decimal numbers. In Problem 6.2, Moving Decimal Points, students analyze the effects of the placement of the decimal point on sums and differences. In Problem 6.3, Multiplying Decimals, students search for patterns in what happens to place value when they systematically multiply by a decimal. In Problem 6.4, Shifting Decimal Points, students shift decimal points in factors to obtain a given product or a product in a given range. The explorations culminate in Problem 6.5, Fencing a Yard, which pulls together computation with fractions and decimals in a real-world, problem-solving context.

Mathematical and Problem-Solving Goals

- **To explore situations that involve operations with decimals**

- **To use strategies for quickly estimating sums and products**

- **To develop strategies for adding and subtracting decimals**

- **To understand when addition or subtraction is the appropriate operation**

- **To look for and to generalize patterns**

- **To develop an understanding of decimal multiplication**

- **To use estimation to help make decisions**

- **To use a problem's context to help reason about answers**

Materials		
Problem	**For students**	**For the teacher**
All	Calculators	Transparencies 6.1 to 6.5 (optional)
6.1	Labsheet 6.1 (1 per pair); markers, tiles, or paper squares (about 15 per student)	
6.5	Grid paper (1 sheet per student; provided as a blackline master)	

Student Pages 64–76   **Teaching the Investigation 76a–76j**

6.1

Buying
School
Supplies

Launch

- Play the School Supply game with the class until they understand the rules.

Explore

- Circulate as pairs play the game, asking them to explain how they found items that add to a particular amount.

- Remind pairs to think about strategies they are employing in playing the game.

Summarize

- Ask students to share strategies they developed during the game.

- Pose an addition problem, such as 12.15 + 3.089, and focus on the role of place value in determining the sum.

Assignment
Choices

ACE questions 1–3, 5, and unassigned choices from earlier problems

Computing
with Decimals

Nearly every day of your life, you use or interpret *decimal* quantities. Because our system of currency is based on the decimal system, you deal with decimals every time you buy something. You use decimals when you measure things in metric units. When you read the newspaper, you often have to interpret statements that involve decimal numbers such as, "The new baseball stadium will cost 7.5 million dollars." or "The average working week in Finland is 38.1 hours."

The problems in this investigation involve adding, subtracting, and multiplying decimals. As you work through the problems, you will learn to make sense of operations with decimals.

6.1 Buying School Supplies

The School Supply game will give you practice in estimating and calculating with decimals. The game involves the prices of items at a school store.

Items Sold at the School Store

Divider page	$0.07	Roll of tape	$0.84
Pencil	$0.28	Pen	$0.98
Eraser	$0.35	Highlighter	$1.05
Note paper	$0.42	Notebook	$2.24
Ruler	$0.70	Scissors	$3.15

School Supply Game Board

$2.24	$1.33	$0.35	$2.31	$1.68	$0.07
$3.43	$0.28	$3.08	$2.59	$1.05	$1.47
$1.26	$1.75	$1.12	$1.61	$1.54	$1.96
$1.40	$3.57	$2.80	$1.89	$0.91	$2.66
$2.03	$0.84	$2.87	$2.73	$0.70	$2.52
$3.15	$0.77	$2.45	$0.98	$0.63	$0.42

Tips for the Linguistically Diverse Classroom

Visual Enhancement The Visual Enhancement technique is described in detail in *Getting to Know Connected Mathematics*. It involves using real objects or pictures to make information comprehensible. Example: While discussing the School Supply Game, you might show real objects for the items sold at the school store.

Moving Decimal Points

Grouping:
Individuals, then Pairs

Launch

- Discuss the introduction and the "Think about this!" box shown in the student edition.

- Make sure students understand the constraints of the problem.

Explore

- Have students work individually on parts A and B and in pairs on parts C and D.

- Assign the follow-up as a challenge for pairs who finish early.

Summarize

- Have students share sum and difference problems found in A and B.

- Talk about the extreme values found in C and D.

Rules for the School Supply Game

Materials
- Labsheet 6.1 (1 per pair)
- Markers, such as squares of paper, marked with each player's initials (about 15 per person)

Playing
- Each player begins each turn assuming he or she has $4.20.

- In turn, each player makes up an addition, subtraction, or multiplication problem that uses the prices of some of the items from the school store. (Assume there is no sales tax.)

- If the answer to the problem is on the grid, the player who made up the problem covers the answer with one of his or her markers. If the answer is not on the grid, the player does not get to cover a square, and the next player takes a turn.

- The first player with four markers in a row—horizontally, vertically, or diagonally—wins the game.

Problem 6.1

Play the School Supply game once or twice with your partner. Keep track of any strategies you find that help you win the game.

Problem 6.1 Follow-Up

1. If you wanted to spend as much of your $4.20 as possible on rulers, how many rulers could you buy and how much money would you have left?
2. Tell what operations you used to do question 1, and explain why you used each operation.

 ## Moving Decimal Points

In a decimal number, the location of the decimal point tells you the place value of every digit in the number. For example, in the numbers 236.5 and 23.65, the 2, 3, 6, and 5 mean different things. The 2 in the first number means 2 hundreds; in the second number, it means 2 tens.

In this problem you will explore the possible sums and differences you can make with the same two sets of digits. You might be surprised by all the possibilities you can make just by changing the location of the decimal point!

Assignment Choices

ACE questions 4, 6, and unassigned choices from earlier problems

Answers to Problem 6.1 Follow-Up

1. 6 rulers; No money would be left.

2. There are several ways students may have solved part 1. They may have repeatedly added 0.70 until they got $4.20. They may have reasoned that, since $7 \times 6 = 42$, $0.70 \times 6 = 4.20$. Or, they may have divided 4.20 by 0.70.

To keep the number of possibilities reasonable, the constraint is added that you may place the decimal point just before, between, or just after the given digits. After placing the decimal point, you may add zeros only if they do not change the value of your number. For example, using the numbers 2, 3, 6, and 5, the numbers 0.002365 and 236,500 are not allowed, but 2.3650 is allowed.

Think about this!

Alice is trying to create different sums by moving the decimal points in two numbers: 236 and 89. Here is her work so far:

a.	**b.**	**c.**	**d.**
236	23.6	23.6	23.6
+ 89	+ 8.9	+89.0	+ 0.089
325	32.5	112.6	23.689

Bill says that the 0 added in problem c is all right, but the 0 added after the decimal point in problem d does not fit the constraint. Bill is correct. Why?

Bill says that she could have written this problem:

$$\begin{array}{r} 23.60 \\ + 0.89 \\ \hline 24.49 \end{array}$$

Why does Bill's problem fit the constraints?

Problem 6.2

Work with the digits 2365 and 894. You may insert a decimal point just before, between, or just after the given set of digits, but you cannot change the order of the digits. After placing the decimal point, you may add zeros only if they do not change the value of your number.

A. Find ways to insert decimal points so you get five different *sums* using these two numbers.

B. Find ways to insert decimal points so you get five different *differences* using these two numbers.

C. What is the largest sum that you can make that fits the constraints of the problem? What is the smallest sum?

D. What is the largest difference that you can make that fits the constraints of the problem? What is the smallest difference?

Answers to Problem 6.2

A. You can make five different numbers from the digits 2365 and four numbers from 894, which means there are 5 × 4 = 20 possible sums. Possible answer:

2365	236.5	23.65	2.365	0.2365
+ 894	+ 89.4	+ 8.94	+ 0.894	+ 0.8940
3259	325.9	32.59	3.259	1.1305

B. There are 20 possible differences (40 if you count negative differences). Possible answer:

2365	236.5	23.65	2.365	89.400
− 894	− 89.4	− 8.94	−.894	− 2.365
1471	147.1	14.71	1.471	87.035

(Answers continued on next page.)

Multiplying Decimals

At a Glance

**Grouping:
Individuals,
then Groups**

Launch

- Help students to analyze the sets of problems given in part A.

Explore

- Have students work on the problem individually and then share answers and search for patterns in groups of two or three.

- As you circulate, encourage groups to test their ideas on other problems.

Summarize

- As a class, explore the patterns in the sets of problems.

- Relate the number of decimal places in a decimal number to the denominator in the equivalent fraction. (*optional*)

■ **Problem 6.2 Follow-Up**

Suppose you can put the digits *in any order* and insert a decimal point at any position, but you cannot add zeros after a decimal point in front of the digits.

1. What is the largest sum you can make? What is the smallest sum?
2. What is the largest difference you can make? What is the smallest difference?

6.3 Multiplying Decimals

You can think of decimals as fractions with denominators of 10, 100, 1000, and so forth. For example, $\frac{1}{10}$ can be written as 0.1 and $\frac{37}{100}$ can be written as 0.37. To write $\frac{2}{5}$ as a decimal, first rewrite it as the equivalent fraction $\frac{4}{10}$, and then write it as the decimal 0.4. Since decimal numbers are fractions, you can use what you know about multiplying fractions to help you think about how to multiply decimals.

The grid on the left is a tenths grid with one strip shaded. This strip represents $\frac{1}{10}$, or 0.1. On the right, the strip representing 0.1 is shown divided into 10 squares, with one of the squares shaded darkly. This single square is $\frac{1}{10}$ of $\frac{1}{10}$, or 0.1×0.1.

 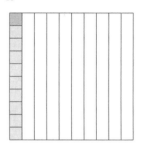

Below the horizontal lines have been extended to make a hundredths grid. This shows that $\frac{1}{10}$ of $\frac{1}{10}$ is one square out of a hundred squares, which is $\frac{1}{100}$, or 0.01 of the whole.

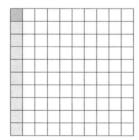

68 Bits and Pieces II

Assignment Choices

ACE questions 5, 7–10, and unassigned choices from earlier problems

---

C. The largest sum is 2365 + 894 = 3259. The smallest sum is 0.2365 + 0.894 = 1.1305.

D. The largest difference is 2365 − 0.894 = 2364.106. The smallest positive difference is 0.894 − 0.2365 = 0.6575. (If you include negative differences, the smallest difference is 0.894 − 2365 = −2364.116.)

Answers to Problem 6.2 Follow-Up

1. The largest sum you can make is 6532 + 984 = 7516. The smallest sum is 0.2356 + 0.489 = 0.7246.

2. The largest difference is 6532 − 0.489 = 6531.511. The smallest positive difference is 0.489 − 0.2356 = 0.2534. (If you include negative differences, the smallest difference is 0.489 − 6532 = − 6531.511.)

When you multiply 0.1 by 0.1 on your calculator, you get 0.01. What is the fraction name for 0.01? It is $\frac{1}{100}$, as you saw with the grid model.

In the next problem, you explore what happens when you multiply decimals on your calculator. Before you use a calculator to find an exact answer, think about how big you expect the answer to be.

Problem 6.3

A. Look at each set of multiplication problems below. Estimate how large you expect the answer to each problem to be. Will the answer be larger or smaller than 1? Will it be larger or smaller than $\frac{1}{2}$?

Set 1	Set 2	Set 3	Set 4
$21 \times 1 =$	$2.1 \times 1 =$	$0.21 \times 1 =$	$2.1 \times 11 =$
$21 \times 0.1 =$	$2.1 \times 0.1 =$	$0.21 \times 0.1 =$	$2.1 \times 1.1 =$
$21 \times 0.01 =$	$2.1 \times 0.01 =$	$0.21 \times 0.01 =$	$2.1 \times 0.11 =$
$21 \times 0.001 =$	$2.1 \times 0.001 =$	$0.21 \times 0.001 =$	$2.1 \times 0.011 =$
$21 \times 0.0001 =$	$2.1 \times 0.0001 =$	$0.21 \times 0.0001 =$	$2.1 \times 0.0011 =$

B. Use your calculator to do the multiplication, and record the answers in an organized way so that you can look for patterns. Describe any patterns that you see.

C. In a multiplication problem, there is a relationship between the number of decimal places in the factors and the number of decimal places in the product. Summarize what you think this relationship is. Show your reasoning.

■ Problem 6.3 Follow-Up

1. Test the relationship you discovered in part C on these two problems:

$0.5 \times 4 =$ $5 \times 0.4 =$

Now do the two problems on your calculator. What does the calculator show? Why?

2. When you multiply a number by 10, do you get a larger number or a smaller number? Why? Give three examples to support your answer.

3. When you multiply a number by 0.1, do you get a larger number or a smaller number? Why? Give three examples to support your answer.

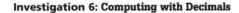

Investigation 6: Computing with Decimals 69

Answer to Problem 6.3

See page 76f.

Answers to Problem 6.3 Follow-Up

1. The two products are the same: $0.5 \times 4 = 2$ and $5 \times 0.4 = 2$. In each problem, you are multiplying the whole numbers 5 and 4, and in each you have one decimal place in the factors, so the answer is 2.
2. You get a larger number; the product is 10 times larger. Multiplying by 10 moves the decimal point one place to the right. For example: $56 \times 10 = 560$, $2.3 \times 10 = 23$, $0.234 \times 10 = 2.34$.
3. You get a smaller number; the product is $\frac{1}{10}$ as large. Multiplying by 0.1 moves the decimal one place to the left. For example: $56 \times 0.1 = 5.6$, $2.3 \times 0.1 = 0.23$, $0.234 \times 0.1 = 0.0234$.

Shifting Decimal Points

At a Glance

Grouping: Pairs or Small Groups

Launch

- Pose an example to the class, asking for two factors that have a given product.

Explore

- Have students work in pairs or groups of three to generate factor pairs that produce a given product or a product in a given range.

Summarize

- As a class, share answers and discuss the patterns students see in the answers.

- Review the follow-up questions to connect multiplication and division.

- Assess students' understanding by posing an additional problem for them.

Now that you have seen how the positions of decimal points affect products, you can use these ideas to build a deeper understanding of multiplication. In this problem, you will work backward to find numbers with products that fit certain constraints.

Problem 6.4

A. **1.** Find two numbers with a product of 1344.
   2. Find two numbers with a product of 134.4.
   3. Find two numbers with a product of 1.344.
   4. Find two numbers with a product of 0.1344.
   5. Explain how you got your answers and why you think they are correct.

B. **1.** Find two numbers with a product between 2000 and 3000.
   2. By moving decimal points, change the value of each of the numbers you found in part 1 so that their product is between 200 and 300.
   3. By moving decimal points, change the value of each of the numbers you found in part 1 so that their product is between 20 and 30.
   4. By moving decimal points, change the value of each of the numbers you found in part 1 so that their product is between 2 and 3.
   5. Explain what you did to get your answers and why you think they are correct.

Problem 6.4 Follow-Up

1. What number times 6 gives the product 0.36? Explain.
2. What number times 0.9 gives the product 2.7? Explain.
3. What number times 1.5 gives the product 0.045? Explain.
4. What number times 0.12 gives the product 24? Explain.

Assignment Choices

ACE questions 11, 12, and unassigned choices from earlier problems

Answers to Problem 6.4

See page 76g.

Answers to Problem 6.4 Follow-Up

See page 76g.

6.5 Fencing a Yard

Kelly has a new Golden Retriever. The dog is full of energy and needs some safe space in which to exercise. Kelly has several friends who have agreed to help her fence in part of her yard—she just needs to buy the materials for the fence.

Problem 6.5

Kelly wants to fence in a rectangular space in her yard, 9 meters by 7.5 meters. The salesperson at the supply store recommends that she put up posts every $1\frac{1}{2}$ meters. The posts cost $2.19 each. Kelly will also need to buy wire mesh to string between the posts. The wire mesh is sold by the meter from large rolls and costs $5.98 a meter. A gate to fit in one of the spaces between the posts costs $25.89. Seven staples are needed to attach the wire mesh to each post. Staples come in boxes of 50, and each box costs $3.99.

A. How much will the materials Kelly needs cost before sales tax? Show how you arrived at your answer.

B. Local sales tax is 7%. How much will Kelly's total bill be?

▦ Problem 6.5 Follow-Up

Using centimeter grid paper, draw a diagram of the fence. Draw the diagram carefully and accurately, and mark the position of each post and the gate.

Answers to Problem 6.5

A. Possible answer: 22 posts × $2.19 = $48.18, 32 meters of wire × $5.98 = $191.36 (31.5 meters cost $188.37), 1 gate = $25.89, and 4 boxes of staples × $3.99 = $15.96 (3 boxes cost $11.97). Therefore, the total cost = $281.39 (or $277.40, or $278.40, or $274.41 if groups took the lesser amount on the wire, staples, or both).

B. Possible answer: $281.39 × 0.07 = about $19.70, so the cost plus tax = about $301.09 (or about $296.82, about $297.89, or about $293.62 if groups took the lesser amount on the wire, staples, or both).

Answer to Problem 6.5 Follow-Up

See page 76h.

Fencing a Yard

Launch

- Read the story of Kelly and her dog.

- Make sure students understand what they are to do.

Explore

- As you circulate, question the assumptions students are making.

- Have each student make his or her own record of the problem and solution.

Summarize

- Ask groups to share their final costs and the assumptions they made.

- Pose additional questions to allow students to practice mental estimation.

Assignment Choices

ACE question 13 and unassigned choices from earlier problems

Assessment

It is appropriate to use Check-Up 3 after this problem.

Answers

Applications

1. $48; Possible explanation: I rounded each amount to whole dollars and added: $24 + $8 + $3 + $13 = $48.

2. $97; Possible explanation: I rounded each amount to whole dollars and subtracted: $120 − $23 = $97.

3. $180.00; Possible explanation: I rounded the dollar amount to whole dollars and multiplied by 10, then by 2, and added the two amounts.

4a. The measures are larger for the second week than for the first week because the plant is growing. During a single week, the teams may not have all measured from the same point on the plant. The measuring devices they used may have had different divisions between the centimeter marks.

4b. First week mean: (3.4 + 3.25 + 3.3 + 3.5 + 3.35) ÷ 5 = 16.8 ÷ 5 = 3.36 cm

Second week mean: (7.95 + 7.8 + 8 + 8.15 + 8.2) ÷ 5 = 40.1 ÷ 5 = 8.02 cm

4c. 8.02 − 3.36 = 4.66 cm

5. (2 × $0.75) + $1.39 + $1.79 + (2 × $1.19) + $1.64 = $8.70

$8.70 × 3% = $8.70 × 0.03 = $0.26

$8.70 + $0.26 = $8.96

As you work on these ACE questions, use your calculator whenever you need it.

Applications

In 1–3, estimate the answer, and explain how you made your estimate.

1. $23.54 + $7.98 + $3.45 + $13.03 ≈

2. $119.56 − $22.90 ≈

3. $15.10 × 12 ≈

4. Mr. Sandival's class is growing a plant. Each of the five teams in his class measured the height of the plant at the end of the first week and at the end of the second week. Here is a table of their measurements.

	Team 1	Team 2	Team 3	Team 4	Team 5
First week	3.4 cm	3.25 cm	3.3 cm	3.5 cm	3.35 cm
Second week	7.95 cm	7.8 cm	8 cm	8.15 cm	8.2 cm

a. All the teams measured the same plant. Why are the measures different?

b. Find the mean of the teams' measures for each week.

c. Using the means, how much did the plant grow from the first week to the second week?

5. Samuel buys the following at the grocery store:

two dozen eggs at $0.75 a dozen

one pound of butter at $1.39

a 5-pound bag of sugar for $1.79

two 5-pound bags of flour at $1.19 each

an 8-ounce package of unsweetened chocolate for $1.64

If Samuel pays 3% sales tax, how much is his bill?

6. Loren is laying decorative brick along both edges of the 21-meter walkway up to his house. Each brick is 0.26 meters long. He is placing the bricks end to end. How many bricks does he need to do the job?

7. Lynette has a beautiful box that she wants to protect. She has been advised to put a strip of molding along each edge of the box to protect it. She measures the edges and finds that the length is 0.75 meters, the width is 0.4 meters, and the height is 0.22 meters.

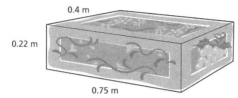

a. Lynette decides she needs four of each of these lengths. Is she correct? Explain.

b. How much molding does Lynette need in all?

c. If the molding costs $0.90 a meter, how much will Lynette's bill be without sales tax?

d. If the sales tax is 4%, how much will her final bill be?

Connections

8. What happens to a decimal number when you multiply it by 10 repeatedly? Use an example to explain your thinking.

9. What happens to a decimal number when you multiply it by 5 repeatedly? Use an example to explain your thinking.

10. Use your calculator to explore what happens to a decimal number when you divide it by 10 repeatedly. Use an example to explain your thinking.

6. 162; 21 ÷ 0.26 = 80.77, so it will take about 81 bricks for each side, which is 162 bricks altogether.

7a. yes; Two edges are lengths on the bottom of the box, and two edges are lengths on the top. Two edges are widths on the bottom of the box, and two edges are widths on the top. Four edges are heights, two on each end of the box.

7b. 4 × 0.4 = 1.6, 4 × 0.75 = 3.0, 4 × 0.22 = 0.88, and 1.6 + 3.0 + 0.88 = 5.48 m

7c. 5.48 × $0.90 = $4.93

7d. $4.93 × 0.04 = $0.20 (rounded to nearest cent), and $4.93 + $0.20 = $5.13

Connections

8. The decimal point moves one place to the right each time you multiply by 10: 0.0392 × 10 = 0.392, 0.392 × 10 = 3.92, and 3.92 × 10 = 39.2.

9. See page 76h.

10. The decimal point moves one place to the left each time you divide by 10: 32.56 ÷ 10 = 3.256, 3.256 ÷ 10 = 0.3256, 0.3256 ÷ 10 = 0.03256, and 0.03256 ÷ 10 = 0.003256.

Investigation 6   73

11a. See below right.

11b. See below right.

11c. See page 76h.

11d. See page 76h.

11e. I found the difference between the two endpoints and divided by 4, since there are four equal divisions between the two numbers. Then I added that amount to the first number on the left, added the same amount to that answer, and then added the amount once more to the next answer.

Extensions

12. See page 76i.

11. In a–d, each mark on the number line is spaced so that the distance between two consecutive marks is the same. Copy each number line and label the marks.

a. 1.8   2

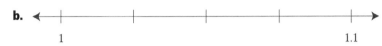

b. 1   1.1

c. 2.93   2.95

d. 1.99   2.01

e. Explain how you figured out what the labels should be.

Extensions

12. The table on the next page lists the winners of the gold medal in nine consecutive Olympic meets in men's springboard diving. The points are awarded for the difficulty and the execution of the dive.

In a–c, give evidence to support your conclusion. You may want to make a table of the differences between each pair of years.

a. Between what two years did the greatest change in winning score occur?

b. Between what two years did the next greatest change in winning score occur?

c. Between what two years did the least change in winning score occur?

d. What is the average of Greg Louganis's scores?

11a.

11b.

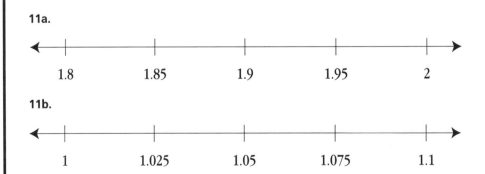

Men's Springboard Diving

Year	Winner (country)	Score
1960	Gary Tobian (USA)	170
1964	Kenneth Stizberger (USA)	150.9
1968	Bernie Wrightson (USA)	170.15
1972	Vladimir Vasin (USSR)	594.09
1976	Phil Boggs (USA)	619.52
1980	Aleksandr Portnov (USSR)	905.02
1984	Greg Louganis (USA)	754.41
1988	Greg Louganis (USA)	730.8
1992	Mark Lenzi (USA)	676.53

13 **a.** Show four *different* ways to fill in the missing numbers on the number line.

2.1

b. Add the five numbers in each of your answers in part a. Do you see a pattern?

c. Can you find four numbers for the blanks on this number line so that the sum of the five numbers will be 10? Why or why not?

2.1

13a. See page 76i.

13b. Possible answer:

0.1 + 1.1 + 2.1 + 3.1 + 4.1 = 10.5

1.1 + 1.6 + 2.1 + 2.6 + 3.1 = 10.5

1.6 + 1.85 + 2.1 + 2.35 + 2.6 = 10.5

1.9 + 2.0 + 2.1 + 2.2 + 2.3 = 10.5

All of the numbers add to 10.5. Since the numbers are equally spaced around 2.1, the average of the two outside numbers that are the same distance from 2.1, but in opposite directions, must be 2.1, and the average of the two inside numbers that are also the same distance from 2.1, but in the opposite direction, must be 2.1. This means that the sum of the numbers will always be 10.5, which is 5 × 2.1. Another way to say this is that the mean of the numbers is 2.1. Since there are 5 numbers, the sum must be 10.5.

13c. no; Since the numbers are evenly spaced around 2.1, the mean will be 2.1. Therefore the sum of the five numbers must be 5 × 2.1 = 10.5.

1. Line up the numbers so that the decimal points are underneath each other. This aligns digits representing like places. Place a decimal point just below the decimal points in the numbers being added, so all three are in a vertical line. Then, simply add the numbers as you would whole numbers. As you add, you are adding digits that represent the same value in terms of their place in the number. You will be adding tenths to tenths and hundreds to hundreds. For example:

```
  2.145
+ 32.74
 34.885
```

(You can add a zero after the 4 if you want to because it does not change the place value of the other digits.)

```
 405.67
+ 33.80
 439.47
```

(The zero after the 8 does not change the place value of the other digits.)

2. The rule handles this case. Notice that two zeros were added to the end of 11.99 to help keep track of the place values.

```
  23.0574
+ 11.9900
  35.0474
```

3–6. See page 76j.

Mathematical Reflections

In this investigation, you explored adding, subtracting, and multiplying decimals. You looked for relationships between whole-number and decimal computation. These questions will help you summarize what you have learned:

(1) Describe in words, and illustrate with one or more examples, how to add two decimal numbers without using a calculator. Explain why your method makes sense.

(2) Test your method from part 1 on this sum: 23.0574 + 11.99. Does your method tell you how to handle this case? If not, adjust your description so that someone reading it would know how to add these two decimals.

(3) Describe in words, and illustrate with one or more examples, how you subtract two decimal numbers without using a calculator. Explain why your method makes sense.

(4) Test your method from part 3 on this difference: 23.05 − 11.9863. Does your method tell you how to handle this case? If not, adjust your description so that someone reading it would know how to subtract these two decimals.

(5) How is the number of decimal places in the product of two decimal numbers related to the number of decimal places in each of the numbers? Why is this so?

(6) **a.** Find or create an example in which the product of two decimals is smaller than either of the numbers that are multiplied.

  b. Find or create an example in which the product of two decimals is smaller than one of the numbers multiplied but larger than the other.

  c. Find or create an example in which the product of two decimals is larger than either of the numbers multiplied.

  d. Look for patterns that will help you predict which of these results—a, b, or c—will be the case with any multiplication problem that you do.

Think about these questions, discuss your ideas with other students and your teacher, and then write a summary of your findings in your journal.

TEACHING THE INVESTIGATION

6.1 • Buying School Supplies

This problem is a game designed to help students practice estimating sums and differences of decimals. In the game, students create addition and subtraction problems that give them a result that is on the gameboard. Students are likely to make several estimates in the process of taking each turn.

Launch

Demonstrate the School Supply game by playing a couple of rounds against the class. During your turn, model what you expect from your students. For example, suppose you want to cover the $1.89 space. You might start by looking for two items that add to $1.89. When you scan the supply list, you might look for numbers with units digits that add to 9. You want to find numbers with a sum that is near, but smaller than, $2.00. For example, a highlighter is $1.05, so you would need to spend 84¢ more—the price of a roll of tape, so you announce that you want to buy a highlighter and a roll of tape. Or, suppose you want to cover the $3.15 space. You could start by choosing a more costly item, such as a notebook, leaving you with $3.15 − $2.24 = 91¢ to spend. Since getting a 1 in the units digit is difficult, you might look for items that could give a 1 here—such as three sets of divider pages for 3×7¢ = 21¢. This leaves 70¢, and a ruler costs exactly this amount.

When students understand the rules, let them play several rounds.

Explore

Have students play the game in pairs. As they play, they will get lots of practice estimating and computing with decimals, and a chance to think about the size of decimals and about place values. Because students want the answer to the problem they pose to be a number that will give them an advantage on the game board, they are likely to make several estimates in the process of taking a turn.

As you visit pairs, point to a number that has been taken on the board, and ask the students to explain how they found a set of items that cost exactly that amount. Remind them to think about strategies they are using to help win the game.

Summarize

Have a class discussion during which students share their strategies for winning the game. Here are some strategies students have used:

- Alisa says she figures out the doubles of each item sold, because those amounts are easy to determine—if they are on the board, she has some quick, easy marks to help her get started.

- Kevin adds two amounts together and sees whether their sum is on the board, since adding only two amounts is easy to do.

- Sharif says that once his opponent has a mark on the board, he tries to add items and get one of the amounts next to the mark so that he can block his opponent.

During the discussion, help students build better strategies by asking questions that focus on estimation and on number facts that help find a set of items that work. Pose a problem that involves adding decimals that are not money values, such as 12.15 + 3.089.

How can we use what we know about money to help us add these numbers?

Why does it make sense to add digits that have the same place value?

Students might reason that in 12.15 + 3.089, you must add the 5 and the 8 because they are both hundredths. This is clearer when we arrange the two numbers vertically, so like place values are aligned:

$$
\begin{array}{r}
12.15 \\
+\ 3.089 \\
\hline
15.239
\end{array}
$$

Now we can see that there are thousandths in only one of the numbers, and the sum is 9 thousandths. The hundredths in the two numbers add to 13 hundredths, which we can think of as (10 + 3) hundredths. This is the same as 10 hundredths (1 tenth) and 3 hundredths, so we have 1 tenth plus another 1 tenth for 2 tenths in the sum. We find the sum of the whole-number parts as we have always found it.

6.2 • Moving Decimal Points

This problem focuses on the meaning of place value in adding and subtracting decimal numbers and introduces the strategy of adding zeros to make decimal numbers with the same number of digits to the right of the decimal point.

Launch

Talk about the introduction and the examples of Alice's work given in the "Think about this!" box. Explain that Alice is trying to build different sums by inserting the decimal points at different places in two given strings of digits without adding any "illegal" zeros.

Be sure students understand that when they add zeros to the number, they must not do it in a way that changes the value of the places for other digits in the number. For example, when working with 2365, the combinations 2365, 236.5, 23.65, 2.365, and 0.2365 are all allowed, but 0.002365 is not allowed. (We add this constraint to make the number of options reasonable.) Zeros can also be added at the end of digits after the decimal point, as in 2.36500. Sometimes we add zeros like this so that the numbers we are adding or subtracting have the same number of digits to the right of the decimal point.

Explore

Have students work on parts A and B individually, then with a partner to share their examples and to work on parts C and D.

As you circulate, check to see whether students' answers are reasonable. Point to one of their sums or differences, and ask them to convince you that it is correct. Ask questions about how the place values of the digits change as the decimal is moved to make a new number.

Assign the follow-up as a challenge for pairs who finish early.

Summarize

Ask students to record some of the examples they got for parts A and B on the board.

Are there any other possibilities that were not recorded on the board?

Allow students to add to the work on the board until they have recorded all their problems. Then, talk about parts C and D. Make the point that in situations in which there are many different answers, it is often interesting to think about the largest and smallest possible answers. These extreme values often give us a lot of information about the situation.

6.3 • Multiplying Decimals

In this problem students explore patterns that occur when a number is systematically multiplied.

Launch

Before introducing the problem, review the introductory material on pages 68 and 69 of the student edition.

Ask students to look over the problems in part A and to describe how the problems in a set are related.

What patterns were used to generate these sets of problems? What would the next two problems be if we added to each of these sets of problems?

When students see how the sets differ, let them use their calculators to see what patterns they can find in the answers for each set.

Explore

Allow students to explore this problem individually for a few minutes before they share in groups of two or three. Comparing their results will help them to clean up their data, and once students agree on what the products are, the search for patterns will be more productive.

As you circulate, encourage students to make up problems on which to test their ideas. When they are ready, ask them to answer the follow-up questions.

Summarize

Focus the summary on the patterns students see in the products and the reasons these patterns make sense. You want students to see that multiplying by a progressively smaller number gives a progressively smaller product. You also want them to begin to develop some sense of the order of magnitude of the answer. For example, recognizing that 0.01 is 10 times bigger than 0.001 can help us to understand why the product of 2.1 and 0.01 is 10 times bigger than the product of 2.1 and 0.001.

Starting with the smallest product in a set and multiplying by 10 to get the product of the factors in the equation above helps to cement the relationships. Moving from the smallest product to the largest product in a set can be followed by starting at the other end—the largest product—and dividing by 10 to get the next smallest product in the set. Time spent experimenting with such patterns helps students to see the relationship between the number of decimal places in the two factors and the number of decimal places in the product. More importantly, it helps them to begin to build an understanding of *why* this relationship exists.

Another way to focus students on the relationship is to express the decimals as fractions and look at the relationship between the denominator in the product expressed as a fraction and the number of decimal places in the product expressed as a decimal. For example, $\frac{21}{10} \times \frac{1}{1000} = \frac{21}{10,000}$ or 0.0021. The four decimal places correspond to the four zeros in ten thousandths.

For the Teacher: Adding Zeros to a Decimal

Students should be careful about adding zeros to the end of a decimal; the zeros do not count since they do not affect the size of the numbers and thus do not affect the answer. Students may need to add zeros and test a few cases to verify that this is so.

6.4 • Shifting Decimal Points

Up to this point, students have been finding products that involve decimals. The challenge in this problem is to work the other way, finding factors that will produce a given product.

Launch

Present an example so students understand the challenge.

> Let's look at the number 1560. Who can tell me a number that is a factor of 1560? Can someone tell me two numbers whose product is 1560?

Students' familiarity with factors and multiples from the *Prime Time* unit can be employed here to help them find a pair of numbers whose product is 1560. They may suggest finding the prime factorization of the number and using it to generate several pairs of numbers whose product is 1560. The prime factorization is $2 \times 2 \times 2 \times 3 \times 5 \times 13$. Some pairs of numbers that give 1560 are 8×195, 24×65, 39×40, and 52×30.

> We have found several pairs of numbers that have 1560 as their product, such as 39×40. Now can you give me a pair of numbers whose product is 156.0? (*3.9 × 40, 39 × 4.0, and so on*)

Can you give me a pair of numbers with a product of 1.560? *(2.4 × 0.65, 0.024 × 65, 0.39 × 4.0, and so on)*

When students understand what the problem is asking them, turn them loose to explore.

Explore

Let students work in pairs or groups of three. For part A, have each student in a group find two different factor pairs for each product. This will generate more examples. As you work with the groups, ask questions that extend their thinking beyond the series given in the problem. For example, ask for two numbers whose product is 0.01344 or 0.001344. You can also extend in the other direction; for example, ask for two numbers whose product is 13,440 or 134,400.

Part B is more difficult, because students are working in a range rather than with a specific product. Again, have each member of the group find two solutions for each part. Once a group finds several pairs that will work for part 1, they must decide how to adjust the place values to get a product within a smaller range. For groups that are struggling, you may need to ask how 200 is related to 2000 and how 300 is related to 3000 to get them to begin to see how they can apply the kind of thinking they developed in part A. The question is how many times smaller must the numbers be to give the new range. Each new range is 10 times smaller, or $\frac{1}{10}$ as large as the numbers in the range before it.

Summarize

As students share their answers to the various parts of the problem, ask what is alike and different among the pairs of numbers in each of the groups of answers. They should see that for each product, the sum of the number of decimal places in the two factors is the same, though the numbers themselves may differ.

Use the follow-up questions to remind students of the connection between division and multiplication: a division problem can be thought of as finding a missing factor.

To assess students' understanding, pose the following question.

> Here is a new product on which to test your skill. (*Write 1105 on the board.*) I will give you a couple of minutes to find two numbers whose product is 1105.

The factorization of 1105 is $5 \times 13 \times 17$, so the possible factors are 65×17, 5×221, and 13×85. Some students may see that they could give variations with decimals, such as 650×1.7. If this idea does not arise, add an example to those your students have generated, and ask whether it works and why.

6.5 • Fencing a Yard

The culminating problem for *Bits and Pieces II* is a multi-step problem in which students need to keep track of each part in order to find the grand total.

Launch

Read the story of Kelly and her dog with your students. Make sure they have a good mental image of the fence and how it is to be constructed, but don't let the discussion go on so long that students have nothing left to think about in their groups.

Explore

As students work in groups of two or three, ask questions about their assumptions, such as how they determined how much of each material Kelly would need.

Encourage each student in each group to make his own record of the solution and the assumptions the group agrees to.

Summarize

Groups' answers will depend on the assumptions they made. Have groups present their argument for the final costs and explain what decisions or assumptions they made. Some students may argue that Kelly only needs 31.5 meters of wire and therefore would buy that amount. Others may argue that the store will only sell in whole meters, so she would have to buy 32 meters. Others may say that she will need a bit of extra wire at the posts where the gate is attached. Some groups may argue for three boxes of staples, reasoning that the two posts at the gate need fewer staples. Others may argue for four boxes, because Kelly must still attach wire to the two posts beside the gate, or because it is likely that some staples will be damaged during construction.

You can use this summary as an opportunity to give students practice with mental estimation.

> How can you find, in your head, the cost of four boxes of staples? How can you quickly estimate how much the wire will cost?

Strategies based on recognizing that prices are often just under a whole-number amount should arise. The staples are $3.99 a box. If they were $4 a box, four boxes would cost $16. These staples would cost 4¢ less, so the cost is $15.96. The wire is about $6 a meter. You need about 30 meters, so the cost is about $180.

Additional Answers

Answers to Problem 6.3

A.

Set 1	Set 2	Set 3	Set 4
larger than 1	larger than 1	smaller than $\frac{1}{2}$	larger than 1
larger than 1	smaller than $\frac{1}{2}$	smaller than $\frac{1}{2}$	larger than 1
smaller than $\frac{1}{2}$	smaller than $\frac{1}{2}$	smaller than $\frac{1}{2}$	smaller than $\frac{1}{2}$
smaller than $\frac{1}{2}$	smaller than $\frac{1}{2}$	smaller than $\frac{1}{2}$	smaller than $\frac{1}{2}$
smaller than $\frac{1}{2}$	smaller than $\frac{1}{2}$	smaller than $\frac{1}{2}$	smaller than $\frac{1}{2}$
smaller than $\frac{1}{2}$	smaller than $\frac{1}{2}$	smaller than $\frac{1}{2}$	smaller than $\frac{1}{2}$

B. In set 1, we are exploring the product of a whole number, 21, and a decimal. The decimal is 10 times smaller as we move from problem to problem. In set 2, we are multiplying a decimal times a decimal, but the first number is kept the same, 2.1, and the second factor is 10 times smaller each time. In set 3, we have the same numbers as in set 2 except the first number is now 10 times smaller, or 0.21. In set 4, the product is a decimal times a decimal, but we are multiplying by a decimal that has something other than a single 1 and 0s as digits.

Set 1	Set 2	Set 3	Set 4
21 × 1 = 21	2.1 × 1 = 2.1	0.21 × 1 = 0.21	2.1 × 11 = 23.1
21 × 0.1 = 2.1	2.1 × 0.1 = 0.21	0.21 × 0.1 = 0.021	2.1 × 1.1 = 2.31
21 × 0.01 = 0.21	2.1 × 0.01 = 0.021	0.21 × 0.01 = 0.0021	2.1 × 0.11 = 0.231
21 × 0.001 = 0.021	2.1 × 0.001 = 0.0021	0.21 × 0.001 = 0.00021	2.1 × 0.011 = 0.0231
21 × 0.0001 = 0.0021	2.1 × 0.0001 = 0.00021	0.21 × 0.0001 = 0.00021	2.1 × 0.0011 = 0.00231

C. The number of decimal places in the answer is the sum of the number of decimal places in the factors.

Answers to Problem 6.4

A. Possible answers:

1. 42 × 32 = 1344; 24 × 56 = 1344

2. 4.2 × 32 = 134.4; 24 × 5.6 = 134.4

3. 0.42 × 3.2 = 1.344; 24 × 0.056 = 1.344

4. 0.42 × 0.32 = 0.1344; 0.024 × 5.6 = 0.1344

5. I factored 1344 to find a factor pair. Once I had two numbers that worked, I used the fact that multiplying by 0.1 makes a number 10 times smaller, which moves the decimal point one place to the left, to find the other pairs.

B. Possible answers:

1. 56 × 48 = 2688

2. 5.6 × 48 = 268.8

3. 5.6 × 4.8 = 26.88

4. 5.6 × 0.48 = 2.688

5. I multiplied two numbers together and used the result to help me find a pair of numbers with a product in the given range. I first thought I would have to have two decimal places in the factors to move the product between 200 and 300. I tried this and it was wrong. Then I realized that the two endpoints on the range were $\frac{1}{10}$ of the original endpoints, so a number in between them would be $\frac{1}{10}$ of the original product.

Answers to Problem 6.4 Follow-Up

1. 0.06; Possible explanation: 0.36 ÷ 6 = 0.06. Or, we can reason that 6 × 6 = 36, and we need 0.36, which is 100 times smaller, so we must move the decimal point in the other factor two places to the left.

2. 3; Possible explanation: 2.7 ÷ 0.9 = 3. Or, we can reason that 3 × 9 = 27. We need 2.7, which is 10 times smaller. We have 0.9, which is already 10 times smaller, so the other factor is 3.

3. 0.03; Possible explanation: 0.045 ÷ 1.5 = 0.03. Or, we can reason that 3 × 15 = 45, and we need 0.045, which is 1000 times smaller. One factor, 1.5, is 10 times smaller, so we need to make the other factor 100 times smaller, or 0.03.

4. 200; Possible explanation: 24 ÷ 0.12 = 200. Or, we can reason that 2 × 12 = 24, and we already have a factor, 0.12, that is 100 times smaller, so we need the other factor to be 100 times bigger to, keep the product the same, or 200.

Answer to Problem 6.5 Follow-Up

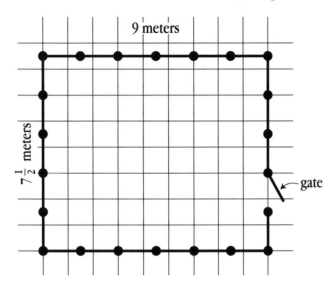

ACE Answers

Connections

9. What students see here depends on the number they use as an example. In the examples below, the original number is even and the first product "lost" a decimal place. In the first example, by the second product the decimals had disappeared. In the second example each product after the first kept the one decimal place. What happened? Notice that when the factor multiplied by 5 is even, the product ends in 0. Hence, we can "lose" a decimal place. If the factor multiplied by 5 is odd, the product cannot end in zero and thus you cannot "lose" a decimal place.

$0.32 \times 5 = 1.6$	$0.26 \times 5 = 1.3$
$1.6 \times 5 = 8$	$1.3 \times 5 = 6.5$
$8 \times 5 = 40$	$6.5 \times 5 = 32.5$
$40 \times 5 = 200$	$32.5 \times 5 = 162.5$

11c.

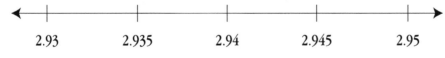

11d.

Extensions

12a. The greatest change occurred between 1968 and 1972.

12b. The next greatest change occurred between 1976 and 1980.

12c. The least change occurred between 1960 and 1964.

For the Teacher: Modeling Change

To find the answers in a systematic way, students could make a table of change from one year to the next. They could also use estimation to pick out the particular change points that look promising. Here we give a table of change from the year before.

Year	Change in score
1964	−19.1
1968	+19.25
1972	+423.94
1976	+25.43
1980	+285.5
1984	−150.61
1988	−23.61
1992	−54.27

12d. 754.41 + 730.8 = 1485.21, and 1485.21 ÷ 2 = 742.605

13a. Possible answer:

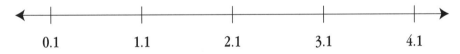

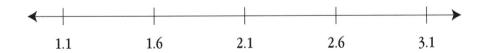

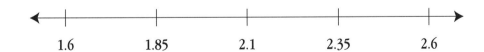

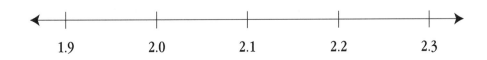

Mathematical Reflections

3. Line up the numbers so that the decimals are underneath each other. This aligns the digits representing like places. Place a decimal point just below the decimal points in the numbers being added, so all three are in a vertical line. Then, simply subtract the numbers as you would whole numbers. As you subtract, you are subtracting digits with the same place value.

4. The rule handles this case. Notice that two zeros were added to the end of 23.0500 to help keep track of the place values.

$$
\begin{array}{r}
23.0500 \\
-\ 11.9863 \\
\hline
11.0637
\end{array}
$$

5. The number of decimal places in the product is equal to the sum of the number of decimal places in the two numbers. This is because the number of decimal places in the two numbers is the same as the power of 10 that tells how many times smaller the product will be than the product of the two numbers without the decimals. For example, $12 \times 34 = 408$, but 0.12×3.4 must be $10 \times 10 \times 10 = 1000$ times smaller since the two numbers are 100 times smaller and 10 times smaller, so the product is 0.408.

6a. Possible answer: $0.23 \times 0.1 = 0.023$

6b. Possible answer: $2.3 \times 0.1 = 0.23$

6c. Possible answer: $2.3 \times 1.1 = 2.53$

6d. If both the numbers are less than 1, the product will be smaller than both. If one of the numbers is less than 1 and one is greater than 1, the product will be smaller than only one of the numbers. If both of the numbers are greater than 1, the product will be larger than either of the multiplied numbers.

Assessment Resources

The final assessment is a unit test consisting of two parts. The first part is done in class. The second part is a take-home portion. For the take-home part, students are to go through catalogs and find three different items they would like to order. Each item they select must cost at least $10.00. You might want to have a collection of catalogs for students who need them; perhaps solicit the help of your colleagues in gathering them.

Check-Up 1

1. Ms. Ngyen has a total of 150 students in her classes. Of these students, 30% eat during the first lunch period, 20% eat during the second lunch period, and the rest eat during the third lunch period. How many of her students eat during each lunch period?

2. Each week, Stewart saves $16 of his $48 paycheck. What percent of his pay does he save?

3. During the T-Shirt Shoppe's Fantastic Fall Sale, customers who buy an $8 t-shirt at the regular price get a second t-shirt at half price. Zahara bought two t-shirts during the sale. What percent did she save off the regular price?

4. Ted has a coupon for 50¢ off a jar of Sticky peanut butter. If a jar of the peanut butter is priced at $1.59, what percent of the cost will Ted save by using the coupon?

5. The total bill for drinks and a large pizza for three people is $14.90 before tax. The sales tax is 5%. The group wants to leave a 15% tip. How much should each person pay if they are to share the bill equally? Indicate whether you figured out the tip before or after the tax was added.

© Dale Seymour Publications

Check-Up 2

1. At D. J.'s Drink Stand, Erika ordered chocolate milk made in the following proportions: $\frac{1}{4}$ chocolate syrup, $\frac{2}{3}$ cold milk, and the rest whipped cream.

   a. What fraction of Erika's drink will be whipped cream?

   b. Erika changes her mind and decides that she wants the whipped cream in her drink replaced with cold milk. What fraction of her drink will be milk?

2. Gregorio made money over his summer vacation by mowing lawns. One week he worked the following schedule:

Monday	$5\frac{1}{2}$ hours
Tuesday	$3\frac{3}{4}$ hours
Wednesday	$4\frac{3}{4}$ hours
Thursday	$6\frac{1}{4}$ hours
Friday	$2\frac{3}{4}$ hours
Saturday	$2\frac{3}{4}$ hours

   How many hours did Gregorio work for the week?

© Dale Seymour Publications®

Check-Up 2

3. Mr. Broadston took his cross-country team out for pizza. He ordered four medium pizzas, which were each cut into 12 pieces. The team ate the following amounts:

Scott ate $\frac{1}{3}$ of a pizza   Rusty ate $\frac{1}{2}$ of a pizza

Josh ate $\frac{7}{12}$ of a pizza   Da-Wei ate $\frac{5}{12}$ of a pizza

Darin ate $\frac{2}{12}$ of a pizza   Alex ate $\frac{2}{3}$ of a pizza

Mr. Broadston ate $\frac{1}{12}$ of a pizza

   a.   How many pizzas did the team eat?

   b.   How many pizzas were left?

   c.   What is the difference between the amount of pizza eaten and the amount of pizza left uneaten?

© Dale Seymour Publications

Check-Up 3

1. On a particular map of Denmark, 1 inch on the map represents 12 miles.

   a. What does $2\frac{1}{2}$ inches on the map represent?

   b. What does $3\frac{3}{4}$ inches on the map represent?

2. A winter sports pass at Wood Middle School costs $15.00. A student without a pass must pay $1.75 for each event. How many sports events would a student have to attend to make the pass a better deal?

3. If each person in North America produces $3\frac{2}{3}$ pounds of garbage a day, how many pounds of garbage does each person produce in a year?

© Dale Seymour Publications®

Check-Up 3

4. Derek and Conor work for two different radio stations. Derek makes $15.75 an hour. Conor makes $12.25 an hour for a 20-hour work week, but he is paid time and a half for any time he works over 20 hours. (*Time and a half* means Conor is paid $1\frac{1}{2}$ times his hourly wage for each overtime hour.) If Derek and Conor both work 30 hours one week, how much does each make?

5. Paula had $\frac{2}{3}$ of a pan of brownies left. She took the brownies to school, and her friends ate $\frac{3}{4}$ of them.

   a. How much of the pan of brownies did her friends eat?

   b. How much of the pan of brownies was left?

Assign these questions as additional homework, or use them as review, quiz, or test questions.

1. Find out what your local sales tax is. Ingrid purchased a product in your area and was charged 63¢ for sales tax. Give three possible amounts the product could have cost.

2. Michel and Benita are making a square dartboard for the school carnival. They want to paint the board so that it is 30% red, 20% green, 40% yellow, and 10% blue.

   a. Design a square dartboard that fits Michel and Benita's requirements.

   b. Benita decided that a circle would be better for the game. Make a circular dartboard that satisfies the same color requirements given above.

   c. Which dartboard would you rather use?

   d. Which dartboard was easier to design? Why?

3. McDonald's farmstand sells eggs for 80¢ a dozen.

   a. How much would $3\frac{1}{2}$ dozen eggs cost?

   b. How much would $\frac{3}{4}$ of a dozen eggs cost?

4. Suppose that the Pizza Pirate ate $\frac{1}{3}$ of a pizza the first night and $\frac{1}{4}$ of what remained every night after that. How many nights would it take until the pizza was half gone? Drawing a picture might help you explain your reasoning.

5. a. What happens to the size of a fraction between 0 and 1 when you add the same number to the numerator and the denominator? For example, if you start with $\frac{1}{2}$ and add 1 to the numerator and the denominator, and you get $\frac{2}{3}$. Choose other fractions between 0 and 1, and add the same number to the numerator and the denominator. How do the new fractions compare to the fractions you started with? What patterns do you notice?

   b. How does the fraction you get by adding the same number to both the numerator and denominator of a fraction *greater than 1* (for example, $\frac{6}{5}$) compare to the fraction you started with?

   c. How does the new fraction you get by multiplying the numerator and denominator of a fraction by the same number compare to the fraction you started with? You may want to try several fractions and look for patterns.

   d. What happens when you add or multiply the numerator and denominator of a fraction that is equivalent to 1 by the same number?

   e. Summarize what you know from the work you did in this problem.

© Dale Seymour Publications®

6. The cost of renting a drum set is a $25 initial fee, plus $35.95 a month. How much will it cost to rent a drum set for a year?

7. The local youth group has decided to run a summer baby-sitting program to earn money for the club and for the individuals in the club. The baby-sitting program will run from 9:00 A.M. to 4:30 P.M. Monday through Friday. The youth-group leader and student officers must develop a plan for the program. (When answering the following questions, show enough of your work so that someone reading it can follow how you solved the problems.)

   a. Jin Lee, Sarah, Jesse, and Alex are assigned to the toddler room for the month of July. Two students must work in this room at all times. They decide to share the workload equally. How many hours will each of them work each week?

   b. If students are paid $3.75 an hour, how much will each of these students be paid for a week of work?

   c. Set up a work schedule for Jin Lee, Sarah, Jesse, and Alex for a week in July.

   d. Jin Lee and Sarah decide to make a pancake breakfast for the six morning workers who work in the toddler room, the preschool room, and the kindergarten room. They found a recipe that will make 12 silver-dollar pancakes per batch. They figure that they need 30 silver-dollar pancakes, 5 per person. How much of each ingredient will they need to make 30 silver-dollar pancakes?

Silver-Dollar Pancakes

$1\frac{1}{4}$ cups flour

1 egg

3 teaspoons baking powder

$1\frac{1}{2}$ tablespoons sugar

$\frac{1}{2}$ teaspoon salt

$\frac{3}{4}$ cup milk

2 tablespoons salad oil

Makes 12 silver-dollar pancakes.

---

8. In stage 1 below, the middle one third of a line segment is covered by a triangle. In stage 2, the middle one third of each of the two parts that were uncovered in stage 1 are covered. In stage 3, the middle one third of each of the parts that were not covered in stage 3 are covered.

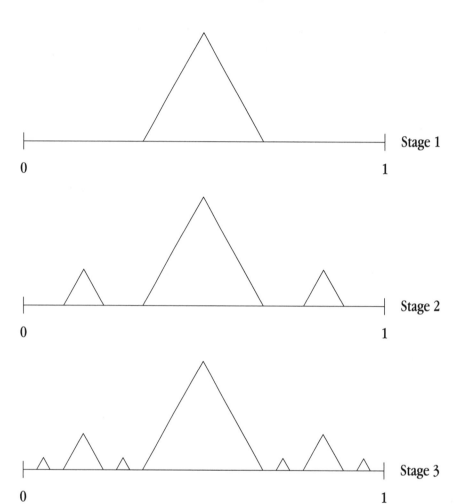

a. What fraction of the line is covered at stage 1? What fraction of the line is *not* covered?

b. What fraction of the line is covered at stage 2? What fraction of the line is *not* covered?

c. What fraction of the line is covered at stage 3? What fraction of the line is *not* covered?

© Dale Seymour Publications®

Unit Test: In-Class Portion

1. Troy is going to basketball camp. Before he goes, he needs to buy some things. He and his parents agree that he can buy two pairs of shorts, four t-shirts, six pairs of socks, and a jacket. Shop Easy has everything they need for the following prices:

   Shorts $7.98 each

   T-shirts $6.35—on sale: buy one at the regular price, and get a second at half price

   Socks $1.98 for two pairs

   Jackets $19.99 each

   a. How much will the total bill for Troy's clothes be, including sales tax? (Figure sales tax based on what is charged in your area.)

   b. Troy had $100 when he started his shopping. Did he have enough money? If so, how much extra? If not, how much was he short?

Unit Test: In-Class Portion

2. Kristine, a high-school student, works part time at the dry cleaners. Her take-home check is $80 every two weeks. She has set up this budget for herself:

$\frac{1}{3}$ of her paycheck goes into her college savings account

$\frac{1}{4}$ of her paycheck is for clothing

$\frac{1}{6}$ of her paycheck is for snacks

$\frac{1}{4}$ of her paycheck is for entertainment and recreational activities with friends

   a. What dollar amount of her paycheck goes to

       savings? _____   clothing? _____

       snacks? _____   entertainment? _____

   b. Make a circle graph showing Kristine's budget.

© Dale Seymour Publications®

Unit Test: In-Class Portion

3. Elizabeth is shopping for a new winter coat. She finds the coat that she likes the best in two different stores.

- In the first store, the coat is priced at $84, but a sale sign states that the coat is $\frac{1}{3}$ off.
- In the second store, the coat is priced at $76, but a sale sign states that the coat is $\frac{1}{4}$ off.

Store 1   Store 2

a. From which store should Elizabeth buy the coat if she wants to spend the least amount of money?

b. Elizabeth's mother finds the same coat in a catalog. The coat is priced the same as the regular price at the store from which Elizabeth has decided to buy (based on your results to part a), but the catalog has the coat on sale for 30% off. In addition, Elizabeth's mother has a coupon for $5.00 off any purchase from the catalog. Any catalog order has a shipping charge of 6% of the price of an item. Which is the better buy, the coat at the store or the coat in the catalog?

Unit Test: In-Class Portion

4. How many bows can you make from 5 meters of ribbon if a bow takes $\frac{1}{4}$ of a meter of ribbon?

5. If a toy store offers an additional 25% discount on board games that have already been reduced by 30%, will the final cost be the same as a discount of 55% on the original price? Work through an example to help explain your answer.

Unit Test: Take-Home Miniproject

Ordering from a Catalog

1. Find three different items you would like to order from a catalog. Each item must cost at least $10.00. On the back of your paper, tape or glue the picture of the item and its description, or draw a picture of the item and write out its description. Include the price.

2. Complete the attached order form as if you were ordering your three items from the C. M. Project catalog. On the back of the order form, show all the work you did to calculate the amounts for shipping and tax.

3. **a.** Choose one of the items you ordered. List the item with a brief description and give its price.

   b. What would this item cost if it were on sale for 25% off? Show how you found your answer.

   c. What would the item cost if it were on sale for $\frac{1}{3}$ off? Show how you found your answer.

4. Suppose another catalog has your first item listed for $5.00 less than the price you have listed. A third catalog has your item marked down 20%. If shipping charges and tax are the same, which is the better deal for you, and why?

C.M. Project Catalog
Order Form

Shipping Address

Name _____
Address _____
City _____ State _____ Zip Code _____
Phone ( ) _____

To speed up your order, use our toll-free number 24 hours a day, 7 days a week—100% of the time! 1-800-PER-CENT

Item No.	Description	Size	Color	Qty.	Price/Unit	Total

Merchandise Total	
Shipping (10% of Merchandise Total)	
Tax (_____%)	
TOTAL	

Method of Payment

☐ Charge to:
_____ VISA _____ MASTERCARD
Credit Card # _____
Expiration Date _____ / _____ / _____

☐ Check or Money Order

Signature _____

© Dale Seymour Publications®

Name _____ Date _____

Journal Organization

_____ Problems and Mathematical Reflections are labeled and dated.

_____ Work is neat and easy to find and follow.

Vocabulary

_____ All words are listed. _____ All words are defined and described.

Quizzes and Check-Ups

_____ Check-Up 1 _____ Check-Up 3

_____ Check-Up 2 _____ Unit Test

Homework Assignments

___ _____

___ _____

___ _____

___ _____

___ _____

___ _____

___ _____

___ _____

___ _____

___ _____

___ _____

___ _____

___ _____

___ _____

___ _____

___ _____

Self-Assessment

Vocabulary

Of the vocabulary words I defined or described in my journal, the word _____ best demonstrates my ability to give a clear definition or description.

Of the vocabulary words I defined or described in my journal, the word _____ best demonstrates my ability to use an example to help explain or describe an idea.

Mathematical Ideas

1. **a.** I learned these things about adding, subtracting, and multiplying fractions and decimals:

    b. I learned these things about working with percents:

    c. Here are page numbers of journal entries that give evidence of what I have learned, along with descriptions of what each entry shows:

2. **a.** These are the mathematical ideas I am still struggling with:

    b. This is why I think these ideas are difficult for me:

    c. Here are page numbers of journal entries that give evidence of what I am struggling with, along with descriptions of what each entry shows:

Class Participation

I contributed to the classroom discussion and understanding of *Bits and Pieces II* when I . . . (Give examples.)

Answers to Check-Up 1

1. In the first lunch period, there are $0.3 \times 150 = 45$ students. In the second lunch period, there are $0.2 \times 150 = 30$ students. This leaves 50% (or half) for the third lunch period, or 75 students.

2. $\frac{16}{48}$ = about 0.3333 or $33\frac{1}{3}$%

3. Normally, the two t-shirts would cost \$16; during the sale, they cost $8 + $4 = $12, a savings of $4. The percent savings is $\frac{4}{16} = 0.25$ or 25%.

4. Using the coupon, Ted would save $\frac{0.50}{1.59}$ = about 0.3144 or about 31.4%.

5. The tip can be figured in two ways, before tax and after tax.

    Evaluating the tip on the food cost before tax: The tip is $14.90 \times 0.15 = $2.235 or $2.24. The tax is $14.90 \times 0.05 = $0.745 or $0.75. The total bill is $14.90 + $0.75 + $2.24 = $17.89. Each person should pay about $17.89 \div 3 = $5.97.

    Evaluating the tip on the food cost after tax: The tax is $14.90 \times 0.05 = $0.745 or $0.75. The check total is $14.90 + $0.75 = $15.65. The tip is $15.65 \times 0.15 = $2.3475 or $2.35. The total bill is $15.65 + $2.35 = $18.00. Each person should pay about $18.00 \div 3 = $6.00.

Answers to Check-Up 2

1. a. $\frac{1}{4} + \frac{2}{3} = \frac{3}{12} + \frac{8}{12} = \frac{11}{12}$, so $\frac{1}{12}$ of the drink will be whipped cream.

    b. $\frac{2}{3} + \frac{1}{12} = \frac{8}{12} + \frac{1}{12} = \frac{9}{12} = \frac{3}{4}$ of the drink will be milk.

2. $25\frac{3}{4}$ hours.

3. a. $\frac{1}{3} + \frac{7}{12} + \frac{2}{12} + \frac{1}{12} + \frac{1}{2} + \frac{5}{12} + \frac{2}{3} = \frac{4}{12} + \frac{7}{12} + \frac{2}{12} + \frac{1}{12} + \frac{6}{12} + \frac{5}{12} + \frac{8}{12} = \frac{33}{12} = 2\frac{3}{4}$ pizzas

    b. $4 - 2\frac{3}{4} = 1\frac{1}{4}$ pizzas

    c. $2\frac{3}{4} - 1\frac{1}{4} = 1\frac{1}{2}$ pizzas

Answers to Check-Up 3

1. a. $12 \times 2\frac{1}{2} = 30$ miles

    b. $12 \times 3\frac{3}{4} = 45$ miles

2. 9; One way to solve this problem is to divide 15 by 1.75 and round the quotient up to the next whole number, since the number of events must be an integer: $15 \div 1.75 = 8.57$, and rounding up to the nearest whole number gives an answer of 9 events (which would cost $15.75 if the tickets were purchased separately).

3. In a 365-day year, a person will produce $3\frac{2}{3} \times 365 =$ about 1338 pounds of garbage.

4. Derek makes $15.75 \times 30 = \$472.50$. Conor makes $(12.25 \times 20) + (1.5 \times 12.25 \times 10) = \$428.75$.

5. Possible answer: In the drawing, the shaded area represents the $\frac{2}{3}$ of a pan that Paula took to school.

Portion left in pan

$\frac{3}{4}$ of the pan eaten by Paula's friends

$\frac{2}{3}$ of pan originally taken to school

a. The lighter shaded area represents the portion eaten by Paula's friends, which is $\frac{6}{12}$ or $\frac{1}{2}$ of the pan.

b. The darker shaded area represents the portion remaining, which is $\frac{2}{12}$ or $\frac{1}{6}$ of the pan.

Answers to Question Bank

1. Answers will depend on the local sales tax.

2. a. Possible answer:

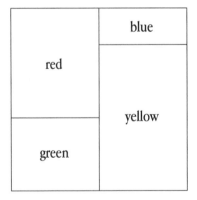

b. Possible answer:

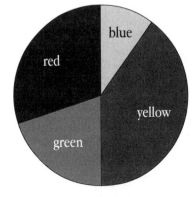

    c.   Answers will vary.

    d.   Answers will vary.

3.   **a.** $3\frac{1}{2} \times 80¢ = \$2.80$

     b. $\frac{3}{4} \times 80¢ = 60¢$

4.   The pizza would be half gone after the second night. In the drawing, the Pizza Pirate's first meal is outlined on the right. The area remaining after the first night is divided into fourths. The top fourth is outlined to show what the Pizza Pirate ate the second night. The remaining region is $\frac{1}{2}$ of the total pizza.

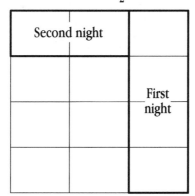

5.   **a.**   If you start with a fraction less than 1, the value of the fraction increases when the same number is added to both the numerator and the denominator. As 1 is repeatedly added to both the numerator and denominator of a fraction between 0 and 1, the value of the fraction increases, getting closer and closer to (but never reaching) the value of 1.

     b.   If you start with a fraction greater than 1, the value of the fraction decreases when a number is added to both the numerator and the denominator.

     c.   If you multiply the numerator and denominator of a fraction by the same number, the value of the fraction stays the same because equivalent fractions are produced.

     d.   If the fraction you start with is equal to 1, multiplying the numerator and the denominator by the same number or adding the same number to both the numerator and the denominator will result in a fraction that is also equal to 1.

     e.   Possible answer:

- Adding the same number to the numerator and denominator of a fraction that is not equal to 1 will always change the value of the fraction.
- Multiplying the numerator and denominator of a fraction by the same number will not change the value of the fraction, because this produces equivalent fractions.
- The value of a fraction that is equal to 1 does not change when a number is added to or multiplied by both the numerator and denominator.

6. Renting a drum set for one year will cost $25 + (12 × $35.95) = $456.40.

7. **a.** The program runs $7\frac{1}{2} \times 5 = 37\frac{1}{2}$ hours per week. Since two people will work at a time, there are $37\frac{1}{2} \times 2 = 75$ hours per each week to be worked. Dividing among four people gives $75 \div 4 = 18\frac{3}{4}$ hours per person.

b. For one week of work, each student will make $3.75 × 18.75 = $70.31.

c. Answers will vary.

> **For the Teacher: Extending Problem**
>
> This is a good exercise in organizing a schedule and working with fractional parts of hours. To make this problem more challenging, additional restrictions may be added—for example, that Jin Lee and Sarah must always work together, as they share a ride; that Alex cannot work past 2:00 P.M. due to his second job; or that Jesse can only work on Mondays, Wednesdays, and Fridays.

d. Since the original recipe yields only 12 pancakes, to mix a batch that would make 30, you must multiply each ingredient by $\frac{30}{12} = \frac{5}{2}$.

$1\frac{1}{4} \times 2\frac{1}{2} = 3\frac{1}{8}$ cups flour

$1 \times 2\frac{1}{2} = 2\frac{1}{2}$ eggs

$3 \times 2\frac{1}{2} = 7\frac{1}{2}$ teaspoons baking powder

$1\frac{1}{2} \times 2\frac{1}{2} = 3\frac{3}{4}$ tablespoons sugar

$\frac{1}{2} \times 2\frac{1}{2} = 1\frac{1}{4}$ teaspoons salt

$\frac{3}{4} \times 2\frac{1}{2} = 1\frac{7}{8}$ cups milk

$2 \times 2\frac{1}{2} = 5$ tablespoons salad oil

8. **a.** At stage 1, $\frac{1}{3}$ of the line is covered and $\frac{2}{3}$ of the line is not covered.

b. At stage 2, $\frac{1}{3} + \frac{2}{9} = \frac{5}{9}$ of the line is covered and $\frac{4}{9}$ of the line is not covered.

c. At stage 3, $\frac{5}{9} + \frac{4}{27} = \frac{19}{27}$ of the line is covered and $\frac{8}{27}$ of the line is not covered.

Answers to Unit Test: In-Class Portion

1. **a.** Answers will vary based on your local sales tax. The cost before tax is $2 \times 7.98 + 2 \times 6.35 + 2 \times \frac{1}{2} \times 6.35 + 3 \times 1.98 + 19.99 = $60.94. At a 6% tax rate, the cost would be $60.94 + 0.06 \times 60.94 = $64.60.

b. Troy had enough money. At a 6% tax rate, he had $35.40 extra.

2. **a.** Out of her $80 paycheck, Kristine devotes the following amounts to these areas: savings, $26.67; clothing, $20.00; snacks, $13.33; entertainment, $20.00.

b.

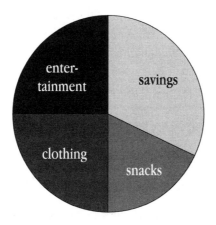

3. **a.** Coat at store 1: $\$84 - \frac{1}{3} \times 84 = \$56$

Coat at store 2: $\$76 - \frac{1}{4} \times 76 = \$57$

The coat at store 1 is the better buy.

b. To calculate the catalog price takes several steps:

Step 1 Find the price after the discount: $\$84.00 - 0.3 \times \$84.00 = \$58.80$

Step 2 Apply the coupon: $\$58.80 - \$5.00 = \$53.80$

Step 3 Add the shipping charge: $\$53.80 + 0.06 \times \$53.80 = \$57.03$

The coat at store 1 is the better buy.

4. Four bows can be made from 1 meter of ribbon, so $4 \times 5 = 20$ bows can be made from 5 meters.

5. No, the final costs will be different. For example, a $10 board game with a 30% discount would cost $7, then when reduced another 25%, would cost $5.25. The same $10 game at a 55% discount would cost only $4.50.

The final assessment for *Bits and Pieces II* consists of an in-class test and a take-home miniproject. The miniproject asks students to select three items from a catalog and fill out an order blank as if they were going to purchase the items. They must find shipping cost (which is a percent of the total cost) and the sales tax (based on the rate for their state). They are also asked to compute what the items would cost if given discounts were applied. The blackline masters for the project and the order blank appear on pages 91 and 92. Below is a scoring rubric. This is followed by samples of student work and a teacher's comments on each sample.

Suggested Scoring Rubric

This rubric for scoring the project employs a scale that runs from 0 to 4 and is used to evaluate the work as a whole. You may use this rubric as presented here or modify it to fit your district's requirements for evaluating and reporting students' work and understanding.

4   **Complete Response—Meets the demands of the task**
   ■ Complete, with clear, coherent explanations
   ■ Shows understanding of the mathematical concepts and procedures
   ■ Satisfies all essential conditions of the problem

3   **Reasonably Complete Response—Needs some revision**
   ■ Reasonably complete; may lack detail in explanations
   ■ Shows understanding of most of the mathematical concepts and procedures
   ■ Satisfies most of the essential conditions of the problem

2   **Partial Response—Student needs some instruction to correct and complete work**
   ■ Gives response; explanation may be unclear or lack detail
   ■ Shows some understanding of some of the mathematical concepts and procedures
   ■ Satisfies some essential conditions of the problem

1   **Inadequate Response—Student needs significant instruction to do the task**
   ■ Incomplete; explanation is insufficient or not understandable
   ■ Shows little understanding of the mathematical concepts and procedures
   ■ Fails to address essential conditions of problem

0   **No Attempt**
   ■ Irrelevant response
   ■ Does not attempt a solution
   ■ Does not address conditions of the problem

Sample 1

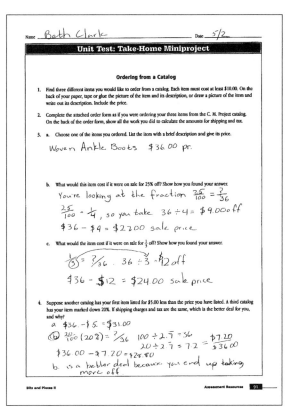

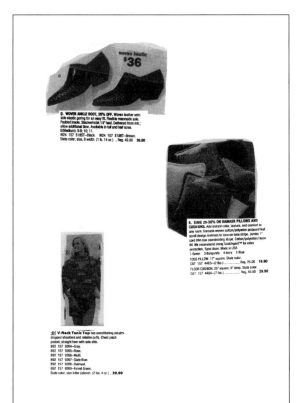

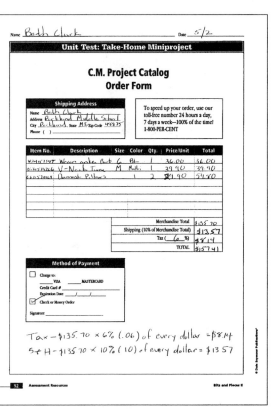

Sample 2

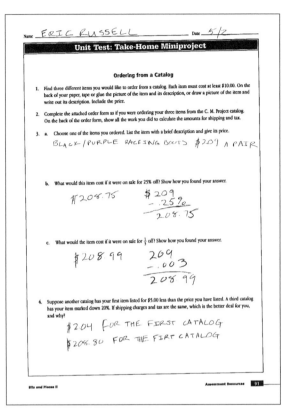

Name ERIC RUSSELL   Date 5/2

Unit Test: Take-Home Miniproject

Ordering from a Catalog

1. Find three different items you would like to order from a catalog. Each item must cost at least $10.00. On the back of your paper, tape or glue the picture of the item and its description, or draw a picture of the item and write out its description. Include the price.

2. Complete the attached order form as if you were ordering your three items from the C. M. Project catalog. On the back for the order form, show all the work you did to calculate the amounts for shipping and tax.

3. a. Choose one of the items you ordered. List the item with a brief description and give its price.

   BLACK/PURPLE RACEING BOOTS $209 A PAIR

   b. What would this item cost if it were on sale for 25% off? Show how you found your answer.

   $208.75

   $209
   −.25%
   208.75

   c. What would the item cost if it were on sale for ⅓ off? Show how you found your answer.

   $208.99

   209
   −.003
   208.99

4. Suppose another catalog has your first item listed for $5.00 less than the price you have listed. A third catalog has your item marked down 20%. If shipping charges and tax are the same, which is the better deal for you, and why?

   $204 FOR THE FIRST CATALOG
   $208.80 FOR THE FIRT CATALOG

$99

$209

$29.95

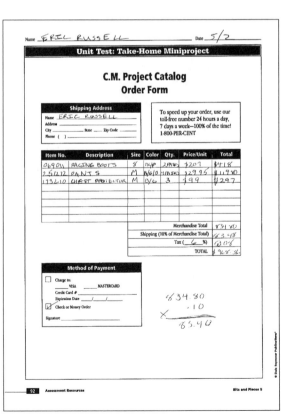

Name ERIC RUSSELL   Date 5/2

Unit Test: Take-Home Miniproject

C.M. Project Catalog
Order Form

Shipping Address

Name ERIC RUSSELL
Address
City _____ State _____ Zip Code _____
Phone ( )

To speed up your order, use our toll-free number 24 hours a day, 7 days a week—100% of the time! 1-800-PER-CENT

Item No.	Description	Size	Color	Qty.	Price/Unit	Total
069011	RACEING BOOTS	8	B4/P	2PAIR	$209	$418
252212	PANTS	M	B/6/0	4PAIR	$2995	$11980
173210	CHEST PROTECTOR	M	B/O	3	$99	$297
				Merchandise Total		834.80
				Shipping (10% of Merchandise Total)		83.48
				Tax (6 %)		50.08
				TOTAL		$968.36

Method of Payment

☐ Charge to:
   _____ VISA _____ MASTERCARD
   Credit Card #
   Expiration Date ___/___/___
☑ Check or Money Order
Signature

834.80
× .10
83.48

A Teacher's Comments on Sample 1

Beth received a 4 for her work. She meets the demands of the task by successfully addressing all the essential conditions of the questions. Her explanations of her reasoning are very clear. For example, when she computes the tax and shipping for her order, she shows how she multiplied the merchandise total by the decimal equivalents of the needed percents. She also clearly shows her thinking in computing the 25%, $\frac{1}{3}$, and 20% discounts. Beth shows a considerable amount of understanding of rational numbers and flexibility in working with them. She uses multiple methods when performing operations involving rational numbers.

A Teacher's Comments on Sample 2

Eric received a 1 for his work. His response is weak. He does find tax and shipping for his order but does not show or explain how he found the 6% sales tax. In the last question, he does not show or explain how he came up with the sales price after a 20% discount. I feel that a student's explanation is as important as the correct answer. The lack of explanation is critical to the quality of Eric's paper. I am also concerned about his misconceptions about discounts. In questions 3 and 4, he subtracts to find the sales price for the discounted item, showing no understanding of rational numbers. It is not clear why he subtracted for these problems when he multiplied to find the 10% shipping charge. Eric's work suggests that he needs additional instruction on working with rational numbers.

Blackline Masters

Larry's Lunch Place

LUNCH SPECIALS

1. Roast Turkey..........................3.95
Succulent slices of turkey breast, savory dressing, homemade gravy, and cranberry sauce

2. Veggie Quesadilla......................3.95
Whole-wheat tortillas stuffed with tomatoes, roasted peppers, and three kinds of cheese

3. Chicken Tenders......................4.50
Strips of tender, all-white-meat chicken baked to a golden brown, served with a baked potato, coleslaw, and barbecue sauce

LARRY'S FAMOUS BURGERS

7. Quarter-Pound Hamburger Platter......3.30

8. Quarter-Pound Cheeseburger Platter...3.60
Topped with your choice of cheese

SEAFOOD

10. Shrimp Cocktail......................6.95
Tender steamed shrimp served on ice with tangy cocktail sauce

4. Baked Meatloaf......................3.95
Tasty homestyle meatloaf with mixed green salad

5. Spaghetti with Tomato Sauce..............3.25
Zesty sauce ladled over a generous portion of pasta with parmesan cheese and hot garlic bread

6. Grilled Chicken Breast..........................5.25
Served over rice with lemon parsley sauce, crisp lettuce, tomato slices, and whole wheat rolls
(low cholesterol)

9. Larry's Special........................4.35
Two patties, with crisp lettuce, Larry's own sauce, and your choice of cheese on a specially baked sesame seed bun

11. Fish and Chips........................4.45
Three batter-dipped filets, deep fried to a golden brown, with French fries, coleslaw, and tartar sauce

DESSERTS

12. Chocolate Cake....................1.50
With ice cream..................1.95

13. Fresh Strawberry Pie..........1.89
With frozen yogurt..........2.25

BEVERAGES
(Free refills on coffee and tea)

14. Coffee, Regular or Decaffeinated.......... .80
15. Hot or Iced Tea.................... .80
16. White or Chocolate Milk........................ .99
17. Lemonade.................... .99

18. Soft Drinks................................. .99
19. Orange Juice................................ .99
20. Hot Chocolate................................. .99
21. Root Beer Float.................... 1.99

Order Check

Larry's Lunch Place Food Order

Item	Price

Date	Server	Table	Guests	Check No.
				354124

Tupelo Township

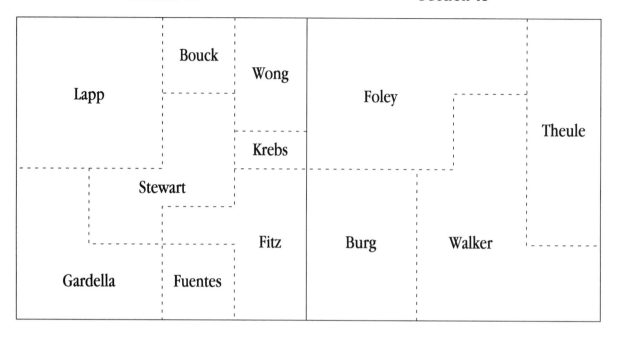

Section 18

Lapp

Bouck

Wong

Krebs

Stewart

Fitz

Gardella

Fuentes

Section 19

Foley

Theule

Burg

Walker

Section 18

Lapp

Bouck

Wong

Krebs

Stewart

Fitz

Gardella

Fuentes

Section 19

Foley

Theule

Burg

Walker

© Dale Seymour Publications®

School Supply Game

Items Sold at the School Store

Divider page	$0.07	Roll of tape	$0.84
Pencil	$0.28	Pen	$0.98
Eraser	$0.35	Highlighter	$1.05
Note paper	$0.42	Notebook	$2.24
Ruler	$0.70	Scissors	$3.15

School Supply Game Board

$2.24	$1.33	$0.35	$2.31	$1.68	$0.07
$3.43	$0.28	$3.08	$2.59	$1.05	$1.47
$1.26	$1.75	$1.12	$1.61	$1.54	$1.96
$1.40	$3.57	$2.80	$1.89	$0.91	$2.66
$2.03	$0.84	$2.87	$2.73	$0.70	$2.52
$3.15	$0.77	$2.45	$0.98	$0.63	$0.42

© Dale Seymour Publications

Jill wants to buy a cassette tape that is priced at $7.50. The sales tax is 6%. What will be the total cost of the tape? Try to find more than one way to solve this problem. Be prepared to explain the different methods you find.

Have each member of your group use the menu your teacher provides to make up a lunch order. Write all the items ordered by your group on the order check. Total the bill, and add your local sales tax.

A. What is your total bill for food and tax?

B. How much will you leave for the tip? (The tip must be between 15% and 20%.)

C. The members of your group decide to share the cost of the meal equally. About how much would each person need to contribute to pay the bill as well as the tip?

Try to find more than one way to solve parts A and B. Be prepared to explain the different methods you used.

Joshua and Jeremy go to Loud Sounds to buy a tape and a CD. They do not have much money, so they have pooled their funds. When they get to the store, they find that there is another discount plan available just for that day—if they buy three or more items, they can save 20% (instead of 10%) on each item.

A. If they buy a CD and a tape, how much money will they spend after the store adds a 6% sales tax on the discounted prices?

B. Jeremy says he thinks they can buy three tapes for less money than the cost of a tape and a CD. Is he correct? Explain your reasoning.

Try to find more than one way to solve these problems. Be prepared to explain the different methods you discover.

© Dale Seymour Publications

At the beginning of the evening, Danny had a twenty-dollar bill, five quarters, seven dimes, three nickels, and eight pennies.

A. Danny went to the Friday night school dance, which cost $2.50 to attend. How much money did she have left after paying for the dance?

B. After the dance, Danny and three friends bought a pizza for $6.99 and four soft drinks for 89¢ each. The bill for the pizza and drinks included a sales tax of 7%. How much was the bill? Show how you found your answer.

C. If Danny and her friends shared the cost of the pizza and drinks equally, how much was Danny's share of the bill?

D. On the way home, Danny stopped at a newsstand and bought a copy of *Stars and Planets* magazine for $2.50 plus 7% sales tax. How much had she spent for the evening?

E. How much money did Danny have left at the end of the evening?

A survey asked cat owners, Does your cat have bad breath? Out of the 200 cat owners surveyed, 80 answered yes to this question. What *percent* of the cat owners answered yes?

Try to find more than one way to solve this problem. For example, you might begin by asking yourself what *fraction* of the cat owners surveyed said their cats have bad breath. Be prepared to explain the different methods you use to solve the problem.

© Dale Seymour Publications®

Here are more questions that involve figuring out what percent of people have answered yes to a survey question. As you work on these questions, try to find a way to describe a general strategy you can use for solving these kinds of problems.

A. If 80 out of 400 cat owners surveyed said their cats have bad breath, what percent of the cat owners is this? Is this percent greater than, equal to, or less than the percent represented by 80 out of 200 cat owners? Explain.

B. If 120 out of 300 seventh graders surveyed said math is their favorite subject, what percent of these seventh graders is this?

C. If 30 out of 50 adults surveyed said they enjoy their jobs, what percent of these adults is this?

D. If 34 out of 125 sixth graders surveyed said they would like to try hang gliding, what percent of these sixth graders is this?

E. If 5 out of 73 middle-school students said they look forward to fire drills, what percent of these middle-school students is this?

F. Write an explanation for how to solve these kinds of problems.

What percent discount do you get with the coupon below?

Try to find more than one way to solve this problem. Be prepared to explain the different methods you discover.

Methods Used by Dog Owners   **Methods Used by Cat Owners**

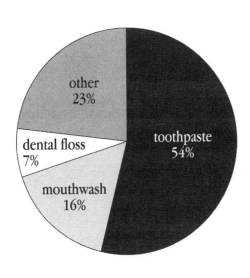

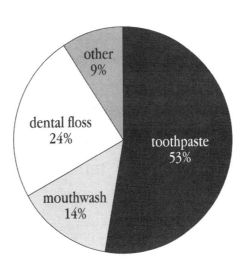

Study the circle graphs above. Use what you know about angle measures, circles, and percents to figure out how they were created. Then work on the problem below.

Cat and dog owners were asked, Do you let your pet lick your face? Here are the results of the survey:

	Cat owners	Dog owners
Yes	40%	75%
No	60%	25%
Total	100%	100%

Create two circle graphs to display this information.

Play Getting Close once or twice. Keep a record of the estimation strategies you find useful.

You may find benchmarks, fraction strips, number lines, hundredths grids, or changing a fraction to a decimal or a decimal to a fraction helpful in making estimates. You may discover other ways of thinking that help.

As you play the game, your group may use a calculator to help check whether a player is correct—but not to estimate the sums!

Play Getting Even Closer once or twice. Keep a record of your strategies for estimating the sums. As before, your group may use a calculator to check whether a player is correct, but not to estimate the sums.

After a round of play, the player who won should explain the strategy he or she used to estimate the sum.

Determine what fraction of a section each person owns. Explain your reasoning.

Section 18   **Section 19**

| Lapp | Bouck |
| Wong |
| Krebs |
| Stewart |
Foley	Theule
Fitz	Burg	Walker
Gardella	Fuentes

Some of the owners of land in sections 18 and 19 sold their land to other people who already owned land in these sections. The clues below describe the results of several transactions.

Clue 1 When all the sales are completed, four people—Theule, Fuentes, Wong, and Gardella—own all of the land in the two sections.

Clue 2 Theule bought from one person and now owns land equivalent to $\frac{1}{2}$ of one section.

Clue 3 Fuentes bought from three people and now owns the equivalent of $\frac{13}{32}$ of one section.

Clue 4 Gardella now owns the equivalent of $\frac{1}{2}$ of a section.

Clue 5 Wong now owns all of the rest of the land in the two sections.

Clue 6 Each of the four owners can walk around all of their land without having to cross onto another person's land.

A. Use the clues to determine what transactions took place. Determine exactly which pieces of land Theule, Fuentes, Wong, and Gardella bought, and explain how you know you are correct.

B. Draw a new map of the two sections, outlining the land belonging to each of the four owners. Tell how many acres each person now owns.

Courtney's class made a gigantic square pizza for a class party to be held the day after the final exam. They made it a week before the party so they would have time to study. To keep the pizza fresh, they stored it in the cafeteria freezer.

Unfortunately, a notorious Pizza Pirate was lurking in the area. That night, the Pizza Pirate disguised himself as a janitor, tiptoed into the cafeteria, and gobbled down half of the pizza! On the second night, he ate half of what was left of the pizza. Each night after that, he crept in and ate half of the pizza that remained.

After the final exam, Courtney's class went to get their pizza to start their celebration—and were stunned by what they found!

What fraction of the pizza was left for the party?

To help you answer this question, make a table or chart showing

- the fraction of the pizza the Pizza Pirate ate each day
- the fraction of the pizza he had eaten so far at the end of each day
- the fraction of the pizza that remained at the end of each day

Write a summary of how your group solved this problem. Draw any diagrams that will help you to show your thinking.

Work with your group to develop at least one algorithm for adding fractions and at least one algorithm for subtracting fractions. You might want to look back over the first three problems in this investigation and discuss how each person in your group thought about them. Look for ideas that you think will help you develop algorithms for adding and subtracting fractions that will always work, even with mixed numbers.

Test your algorithms on a few problems, such as these:

$\frac{5}{8} + \frac{7}{8}$ $\qquad$ $\frac{3}{5} + \frac{5}{3}$ $\qquad$ $3\frac{3}{4} + 7\frac{2}{9}$

$\frac{3}{4} - \frac{1}{8}$ $\qquad$ $5\frac{4}{6} - 2\frac{1}{3}$ $\qquad$ $\frac{5}{6} - \frac{1}{4}$

If necessary, make adjustments to your algorithms until you think they will work all the time. Write up a final version of each algorithm. Make sure they are neat and precise so others can follow them.

The brownies are baked in square pans, and they are sold as fractional parts of a pan. A whole pan of brownies costs $24 dollars. The cost of any fractional part of a pan is that fraction of $24.

A. One pan of brownies was $\frac{2}{3}$ full. Mr. Sims bought $\frac{1}{2}$ of what was in the pan. What fraction of a full pan did Mr. Sims buy? How much did he pay?

B. Paulo's aunt Serena asked to buy $\frac{3}{4}$ of what was left in another pan. The pan was half full. How much of a whole pan did Aunt Serena buy? How much did she pay?

The school fair was almost over. Paulo and Paula wanted to sell all the remaining brownies in a hurry, so they decided to offer a discount of 20% on all sales. They had $2\frac{1}{4}$ pans of brownies left. Remember, they originally sold a pan of brownies for $24.

Mr. Vargas offered to buy half of all that they had left.

A. How much will Mr. Vargas purchase?

B. How much should Paulo and Paula charge Mr. Vargas?

A. Which lot should Miguel's mother buy if she wants the biggest lot? Explain your reasoning.

B. If land in this area sells for $750,000 a square mile, about how much should Miguel's mother expect to pay?

Work with your group to develop at least one algorithm for multiplying fractions. You might want to look back over the first three problems in this investigation and discuss how each person in your group thought about them. Look for ideas that you think will help you develop an algorithm for multiplying fractions that will always work, even with mixed numbers.

Test your algorithm on a few problems, such as these:

$\frac{1}{5} \times 25$ $\qquad$ $24 \times \frac{2}{3}$ $\qquad$ $\frac{5}{8} \times 12$

$\frac{3}{8} \times \frac{3}{4}$ $\qquad$ $\frac{1}{2} \times 2\frac{2}{3}$ $\qquad$ $3\frac{1}{3} \times 2\frac{4}{5}$

If necessary, make adjustments to your algorithm until you think it will work all the time. Write up a final version of the algorithm. Make sure it is neat and precise so others can follow it.

Play the School Supply game once or twice with your partner. Keep track of any strategies you find that help you win the game.

Items Sold at the School Store

Divider page	$0.07	Roll of tape	$0.84
Pencil	$0.28	Pen	$0.98
Eraser	$0.35	Highlighter	$1.05
Note paper	$0.42	Notebook	$2.24
Ruler	$0.70	Scissors	$3.15

School Supply Game Board

$2.24	$1.33	$0.35	$2.31	$1.68	$0.07
$3.43	$0.28	$3.08	$2.59	$1.05	$1.47
$1.26	$1.75	$1.12	$1.61	$1.54	$1.96
$1.40	$3.57	$2.80	$1.89	$0.91	$2.66
$2.03	$0.84	$2.87	$2.73	$0.70	$2.52
$3.15	$0.77	$2.45	$0.98	$0.63	$0.42

Work with the digits 2365 and 894. You may insert a decimal point just before, between, or just after the given set of digits, but you cannot change the order of the digits. After placing the decimal point, you may add zeros only if they do not change the value of your number.

A. Find ways to insert decimal points so you get five different *sums* using these two numbers.

B. Find ways to insert decimal points so you get five different *differences* using these two numbers.

C. What is the largest sum that you can make that fits the constraints of the problem? What is the smallest sum?

D. What is the largest difference that you can make that fits the constraints of the problem? What is the smallest difference?

A. Look at each set of multiplication problems below. Estimate how large you expect the answer to each problem to be. Will the answer be larger or smaller than 1? Will it be larger or smaller than $\frac{1}{2}$?

Set 1	Set 2	Set 3	Set 4
$21 \times 1 =$	$2.1 \times 1 =$	$0.21 \times 1 =$	$2.1 \times 11 =$
$21 \times 0.1 =$	$2.1 \times 0.1 =$	$0.21 \times 0.1 =$	$2.1 \times 1.1 =$
$21 \times 0.01 =$	$2.1 \times 0.01 =$	$0.21 \times 0.01 =$	$2.1 \times 0.11 =$
$21 \times 0.001 =$	$2.1 \times 0.001 =$	$0.21 \times 0.001 =$	$2.1 \times 0.011 =$
$21 \times 0.0001 =$	$2.1 \times 0.0001 =$	$0.21 \times 0.0001 =$	$2.1 \times 0.0011 =$

B. Use your calculator to do the multiplication, and record the answers in an organized way so that you can look for patterns. Describe any patterns that you see.

C. In a multiplication problem, there is a relationship between the number of decimal places in the factors and the number of decimal places in the product. Summarize what you think this relationship is. Show your reasoning.

A. 1. Find two numbers with a product of 1344.

2. Find two numbers with a product of 134.4.

3. Find two numbers with a product of 1.344.

4. Find two numbers with a product of 0.1344.

5. Explain how you got your answers and why you think they are correct.

B. 1. Find two numbers with a product between 2000 and 3000.

2. By moving decimal points, change the value of each of the numbers you found in part 1 so that their product is between 200 and 300.

3. By moving decimal points, change the value of each of the numbers you found in part 1 so that their product is between 20 and 30.

4. By moving decimal points, change the value of each of the numbers you found in part 1 so that their product is between 2 and 3.

5. Explain what you did to get your answers and why you think they are correct.

Kelly wants to fence in a rectangular space in her yard, 9 meters by 7.5 meters. The salesperson at the supply store recommends that she put up posts every $1\frac{1}{2}$ meters. The posts cost $2.19 each. Kelly will also need to buy wire mesh to string between the posts. The wire mesh is sold by the meter from large rolls and costs $5.98 a meter. A gate to fit in one of the spaces between the posts costs $25.89. Seven staples are needed to attach the wire mesh to each post. Staples come in boxes of 50, and each box costs $3.99.

A. How much will the materials Kelly needs cost before sales tax? Show how you arrived at your answer.

B. Local sales tax is 7%. How much will Kelly's total bill be?

Dear Family,

The next unit in your child's course of study in mathematics class this year is *Bits and Pieces II.* This unit continues the study of fractions, decimals, and percents begun in *Bits and Pieces I.* In the last two units, *Covering and Surrounding* and *How Likely Is It?,* your child has used rational numbers in many different contexts to solve problems. In this unit, the focus is on operations with rational numbers, and students develop systematic ways to add, subtract, multiply, and divide fractions and decimals. In addition, students learn to use percents to compute discounts, taxes, and tips.

While working on this unit, students investigate many interesting problem situations. Out of these experiences, they will develop algorithms for computation. Throughout the unit, the focus is on *understanding* and making sense of these algorithms.

The homework problems reflect the variety of contexts that students experience in class. Although students will not see dozens of problems of the same kind, they *will* return to important ideas again and again as they proceed through this and other units. Many homework problems require students to read, think, try different approaches, and evaluate the solutions.

You can help your child with his or her work in this unit in several ways:

- When shopping or eating in a restaurant with your child, ask him or her to estimate what the tax will be on a purchase or what the tip should be for dinner.

- Ask your child to tell you about a problem that he or she enjoyed working on. Ask for an explanation of the ideas in the problem.

- Look over your child's homework and make sure all questions are answered and explanations are clear.

As always, if you have any questions or concerns about this unit or your child's progress in the class, please feel free to call. All of us here are interested in your child and want to be sure that this year's mathematics experiences are enjoyable and promote a firm understanding of mathematics.

Sincerely,

Estimada familia,

La próxima unidad del programa de matemáticas de su hijo o hija para este curso se llama *Bits and Pieces II* (*Trocitos y pedacitos II*). En ella se continúa con el estudio de las fracciones, los decimales y los porcentajes que fue iniciado en *Bits and Pieces I*. En las dos últimas unidades, *Covering and Surrounding* y *How Likely Is It?*, su hijo o hija usó números racionales en una diversidad de contextos a fin de resolver problemas. La presente unidad trata principalmente sobre operaciones con números racionales; en ella los alumnos crearán formas sistemáticas de sumar, restar, multiplicar y dividir fracciones y decimales. Asimismo, aprenderán a utilizar porcentajes para calcular descuentos, impuestos y propinas.

A lo largo de la unidad los alumnos examinarán numerosas e interesantes situaciones relacionadas con problemas. Y a partir de dichas experiencias desarrollarán algoritmos para los cálculos. En todo momento se enfatizará el sentido y la *comprensión* de los algoritmos.

Los problemas de la tarea reflejan toda la variedad de contextos que se examinan en clase. El número de veces que los alumnos tratarán cada tipo específico de problema será limitado, aunque sin embargo sí que volverán una y otra vez a las ideas más importantes a medida que estudien esta unidad y las que le siguen. Para resolver los problemas de la tarea, los alumnos se verán obligados a leer, pensar, probar diversos enfoques y evaluar las soluciones.

Para ayudar a su hijo o hija con el trabajo de esta unidad, ustedes pueden hacer lo siguiente:

- Cuando vayan de compras o a un restaurante con su hijo o hija, pídanle que estime el importe del impuesto sobre alguna compra o la propina de la comida.

- Pídanle que les hable de alguno de los problemas que le haya gustado resolver y que les explique las ideas expuestas en el mismo.

- Repasen su tarea para asegurarse de que conteste todas las preguntas y escriba con claridad las explicaciones.

Y como de costumbre, si ustedes necesitan más detalles o aclaraciones respecto a esta unidad o sobre los progresos de su hijo o hija en esta clase, no duden en llamarnos. A todos nos interesa su hijo o hija y queremos asegurarnos de que las experiencias matemáticas que tenga este año sean lo más amenas posibles y ayuden a fomentar en él o ella una sólida comprensión de las matemáticas.

Atentamente,

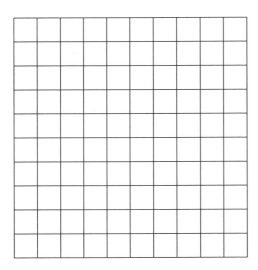

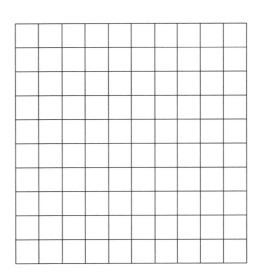

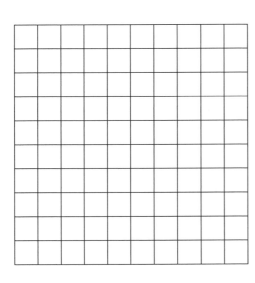

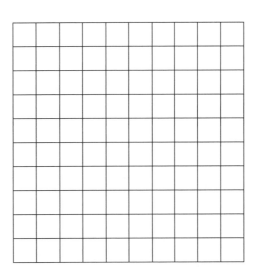

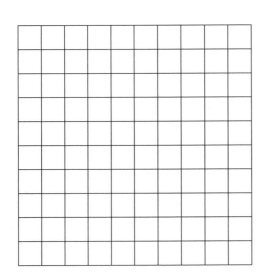

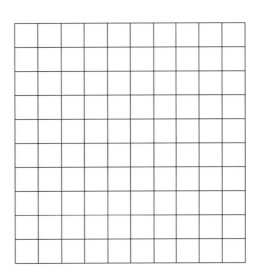

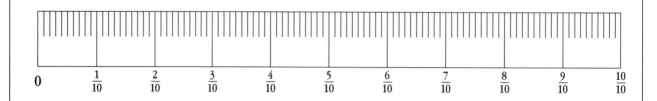

$$0 \quad \frac{1}{10} \quad \frac{2}{10} \quad \frac{3}{10} \quad \frac{4}{10} \quad \frac{5}{10} \quad \frac{6}{10} \quad \frac{7}{10} \quad \frac{8}{10} \quad \frac{9}{10} \quad \frac{10}{10}$$

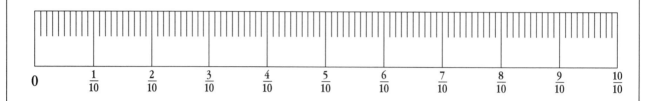

$$0 \quad \frac{1}{10} \quad \frac{2}{10} \quad \frac{3}{10} \quad \frac{4}{10} \quad \frac{5}{10} \quad \frac{6}{10} \quad \frac{7}{10} \quad \frac{8}{10} \quad \frac{9}{10} \quad \frac{10}{10}$$

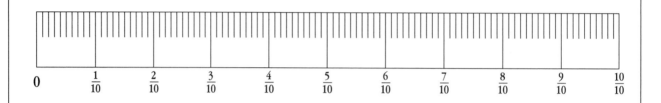

$$0 \quad \frac{1}{10} \quad \frac{2}{10} \quad \frac{3}{10} \quad \frac{4}{10} \quad \frac{5}{10} \quad \frac{6}{10} \quad \frac{7}{10} \quad \frac{8}{10} \quad \frac{9}{10} \quad \frac{10}{10}$$

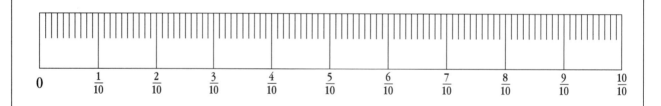

$$0 \quad \frac{1}{10} \quad \frac{2}{10} \quad \frac{3}{10} \quad \frac{4}{10} \quad \frac{5}{10} \quad \frac{6}{10} \quad \frac{7}{10} \quad \frac{8}{10} \quad \frac{9}{10} \quad \frac{10}{10}$$

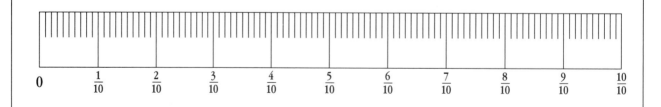

$$0 \quad \frac{1}{10} \quad \frac{2}{10} \quad \frac{3}{10} \quad \frac{4}{10} \quad \frac{5}{10} \quad \frac{6}{10} \quad \frac{7}{10} \quad \frac{8}{10} \quad \frac{9}{10} \quad \frac{10}{10}$$

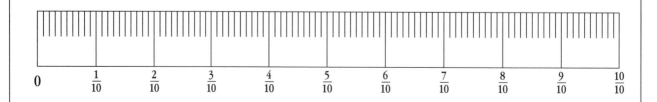

$$0 \quad \frac{1}{10} \quad \frac{2}{10} \quad \frac{3}{10} \quad \frac{4}{10} \quad \frac{5}{10} \quad \frac{6}{10} \quad \frac{7}{10} \quad \frac{8}{10} \quad \frac{9}{10} \quad \frac{10}{10}$$

$\frac{1}{10}$	$\frac{1}{8}$	$\frac{1}{5}$	$\frac{1}{4}$	$\frac{1}{3}$
$\frac{1}{2}$	$\frac{3}{10}$	$\frac{7}{10}$	$\frac{9}{10}$	$\frac{2}{5}$
$\frac{3}{5}$	$\frac{4}{9}$	1	$\frac{3}{4}$	$1\frac{4}{10}$
$1\frac{1}{5}$	$1\frac{3}{4}$	$1\frac{2}{3}$	$1\frac{1}{3}$	$\frac{2}{3}$
$\frac{6}{8}$	$\frac{3}{8}$	$\frac{5}{8}$	$\frac{7}{8}$	$\frac{5}{9}$

$\dfrac{4}{7}$	0.5	0.75	0.6	0.9
0.125	0.375	0.875	1.5	1.75
1.125	0.2	0.8	1.33	1.67
0.33	0.67	1.875	0.1	1.9
1.1	2	1.45	1.25	1.6

0	0.5	1	1.5	2	2.5
0	0.5	1	1.5	2	2.5
0	0.5	1	1.5	2	2.5
0	0.5	1	1.5	2	2.5
0	0.5	1	1.5	2	2.5
0	0.5	1	1.5	2	2.5
0	0.5	1	1.5	2	2.5
0	0.5	1	1.5	2	2.5

Additional Practice

Investigation 1

1. The Oceanview Middle School sixth-grade class voted on whether to hold their class party on the second or third of April. Holding the party on the third won with 62% of the vote.

    a. What percent of the sixth-grade class voted to have the party on the second?

    b. There are 355 sixth graders at Oceanview Middle School.

        i. How many voted for having the party on the third?

        ii. How many voted for having the party on the second?

    c. The planning committee is expecting 80% of the class to attend the party. How many students are they expecting?

2. The number of registered voters in the town of Cedarville is 8916. In the last election, Mayor Burgis won reelection with 72% of the vote.

    a. If 52% of registered voters voted in the election, how many people voted?

    b. Based on your answer to part a, how many voters voted for Mayor Burgis?

    c. Based on your answers to parts a and b, how many voters did not vote for Mayor Burgis?

    d. How many registered voters would need to vote in the next election for voter turnout to be 75%? Explain your reasoning.

3. Last Saturday, Aaron had lunch at a fast-food restaurant. He ordered the lunch special for $3.29. If sales tax is 6%, how much did Aaron pay for the lunch special?

4. Skateboards are on sale at Susan's Skateshop for 30% off.

    a. Express the discount as a fraction.

    b. If the regular price of a skateboard is $89, what is the discounted price?

    c. What is the total cost of the discounted skateboard in part b if sales tax is 4.5%?

5. The Midtown Middle School cheerleaders earned $175 at a car wash. If this amount is 25% of the cost of a new set of uniforms, what is the total cost for a set of uniforms? Explain your reasoning.

6. Karen has completed 9 of the 15 problems assigned for math homework.

    a. What percent of her math homework has Karen finished?

    b. What fraction of her homework does Karen still have to do?

7. Mary and Ms. Miller are ordering merchandise to sell in the student store. Ms. Miller says that the cost of notebooks is 125% of last year's cost.

    a. Explain what Ms. Miller means.

    b. If a notebook cost $2.00 last year, what will a notebook cost this year? Explain how you found your answer.

© Dale Seymour Publications®

Investigation 2

1. The student council at Metropolis Middle School conducted a survey to see whether students would prefer blue, red, or green as the new color for the school logo. The results of the survey are shown in the bar graph below.

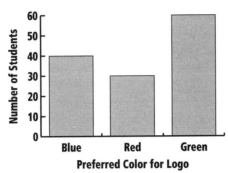

a. What is the total number of students who were surveyed? Explain how you found your answer.

b. What percent of students surveyed preferred blue?

c. What percent of students surveyed preferred red?

d. What percent of students surveyed preferred green?

e. If 970 students attend Metropolis Middle School, what percent of the students were surveyed? Explain how you found your answer.

2. What percent of 75 is 40? Explain your reasoning.

3. What percent of 45 is 135? Explain your reasoning.

4. 3.5 is what percent of 14? Explain your reasoning.

5. What is 60% of 115? Explain your reasoning.

6. What is 42.2% of 635.4? Explain how you found your answer.

7. Stacey's batting average on her softball team is 0.420. Becky has made 47 hits in 119 times up at bat.

a. What percent of the time did Stacey get a hit? Show how you found your answer.

b. What percent of the time did Becky get a hit? Show how you found your answer.

c. During a double-header, Stacey and Becky each bat 18 times.

i. How many hits would you expect Stacey to make?

ii. How many hits would you expect Becky to make?

d. Suppose Becky gets 11 hits during the double-header. Express Becky's new batting average as a decimal. Show how you found your answer.

Investigation 3

1. Josh and his father are estimating how much gas they will need for a car trip. They know that the car gets 39 miles per gallon. Estimate how many gallons of gas they will need for a trip of 778 miles. Explain how you made your estimate.

2. Rosa and Tony need to estimate how much it will cost to purchase the following supplies for their class project.

   4 pieces of posterboard at $2.89 each
   1 bottle of glue at $1.19
   2 booklets of construction paper at $4.99 each
   2 pairs of scissors at $0.59 each

   a. Estimate the cost of the supplies that Rosa and Tony need to buy. Explain your reasoning.

   b. In this situation, would it be better to overestimate or underestimate? Explain.

3. For each of the following problems, state whether the sum of the fractions is less than, greater than, or equal to 1.

   a. $\frac{3}{8} + \frac{2}{5}$ b. $\frac{5}{10} + \frac{3}{4}$ c. $\frac{3}{12} + \frac{3}{6}$

   d. $\frac{1}{2} + \frac{4}{8}$ e. $\frac{4}{7} + \frac{7}{12}$ f. $\frac{4}{3} + \frac{1}{100}$

   g. $\frac{1}{4} + \frac{2}{3}$ h. $\frac{9}{20} + \frac{5}{11}$ i. $\frac{9}{12} + \frac{2}{8}$

4. In a recent election for student council president at Harrison Middle School, one candidate received 39% of the vote, a second received 32%, and the third received 29%. A total of 805 students voted in the election.

   a. How many votes did each of the three candidates receive?

   b. Describe a strategy you could use to estimate the number of votes each candidate received.

   c. Using your estimation strategy, estimate the number of votes each candidate received.

   d. How do your estimates in part c compare to the exact numbers of votes you found in part a? In what election situations are estimates of the numbers of votes adequate? In what election situations are exact counts needed? Explain.

© Dale Seymour Publications®

Investigation 4

1. Jack and Helen are making cookies. The recipe says to combine $\frac{1}{2}$ cup of butter with $\frac{3}{4}$ cup chocolate chips and $\frac{3}{8}$ cup chopped nuts.

   a. When these three ingredients are mixed together, how many cups of the mixture will Jack and Helen have? Show your work.

   b. Jack and Helen decide to triple the recipe.

      i. How many cups of butter will be needed?

      ii. How many cups of chocolate chips will be needed?

      iii. How many cups of chopped nuts will be needed?

   c. When the ingredients for the tripled recipe are combined, how many cups of the mixture will Jack and Helen have?

2. Mr. Larson is planning the seating for a school recital. He needs to reserve $\frac{1}{3}$ of the seats for students and $\frac{1}{6}$ of the seats for parents.

   a. After reserving seats for students and parents, what fraction of the seats in the auditorium are left?

   b. Mr. Larson's principal tells him that he also needs to reserve $\frac{1}{8}$ of the seats for teachers and school officials. The remainder can be used for open seating. What fraction of the seats are now left for open seating?

   c. Later, Mr. Larson's principal says that he should reserve $\frac{1}{4}$ of the seats for students from other middle schools. Are there enough seats left? If not, explain why not; otherwise, state what fraction of the seats will be available for open seating.

3. Find the missing fractions. Show your work.

   a. $\frac{3}{4} + ? = \frac{19}{20}$ b. $? - \frac{1}{2} = \frac{3}{8}$ c. $\frac{1}{6} + \frac{5}{12} = ?$ d. $? - \frac{1}{5} = \frac{7}{20}$ e. $\frac{7}{9} - \frac{2}{3} = ?$

   f. $\frac{3}{2} + ? = \frac{9}{4}$ g. $\frac{4}{5} + \frac{1}{6} = ?$ h. $\frac{1}{2} - ? = \frac{1}{5}$ i. $\frac{3}{7} + \frac{4}{21} = ?$

4. In the diagram below, the shaded portion is the whole. Use the diagram to answer each of the following questions.

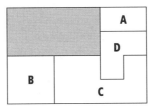

   a. What fraction of the whole are each of the other four regions A, B, C, and D?

   b. Based on your answers to part a, find the area of each of the following:

      i. region A + region B   ii. region C + region D

      iii. region B – region D   iv. region C – region A

   c. If the entire outer rectangle is considered the whole, what fraction of the whole would the shaded grey area be? Explain your reasoning.

Investigation 5

1. Find each product. Show your work.

   a. $\frac{2}{3} \times \frac{1}{2}$ b. $\frac{3}{5} \times \frac{10}{9}$ c. $\frac{3}{4} \times \frac{8}{9}$

   d. $\frac{3}{2} \times \frac{5}{6}$ e. $\frac{2}{7} \times \frac{1}{3}$ f. $\frac{3}{8} \times \frac{12}{15}$

   g. $\frac{9}{10} \times \frac{1}{6}$ h. $\frac{1}{2} \times \frac{6}{7}$ i. $360 \times \frac{7}{9}$

2. In a recent survey of 440 people, $\frac{1}{4}$ said that they watched television every evening, $\frac{2}{5}$ said they watched five or six nights each week, and the remainder said they watched four nights a week or less.

   a. How many people in the survey watch television every evening? Explain how you found your answer.

   b. How many people surveyed watch television five or six nights each week?

   c. What fraction of the people surveyed watch television four nights each week or less? Explain how you found your answer.

   d. How many people surveyed watch television four nights each week or less?

3. Jack and Phil are selling advertisements for the yearbook. A full-page ad will cost $240. Advertisers who want only a fraction of a page will be charged that fraction of $240. Jack and Phil's layout for one page is shown at right.

   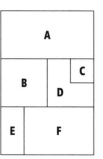

   a. What fraction of the whole page do each of the six regions occupy?

   b. How much should Jack and Phil charge an advertiser who wants to place an ad that fills area A? Explain how you found your answer.

   c. How much should Jack and Phil charge an advertiser who wants to place an ad that fills area D?

   d. How much should an ad that fills area F cost?

   e. Jack and Phil have sold advertising space in areas B, E, and C.

      i. How much did they collect for the three ads?

      ii. What fraction of the page is left for other advertisers?

4. A recipe for granola cookies calls for $\frac{1}{2}$ cup of butter and $\frac{1}{4}$ cup of chopped nuts. Because Jane likes moist cookies without too many nuts, she decides to increase the amount of butter by half and decrease the amount of chopped nuts by half.

   a. How much butter is required for Jane's new recipe? Explain how you got your answer.

   b. What amount of chopped nuts is required for Jane's new recipe? Explain your reasoning.

   c. Since Jane increased the butter by half and decreased the nuts by half, is the combined amount of butter and nuts the same as in the original recipe? Explain why or why not.

5. Paul has $\frac{3}{5}$ of a roll of speaker wire left. His sister uses $\frac{1}{4}$ of it to set up speakers in her room.

   a. How much of the whole roll of speaker wire did Paul's sister use?

   b. What fraction of the whole roll is left? Explain your answer.

Investigation 6

1. Jason and his mother are re-tiling the kitchen floor. The area of the kitchen floor is 96.75 square feet. Each tile has an area of 1.25 square feet. How many tiles will Jason and his mother need to tile the kitchen? Explain how you found your answer.

2. The student concession stand buys 6.5 pounds of unpopped popcorn for $12.75. What is the price per pound of the popcorn?

3. Atul's batting average for the season was 0.388. He was at bat 181 times. How many hits did he get? Explain how you found your answer.

4. The diagram below shows a rectangular plot of land cut into squares of 2.65 acres each.

    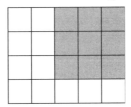

    a. What is the acreage of the shaded region? Explain your reasoning.

    b. What is the acreage of the unshaded region? Explain your reasoning.

    c. In this area, land sells for $2475 per acre.

        i.   What would the price of the shaded region be?

        ii. What would the price of the unshaded region be?

    d. In this area, owners pay property taxes of $13.50 per thousand dollars of property value. What is the total annual property tax for the shaded and unshaded regions combined? Explain your reasoning.

5. What is the cost of $4\frac{3}{8}$ pounds of bananas at $0.79 per pound if sales tax is 6%?

6. In an election among three candidates for school council, the first candidate received 286 votes, the second candidate received 251 votes, and the third candidate received 194 votes.

    a. How many votes were cast altogether?

    b. Express as a decimal the portion of the vote each of the three candidates received. Explain how you found your answers.

    c. What is the sum of the three decimals you found in part b? Does the sum surprise you? Explain.

Investigation 1

1. **a.** 38% **b.** **i.** 220 **ii.** 135 **c.** 284

2. **a.** 4636 **b.** 3337 **c.** 1299 **d.** 6687

3. $3.49

4. **a.** $\frac{3}{10}$ **b.** $62.30 **c.** $65.10

5. They need to raise $175 \times 4 = $700.

6. **a.** 60% **b.** $\frac{2}{5}$

7. **a.** The cost is 1.25 times what the cost was last year. **b.** $2 \times 1.25 = $2.50

Investigation 2

1. **a.** 130 **b.** 31% **c.** 23% **d.** 46% **e.** 13.4%

2. 53.33%

3. 300%, since 45 is 100% of 45, and 135 is 3 times 45.

4. 25%

5. 69

6. 268.14

7. **a.** 42% **b.** 39.5% **c.** **i.** 7 or 8 **ii.** 7 or 8

   d. Becky would now have 58 hits for 137 times at bat so new BA = $\frac{58}{137}$ = 0.423.

Investigation 3

1. Possible answer: Use 40 miles per gallon as an estimate of the gas mileage and 800 miles as an estimate for the trip distance. Then they will need $\frac{800}{40}$ = about 20 gallons of gas.

2. **a.** $24 **b.** It would be better to overestimate to make sure they have enough money.

3. **a.** $\frac{3}{8} + \frac{2}{5} < 1$ **b.** $\frac{5}{10} + \frac{3}{4} > 1$ **c.** $\frac{3}{12} + \frac{3}{6} < 1$
   d. $\frac{1}{2} + \frac{4}{8} = 1$ **e.** $\frac{4}{7} + \frac{7}{12} > 1$ **f.** $\frac{4}{3} + \frac{1}{100} > 1$
   g. $\frac{1}{4} + \frac{2}{3} < 1$ **h.** $\frac{9}{20} + \frac{5}{11} < 1$ **i.** $\frac{9}{12} + \frac{2}{8} = 1$

4. **a.** 314, 258, 233 **b.** Possible answer: Round the candidates' percentages to 40%, 30% and 30%, respectively, and round number of students to 800.

   c. 320, 240, 240 **d.** The estimates indicate that the second and third candidates tied. The actual counts show that the second candidate received 25 more votes than the third candidate. In close elections, estimates are not sufficient.

Answer Keys

Investigation 4

1. a. $1\frac{5}{8}$ cups **b. i.** $1\frac{1}{2}$ **ii.** $2\frac{1}{4}$ **iii.** $1\frac{1}{8}$

    c. $4\frac{7}{8}$

2. a. $\frac{1}{2}$ **b.** $\frac{3}{8}$ **c.** Yes, there are enough seats, and $\frac{1}{8}$ are left for open seating.

3. a. $\frac{3}{4}+\frac{1}{5}=\frac{19}{20}$ **b.** $\frac{7}{8}-\frac{1}{2}=\frac{3}{8}$ **c.** $\frac{1}{6}+\frac{5}{12}=\frac{7}{12}$
    d. $\frac{11}{20}-\frac{1}{5}=\frac{7}{20}$ **e.** $\frac{7}{9}-\frac{2}{3}=\frac{1}{9}$ **f.** $\frac{3}{2}+\frac{3}{4}=\frac{9}{4}$
    g. $\frac{4}{5}+\frac{1}{6}=\frac{29}{30}$ **h.** $\frac{1}{2}-\frac{3}{10}=\frac{1}{5}$ **i.** $\frac{3}{7}+\frac{4}{21}=\frac{13}{21}$

4. a. $\frac{1}{4},\frac{1}{2},\frac{7}{8},\frac{3}{8}$
    b. **i.** $\frac{3}{4}$ **ii.** $1\frac{1}{4}$ **iii.** $\frac{1}{8}$ **iv.** $\frac{5}{8}$
    c. $\frac{1}{3}$ since it takes 3 of the shaded grey region to fill the entire rectangle.

Investigation 5

1. a. $\frac{2}{3}\times\frac{1}{2}=\frac{1}{3}$ **b.** $\frac{3}{5}\times\frac{10}{9}=\frac{2}{3}$ **c.** $\frac{3}{4}\times\frac{8}{9}=\frac{2}{3}$
    d. $\frac{3}{2}\times\frac{5}{6}=\frac{5}{4}$ **e.** $\frac{2}{7}\times\frac{1}{3}=\frac{2}{21}$ **f.** $\frac{3}{8}\times\frac{12}{15}=\frac{3}{10}$
    g. $\frac{9}{10}\times\frac{1}{6}=\frac{3}{20}$ **h.** $\frac{1}{2}\times\frac{6}{7}=\frac{3}{7}$ **i.** $360\times\frac{7}{9}=280$

2. a. 110 **b.** 176 **c.** $\frac{7}{20}$ **d.** 154

3. a. $A=\frac{1}{3}$, $B=\frac{1}{6}$, $C=\frac{1}{24}$, $D=\frac{1}{8}$, $E=\frac{1}{12}$, $F=\frac{1}{4}$
    b. $80 **c.** $30 **d.** $60
    e. **i.** $70 **ii.** $\frac{17}{24}$

4. a. $\frac{3}{4}$ cup **b.** $\frac{1}{8}$ cup **c.** No—original recipe would give $\frac{3}{4}$ cup combined, Jane's recipe gives $\frac{7}{8}$ cup combined.

5. a. $\frac{3}{20}$ **b.** $\frac{3}{5}\times\frac{3}{4}=\frac{9}{20}$

Investigation 6

1. 77.4 tiles **2.** $1.96 **3.** $0.388\times181=$ about 70

4. a. 23.85 **b.** 29.15
    c. **i.** $59,028.75 **ii.** $72,146.25
    d. $1770.86

5. $3.66

6. a. 731 **b.** 0.391, 0.343, 0.265
    c. The sum is 0.999. The sum should be 1, or 100% of the voters. However, because we rounded the decimals in part b, we found an answer slightly less than 1.

Dividing Fractions

Have you ever been with a group of your friends and shared a pizza or cookies or some other kind of food? Perhaps you looked for a way to share the food so that all portions were equal. For a similar type of situation, suppose a large supply of new math books is delivered to your school. The assistant principal hires you and a friend to assemble groups of 30 books to be delivered to each classroom. He asks you to figure out how many classroom sets you can make with the supply you have.

Mathematics can be used in such situations to help determine what an equal share is and how many rooms can receive a set of 30 books. In each of these situations, you can use the operation of division to help find an answer. As you explore the problems in this investigation, you will learn to decide when division is useful, and you will learn to make sense of division of fractions.

Fractions in Fund-Raising

7.1

In earlier investigations of this unit, you've learned how to use the operations of addition, subtraction, and multiplication of fractions to solve a variety of problems. Sometimes problems involving fractions can be solved by using the operation of division. Reviewing the meaning of division in problems involving only whole numbers will help to develop ideas about when and how to divide fractions.

Assignment Choices

ACE questions 1–8, 19, 27–29, 44, 45*, and unassigned choices from earlier problems

*Do not skip.

Note to the Teacher

We discuss several pictorial representations of a solution to a problem to aid student thinking. Since the students have used strip models for fractions in *Bits and Pieces I*, working with a strip model for fraction computation is a natural extension. Some students will probably invent representations you may not have thought about. Among student-invented representations may be jewels that will help other students represent their ideas. Continually ask students to share the diagrams they used to explain their thinking to exploit all options so that all students will have ways to visually organize and think through problems involving division.

Think about this!

Students at Spartan Middle School take a special field trip each spring. But they must raise funds to support the trip. Write number sentences showing the calculations required to solve some of the problems that occurred in one year's plans for fund-raising. Then explain how you recognized what operations to use in each case.

- The 24 members of the school swim team planned to raise money by getting pledges for miles in a swim marathon. If the team goal is to swim 120 miles, how many miles should each swimmer swim?
- Members of the school band plan to sell 600 boxes of cookies in the fund-raising project. There are 20 members in the band. How many boxes should each member sell to reach the goal if all members sell the same number of boxes?
- There will be 360 students going on the field trip, and each school bus carries 30 students. How many buses will be needed?
- Fifteen students in one homeroom earned money for the trip by helping their teacher pick apples in her orchard. She gave them one bushel of apples to split equally. The students counted 125 apples in their bushel. How many apples should each student get?

Compare your number sentences and reasoning about these problems with the ideas of others. If there are different ideas for solving the problems, decide which are correct and why.

Sometimes the amounts given in a situation are not whole numbers but fractions. To deal with those problems, you need to understand what division of fractions means and how to calculate the quotients when a fraction appears as the divisor or the dividend or both. The following problems challenge you to use your understanding of division with whole numbers to make sense of situations involving fractions.

Solutions to Problem 7.1

See text of the **Summarize** on pages 162f, g for supporting drawings.

A. **1.** $9 \div \frac{1}{3} = 27$

2. $9 \div \frac{1}{6} = 9 \times \frac{6}{1} = 54$

3. $9 \div \frac{1}{4} = 9 \times \frac{4}{1} = 36$

4. $9 \div \frac{3}{4} = 9 \times \frac{4}{3} = 12$
(Note that this is $\frac{1}{3}$ of the answer to part 3.)

B. **1.** $12 \div \frac{1}{5} = 12 \times \frac{5}{1} = 60$

2. $12 \div \frac{3}{5} = 12 \times \frac{5}{3} = 20$
(Note that this is $\frac{1}{3}$ of the answer to part 1.)

3. $12 \div \frac{1}{8} = 12 \times \frac{8}{1} = 96$

4. $12 \div \frac{5}{8} = 12 \times \frac{8}{5} = 19\frac{1}{5}$
(Note that this is $\frac{1}{5}$ of the answer to part 3.)

Solutions to Problem 7.1 Follow-Up

1. **a.** $12 \div \frac{1}{4} = 48$

b. $12 \div \frac{1}{3} = 36$

c. $12 \div \frac{2}{3} = 18$

d. $15 \div \frac{5}{3} = 9$

e. $18 \div \frac{5}{6} = 21\frac{3}{5}$

f. $21 \div \frac{7}{1} = 3$

g. There are 3 thirds in each whole, so there are 8×3 thirds in 8. This gives 24. Since $8 \div \frac{2}{3}$ asks how many $\frac{2}{3}$s there are in 8, there would be half as many as the number of $\frac{1}{3}$s, so the answer will be half the answer to $8 \div \frac{1}{3}$. This would give $24 \div 2$ or 12 two-thirds in 8.

Problem 7.1

In preparing food for sale at a school fund-raising event, several students faced questions that involved fractions. Answer the questions and give written explanations or diagrams that show your reasoning. Write a number sentence that shows all calculations that you performed to find your solution.

A. Naylah plans to make small cheese pizzas to sell at the fund-raiser. She has 9 packages of cheddar cheese. How many pizzas can she make if each uses

1. $\frac{1}{3}$ package of cheese? **2.** $\frac{1}{6}$ package of cheese?

3. $\frac{1}{4}$ package of cheese? **4.** $\frac{3}{4}$ package of cheese?

B. A local coffeehouse donated twelve pounds of fresh-roasted gourmet coffee. The students running the fund-raiser decided to sell the coffee in small bags. How many bags can be made if each contains

1. $\frac{1}{5}$ pound? **2.** $\frac{3}{5}$ pound?

3. $\frac{1}{8}$ pound? **4.** $\frac{5}{8}$ pound?

Problem 7.1 Follow-Up

1. Use ideas from your work on the questions about cheese pizzas and coffee bags to complete the following calculations

a. $12 \div \frac{1}{4} =$ **b.** $12 \div \frac{1}{3} =$

c. $12 \div \frac{2}{3} =$ **d.** $15 \div \frac{5}{3} =$

e. $18 \div \frac{5}{6} =$ **f.** $21 \div \frac{7}{1} =$

g. Explain in words why $8 \div \frac{1}{3} = 24$ and $8 \div \frac{2}{3} = 12$. How are these two calculations related? Why is the answer to $8 \div \frac{2}{3}$ exactly half of the answer to $8 \div \frac{1}{3}$?

2. Describe a procedure that seems to make sense for dividing any whole number by any fraction.

3. Write a story problem that can be solved by the division $12 \div \frac{2}{3}$, and explain why the calculation matches the story.

---

2. Answers will vary. One explanation is to multiply the whole number dividend by the denominator of the fraction divisor and then divide that product by the numerator of the fraction divisor. Another way to say this is to multiply by the reciprocal of the fraction divisor. The reason this works is, for example in $8 \div \frac{2}{3}$, multiplying by the denominator 3 finds out how many $\frac{1}{3}$s there are in 8. Then dividing by the numerator 2, recognizes that $\frac{2}{3}$ is twice $\frac{1}{3}$, so the quotient will be half as large.

3. Answers will vary. A sample is given. *Sam has 12 cups of milk. He is making individual custards that take $\frac{2}{3}$ of a cup of milk each. How many custards can he make?*
To solve the problem we need to find out how many $\frac{2}{3}$s there are in 12. To do this grouping problem, we need to divide 12 by $\frac{2}{3}$.

7.2 **Share and Share Alike**

At their special fund-raising event, Spartan Middle School students operated a number of games. Figuring prize amounts for the games led to more questions involving fractions.

Problem 7.2

Answer the following questions and give written explanations or diagrams that show your reasoning. Write a number sentence that shows the calculations that you performed to find your solution.

A. Ms. Phillips brought jars of jellybeans to be shared by members of the student teams winning each game. How much of a pound of candy will each student get if

  1. a four-person team wins $\frac{1}{2}$ pound of jellybeans?

  2. a three-person team wins $\frac{1}{4}$ pound of jellybeans?

  3. a three-person team wins $\frac{1}{3}$ pound of jellybeans?

  4. a two-person team wins $\frac{1}{5}$ pound of jellybeans?

B. A local candy store donated long chocolate bars that were used for prizes in a team competition. What fraction of a whole bar will each team member get if

  1. a two-person team wins $\frac{3}{4}$ of a bar as a prize and shares it equally?

  2. a four-person team wins $\frac{7}{8}$ of a bar and shares it equally?

  3. a four-person team wins $1\frac{1}{2}$ bars and shares the prize equally?

■ **Problem 7.2 Follow-Up**

1. Complete the following calculations based on your work on the questions about jellybeans and chocolate bars. Be prepared to explain how you thought about each problem.

  a. $\frac{1}{2} \div 4 =$ **b.** $\frac{3}{2} \div 2 =$

  c. $\frac{2}{5} \div 3 =$ **d.** $\frac{4}{5} \div 4 =$

  e. $\frac{7}{10} \div 2 =$ **f.** $1\frac{4}{5} \div 3 =$

2. What procedure seems to make sense for dividing a fraction by a whole number?

3. Write a story problem that can be solved by the division $\frac{8}{3} \div 4$, and explain why the calculation matches the story.

Answers to Problem 7.2

See text of the **Summarize** on pages 162j–l for supporting drawings.

A. 1. $\frac{1}{2} \div 4 = \frac{1}{8}$ lb

  2. $\frac{1}{4} \div 3 = \frac{1}{12}$ lb

  3. $\frac{1}{3} \div 3 = \frac{1}{9}$ lb

  4. $\frac{1}{5} \div 2 = \frac{1}{10}$ lb

B. 1. $\frac{3}{8}$

  2. $\frac{7}{32}$

  3. $\frac{3}{8}$

 Answers to Problem 7.2 Follow-Up

1. a. $\frac{1}{8}$ **b.** $\frac{3}{4}$ **c.** $\frac{2}{15}$ **d.** $\frac{4}{20}$ or $\frac{1}{5}$ **e.** $\frac{7}{20}$ **f.** $\frac{9}{15}$ or $\frac{3}{5}$

2. Multiply the dividend by the reciprocal of the divisor.
Multiply by the denominator of divisor and divide by the numerator.

3. Answers will vary. A sample is included.
Four brothers are sharing pizza. Their grandmother made three pizzas and ate $\frac{1}{3}$ of one pizza before the boys got home. The brothers shared the rest equally. How much pizza did each brother get?

Here you have $\frac{8}{3}$ pizza to share among four brothers. You had to realize that 3 whole pizzas minus the $\frac{1}{3}$ the grandmother ate leaves $\frac{8}{3}$ to share.

Assignment Choices

ACE questions 9–13, 18, 20–23, 30–35, 43, and unassigned choices from earlier problems

Answers to Problem 7.3

See text of the **Summarize** on pages 162n, o for supporting drawings.

A. **1.** 3 badges

 2. $4\frac{1}{2}$ badges

 3. $3\frac{3}{4}$ badges

 4. 16 badges

B. **1.** $1\frac{2}{10}$ bows

 2. $\frac{24}{18} = \frac{4}{3} = 1\frac{1}{3}$ bows

 3. $\frac{21}{8} = 2\frac{5}{8}$ bows

 4. $\frac{21}{6}$ or $\frac{7}{2} = 3\frac{1}{2}$ bows

Assignment Choices

ACE questions 14–17, 24–26, 36–42, 46–48, and unassigned choices from earlier problems

7.3 Summer Work

In Problems 7.1 and 7.2, you developed ways of thinking about and solving division problems involving a whole number and a fraction. The questions in this problem involve dividing a fraction by another fraction. Use what you have learned to answer the questions.

Problem 7.3

Rasheed and Jade have a summer job at a kiosk called *Ribbon Remnants*. They sell small amounts of ribbon very inexpensively from end-of-bolt pieces of ribbon. In each situation that follows, give written explanations or diagrams that show your reasoning, and write a number sentence that shows the calculations that you performed to find your solution.

A. Rasheed takes a customer order to provide ribbons for conference badges. Each badge requires $\frac{1}{6}$ of a yard of ribbon. How many badge ribbons can he make from the given remnants of ribbon? For each answer that has a remainder, tell what fractional part of another badge ribbon he could make with that leftover amount of ribbon.

 1. $\frac{1}{2}$ yard

 2. $\frac{3}{4}$ yard

 3. $\frac{5}{8}$ yard

 4. $2\frac{2}{3}$ yards (Remember, $2\frac{2}{3} = \frac{8}{3}$.)

B. Jade is working on an order for bows for the conference workers to wear. She uses $\frac{2}{3}$ of a yard of ribbon to make one bow. How many bows can Jade make from each of the following remnants?

 1. $\frac{4}{5}$ yard

 2. $\frac{8}{9}$ yard

 3. $1\frac{3}{4}$ yards

 4. $2\frac{1}{3}$ yards

■ Problem 7.3 Follow-Up

1. Based on your work in Problems 7.1–7.3, what general procedure makes sense for division of fractions? Remember that a set of steps to do a computation is called an *algorithm*. So this procedure should be your algorithm for dividing fractions.

2. Test your algorithm on these division calculations.

   a. $\frac{2}{5} \div 2$ **b.** $6 \div \frac{2}{3}$ **c.** $\frac{3}{4} \div \frac{2}{3}$

   d. $1\frac{3}{4} \div \frac{1}{2}$ **e.** $7 \div 3$ **f.** $\frac{2}{3} \div 1\frac{1}{4}$

3. Write a story problem that can be solved by the division $1\frac{3}{4} \div \frac{1}{2}$, and explain why the calculation matches the story.

Note to the Teacher

The Follow-Up is essential. Assign it as either class work or homework, but be sure to discuss the problems.

Answers Problem 7.3 Follow-Up

1. Possible Answers

- Find a common denominator for the dividend and divisor (the given quantities). Then divide the numerator of the dividend by the numerator of the divisor.

- Multiply the dividend by the denominator of the divisor and divide the result by the numerator of the dividend.

- Multiply the dividend by the reciprocal of the divisor.

2. a. $\frac{2}{10}$ or $\frac{1}{5}$

   b. 9

   c. $\frac{9}{8}$ or $1\frac{1}{8}$

   d. $\frac{14}{4}$ or $\frac{7}{2}$ or $3\frac{1}{2}$

   e. $2\frac{1}{3}$

   f. $\frac{8}{15}$

3. Answers will vary. One possibility is given.
Josh is cooking for his nephews and wants to make as many recipes of chili as he can from $1\frac{3}{4}$ pounds of dried beans. Each recipe takes $\frac{1}{2}$ pound of dried beans. How many recipes can he make?
Here you must find $1\frac{3}{4} \div \frac{1}{2}$ or how many $\frac{1}{2}$ s are in $1\frac{3}{4}$. There are $3\frac{1}{2}$, so he can make 3 full batches and half of another.

ACE

Answers

Applications

1. 80
2. 160
3. 320
4. 100
5. 50
6. 70
7. 45
8. See below.
9. $\frac{1}{16}$ lb
10. $\frac{1}{16}$ lb
11. $\frac{1}{4}$ lb
12. $\frac{4}{50}$ or $\frac{2}{25}$ lb
13. $\frac{3}{4}$ lb

Applications

Lee's group in Home Arts class purchased ingredients in large quantities to make different sizes of muffins for a bake sale. Each bag of sugar contains approximately 20 cups. In 1–7, find how many muffins can be made from a bag of sugar if each of the different-sized muffins needs the amount of sugar given.

1. $\frac{1}{4}$ cup of sugar
2. $\frac{1}{8}$ cup of sugar
3. $\frac{1}{16}$ cup of sugar
4. $\frac{1}{5}$ cup of sugar
5. $\frac{2}{5}$ cup of sugar
6. $\frac{2}{7}$ cup of sugar
7. $\frac{4}{9}$ cup of sugar

8. Explain in words how the answers for $20 \div \frac{1}{5}$ and $20 \div \frac{2}{5}$ are related. Show why this makes sense.

Sam is in charge of awarding prizes to teams that win medals at an all-state mathematics competition. He decided to give each team member a little bag of chocolate drops with each prize. In 9–13, find how many pounds of candy each member on each of the winning teams receives.

9. The team of 8 students shares $\frac{1}{2}$ pound of the chocolate drops.
10. The team of 4 students shares $\frac{1}{4}$ pound of the chocolate drops.
11. The team of 3 students shares $\frac{3}{4}$ pound of the chocolate drops.
12. The team of 10 students shares $\frac{4}{5}$ pound of the chocolate drops.
13. The team of 2 students shares $1\frac{1}{2}$ pound of the chocolate drops.

Investigation 7: Dividing with Fractions 83

---

8. Since $\frac{2}{5}$ of a cup is two times as large as $\frac{1}{5}$ of a cup, the number of muffins you can make will be half as many.

This shows ten divided into 5 equal sized pieces so that each piece is $\frac{1}{5}$ of a whole.

There are fifty $\frac{1}{5}$ pieces in the strip of ten, so there would be 100 in a strip of 20.

But if it takes two of the $\frac{1}{5}$ pieces to make a $\frac{2}{5}$ piece, we would only have 25 in the strip of 10 and 50 in a strip of 20. This means that $20 \div \frac{1}{5}$ will be twice as large as $20 \div \frac{2}{5}$.

A latte is the most popular coffee drink made at Jean's Beans Coffee Shop. Each latte requires $\frac{1}{3}$ cup of milk. In 14–16, find how many lattes can be made with the given amounts of milk. Be sure to explain what the remainder means in each case.

14. $\frac{7}{9}$ cup of milk

15. $\frac{5}{6}$ cup of milk

16. $3\frac{2}{3}$ cups of milk

Solve 17–19 and show why your answer is correct. Drawings may be used to explain your reasoning. Write a number sentence that can be used to solve each problem.

17. It takes $18\frac{2}{3}$ inches of molding to make a small picture frame for a snapshot. Ms. Jones has 3 yards of molding. How many small picture frames can she make? If there is a remainder, tell what this remainder means.

18. At the pet store, there are 12 cages with a rabbit in each. Sarah's mother owns the pet store and allows Sarah to feed the rabbits special treats. She has $1\frac{1}{3}$ pounds of treats for today. How much should Sarah give to each rabbit?

19. Bill wants to make 22 small pizzas for a party. He has 16 cups of flour, and $\frac{3}{4}$ cup of flour is needed for each crust. Does he have enough flour? Explain your answer.

In 20–25, complete each division. If there is a mixed number equivalent to your quotient, find it.

20. $10 \div \frac{2}{3} =$

21. $5 \div 37 =$

22. $\frac{6}{7} \div 4 =$

23. $\frac{3}{10} \div 2 =$

24. $\frac{2}{5} \div \frac{1}{3} =$

25. $2\frac{1}{2} \div 1\frac{1}{3} =$

26. Choose any two of ACE 20–25 and write a story problem to fit the computation.

Connections

27. Betty jogged $2\frac{2}{5}$ km on a trail and then sat down to wait for her friend, Glenda. Glenda has jogged $1\frac{1}{2}$ km on the trail. How much farther will Glenda have to jog to reach Betty?

Bits and Pieces II

---

14. $2\frac{1}{3}$ which means 2 lattes and $\frac{1}{3}$ of another

15. $2\frac{1}{2}$ which means 2 lattes and $\frac{1}{2}$ of another

16. 11 lattes

17. 3 yards is 108 inches. $108 \div 18\frac{2}{3} = 108 \div \frac{56}{3} = \frac{324}{3} \div \frac{56}{3}$ which is $5\frac{44}{56}$ or $5\frac{11}{14}$.

5 complete frames and $\frac{11}{14}$ of another frame

18. $1\frac{1}{3} \div 12 = \frac{4}{3} \div 12 = \frac{4}{3} \div \frac{36}{3} = \frac{4}{36}$ or $\frac{1}{9}$ pound of treats

19. No. He needs $16\frac{1}{2}$ cups of flour. The amount of flour he has will make $21\frac{1}{3}$ pizzas.

20. 15

21. $\frac{5}{37}$

22. $\frac{6}{28}$ or $\frac{3}{14}$

23. $\frac{3}{20}$

24. $\frac{6}{5}$ or $1\frac{1}{5}$

25. $\frac{15}{8}$ or $1\frac{7}{8}$

26. Answers will vary; samples are given for ACE 20 and ACE 22.

20. I have a ten foot roll of paper to make signs. If each sign takes $\frac{2}{3}$ ft of paper, how many signs can I make?

22. I bought $\frac{6}{7}$ of a pound of jelly beans. If I wanted to share them with 3 other people, how much of a pound would each of us get?

Connections

27. $\frac{9}{10}$ km

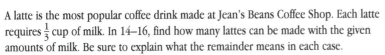

28. $1\frac{1}{4}$ hours

29. $\frac{7}{20}$ left

30. $\frac{11}{10}$ or $1\frac{1}{10}$

31. $\frac{41}{24}$ or $1\frac{17}{24}$

32. $\frac{3}{12}$ or $\frac{1}{4}$

33. $\frac{5}{12}$ or $\frac{10}{24}$

34. 4 or $\frac{12}{3}$

35. $\frac{19}{12}$ or $1\frac{7}{12}$

36. $\frac{7}{2}$ or $3\frac{1}{2}$

37. $\frac{12}{5}$ or $2\frac{2}{5}$

38. $\frac{2}{21}$

39. $\frac{21}{32}$

40. $\frac{3}{6}$ or $\frac{1}{2}$

41. $\frac{154}{12}$ or $12\frac{10}{12}$ or $12\frac{5}{6}$

42. Answers vary. In ACE 36, for example, $\frac{1}{2} \times 7 = 3\frac{1}{2}$. You could think of this as $\frac{1}{2}$ of the amount in 7 which is $3\frac{1}{2}$ or you could think of this as 7 groups of $\frac{1}{2}$ which again totals $3\frac{1}{2}$. For ACE 37, $4 \times \frac{3}{5} = 2\frac{2}{5}$. You could think of this as 4 groups of $\frac{3}{5}$ or $\frac{3}{5} + \frac{3}{5} + \frac{3}{5} + \frac{3}{5}$ which is $\frac{12}{5}$ or $2\frac{2}{5}$.

43. $\frac{1}{5} \div \frac{3}{5} = \frac{1}{3}$ and $\frac{1}{5} \div \frac{1}{3} = \frac{3}{5}$

44. Sample answers are given.

   a. $\frac{2}{3}$ and $\frac{8}{12}$

   b. $\frac{5}{6}$ and $\frac{20}{24}$

   c. $\frac{4}{3}$ and $\frac{24}{18}$

---

28. John is scheduled to work at the car wash for 3 hours. He has already worked $1\frac{3}{4}$ hours. How many more hours must he work?

29. Jenny and her sister are paid to mow their lawn. Jenny mowed $\frac{2}{5}$ of the lawn and her sister mowed $\frac{1}{4}$ of it. How much of the lawn is left to be mowed?

Add or subtract. Write another fraction that is equivalent to each answer.

30. $\frac{9}{10} + \frac{1}{5} =$ **31.** $\frac{5}{6} + \frac{7}{8} =$ **32.** $\frac{2}{3} - \frac{5}{12} =$

33. $\frac{3}{4} - \frac{1}{3} =$ **34.** $2\frac{2}{3} + 1\frac{1}{3} =$ **35.** $2\frac{5}{6} - 1\frac{1}{4} =$

In 36–41, compute each product.

36. $\frac{1}{2} \times 7 =$ **37.** $4 \times \frac{3}{5} =$ **38.** $\frac{2}{7} \times \frac{1}{3} =$

39. $\frac{3}{4} \times \frac{7}{8} =$ **40.** $1\frac{1}{2} \times \frac{1}{3} =$ **41.** $4\frac{2}{3} \times 2\frac{3}{4} =$

42. Choose any two of ACE 36–41 and explain why your answer makes sense. You may use a drawing to support your answer.

43. Show how multiplication and division are connected. Use the multiplication fact that $\frac{1}{3} \times \frac{3}{5} = \frac{1}{5}$ to write two division statements that use the same three numbers.

44. You learned in *Bits and Pieces I* that every fraction can be written in many equivalent forms. For example, the fraction $\frac{12}{15}$ is equivalent to any other fraction that results from multiplying the numerator and the denominator by the same number. If we multiply the numerator and the denominator by 2, we get $\frac{24}{30}$, which is equivalent to $\frac{12}{15}$. When we multiply the numerator by 2 and the denominator by 2, we are multiplying the fraction by $\frac{2}{2}$, which is equal to 1.

Write two fractions that are equivalent to each of the following fractions. Find one with a greater numerator and one with a smaller numerator.

   a. $\frac{4}{6}$ **b.** $\frac{10}{12}$ **c.** $\frac{12}{9}$

Extensions

45. When working with fractions, you sometimes need to find what to multiply a given number by to get a product of 1. For example, you multiply $\frac{1}{6}$ by 6 to get a product of 1. We can show this in symbols as $\frac{1}{6} \times 6 = 1$ or, since $6 = \frac{6}{1}$, we could write $\frac{1}{6} \times \frac{6}{1} = 1$.

In a-i write a factor that will make each number sentence true.

a. $2 \times$ ___ $= 1$ **b.** $\frac{1}{2} \times$ ___ $= 1$ **c.** $3 \times$ ___ $= 1$

d. $\frac{1}{3} \times$ ___ $= 1$ **e.** ___ $\times \frac{2}{3} = 1$ **f.** $\frac{3}{4} \times$ ___ $= 1$

g. ___ $\times \frac{5}{2} = 1$ **h.** $1\frac{1}{4} \times$ ___ $= 1$ **i.** $\frac{7}{12} \times$ ___ $= 1$

In each case, the factor by which you multiply a number so their product is 1 is called the **reciprocal** of the number.

For example, $\frac{1}{2}$ is the **reciprocal** of 2 and 2 is the **reciprocal** of $\frac{1}{2}$ because $\frac{1}{2} \times 2 = 1$ and $2 \times \frac{1}{2} = 1$.

46. Find a number by which to multiply the numerator and the denominator of the fraction so that the resulting denominator equals 1.

a. $\dfrac{1}{\frac{1}{2}}$ **b.** $\dfrac{\frac{2}{3}}{3}$

47. Find a number by which to multiply the numerator and the denominator of the fraction so that the resulting numerator equals 1.

a. $\dfrac{\frac{2}{4}}{\frac{3}{5}}$ **b.** $\dfrac{\frac{5}{2}}{\frac{1}{3}}$

48. Find the missing numbers in each number sentence. Describe the relationship between each pair of number sentences.

a. $3 \div$ _____ $= 9$ $3 \times$ _____ $= 9$

b. $3 \div$ _____ $= 12$ $3 \times$ _____ $= 12$

c. $2\frac{1}{2} \div$ _____ $= 5$ $2\frac{1}{2} \times$ _____ $= 5$

---

45. Simplest form answers are given. Equivalent answers may be accepted.

  a. $\frac{1}{2}$

  b. 2

  c. $\frac{1}{3}$

  d. 3

  e. $\frac{3}{2}$

  f. $\frac{4}{3}$

  g. $\frac{2}{5}$

  h. $\frac{4}{5}$

  i. $\frac{12}{7} = 1\frac{5}{7}$

46a. Multiply both numerator and denominator by 2.

  b. Multiply both the numerator and the denominator by $\frac{1}{3}$.

47a. Multiply the numerator and the denominator by $\frac{4}{2}$.

  b. Multiply the numerator and the denominator by $\frac{2}{5}$.

48. The numbers in each pair are reciprocals of each other.

  a. $\frac{1}{3}$ and 3

  b. $\frac{1}{4}$ and 4

  c. $\frac{1}{2}$ and 2

Possible Answers

1. Students may have different algorithms at this stage. Two algorithms that many students develop are included.

Find a common denominator and then divide the numerators.
Examples:

a. $5 \div \frac{1}{3} = \frac{15}{3} \div \frac{1}{3} = 15$

b. $\frac{2}{3} \div 4 = \frac{2}{3} \div \frac{12}{3} = 2 \div 12 = \frac{2}{12}$ or $\frac{1}{6}$

c. $\frac{2}{3} \div \frac{1}{2} = \frac{4}{6} \div \frac{3}{6} = 4 \div 3 = \frac{4}{3}$ or $1\frac{1}{3}$

d. $1\frac{1}{2} \div \frac{2}{7} = \frac{3}{2} \div \frac{2}{7} = \frac{21}{14} \div \frac{4}{14} = 21 \div 4 = 5\frac{1}{4}$

Recognize that dividing by a number is the same as multiplying by its reciprocal.
Examples:

a. $5 \div \frac{1}{3} = 5 \times 3 = 15$

b. $\frac{2}{3} \div 4 = \frac{2}{3} \times \frac{1}{4} = \frac{2}{12}$ or $\frac{1}{6}$

c. $\frac{2}{3} \div \frac{1}{2} = \frac{2}{3} \times 2 = \frac{4}{3}$ or $1\frac{1}{3}$

d. $1\frac{1}{2} \div \frac{2}{7} = \frac{3}{2} \div \frac{2}{7} = \frac{3}{2} \times \frac{7}{2} = \frac{21}{4} = 5\frac{1}{4}$

2. Since it takes three $\frac{1}{5}$s to make $\frac{3}{5}$, the answer to $20 \div \frac{1}{5}$ is three times as large as the answer to $20 \div \frac{3}{5}$. So, take the answer to $20 \div \frac{1}{5}$ (which is the same as $20 \times 5 = 100$) and divide this by three to get the answer to $20 \div \frac{3}{5}$. That quotient is $\frac{100}{3}$ or $33\frac{1}{3}$.

Mathematical Reflections

In this investigation, you explored situations in which you needed to divide fractions. You developed an algorithm for dividing fractions and used division to solve problems. These questions will help you to summarize what you have learned.

① Explain your algorithm for dividing fractions. Demonstrate the algorithm on a problem for each situation given.

    a. a whole number divided by a fraction

    b. a fraction divided by a whole number

    c. a fraction divided by a fraction

    d. a mixed number divided by a fraction

② How is the quotient of $20 \div \frac{1}{5}$ related to the quotient of $20 \div \frac{3}{5}$? Explain your answer.

③ You considered two different types of situations that call for division—sharing and grouping. Write a story problem for each type of situation and explain why you think it is a sharing problem or a grouping problem.

④ Can the answer to a division problem be greater than, less than, or between the two numbers you are dividing? In each case explain why or why not and show an example to illustrate your answer.

---

3. The answers will vary. The important consideration is what information is given in each problem. In sharing, the total quantity and the number that will share that quantity are given. The portion each receives must be determined. In grouping, the total and the portion size are given. The number of groups that can be formed is what must be determined.

4. See page 162a.

4. The answer to all three is yes. Examples for each are included.

Answer is greater:

$\frac{2}{3} \div \frac{1}{5} = \frac{10}{3} = 3\frac{1}{3}$ which is larger than either number. The answer means that there are 3 one-fifths plus another third of a one-fifth in $\frac{2}{3}$.

Note: A number between zero and one divided by a smaller number between zero and one will give an answer greater than one and thus even greater than the greater of the two original numbers.

Answer is less:

$\frac{2}{3} \div 2 = \frac{1}{3}$ or $6 \div 3 = 2$. In each, the quotient is less than either of the original numbers.

Case I: If a number between zero and one is divided by a number greater than one, the result is a fraction less than either of the original numbers. For example, $\frac{2}{3} \div 2 = \frac{1}{3}$. This division is the same as multiplying the dividend by the reciprocal of a number greater than one ($\frac{2}{3} \times \frac{1}{2}$), which results in a number less than one. Since less than the whole of the dividend is being considered, the answer must be less than the dividend and, of course, less than the divisor.

Case II: If the dividend and the divisor are each greater than one, the divisor must be the greater of two factors whose product is equal to the dividend. This means that the divisor must be larger than the square root of the dividend. For example, in $6 \div 3 = 2$, the divisor, 3, is greater the greater of the two factors whose product equals the dividend, 6.

Answer is between:

$\frac{2}{3} \div \frac{10}{12} = \frac{8}{10}$ or $\frac{4}{5}$. If the three values are rewritten with a common denominator to compare the values, the problem is $\frac{40}{60} \div \frac{50}{60} = \frac{48}{60}$. The answer is between the two fractions. Two more examples are $4 \div \frac{3}{2} = \frac{8}{3}$ and $\frac{1}{4} \div \frac{3}{4} = \frac{1}{3}$.

Note: There are pairs of numbers greater and less than one whose quotient is between the two numbers. Remember that $A \div B = C$ means that $B \times C = A$. Thus, if B and C are not equal, then one is greater and one is less than the square root of A.

Case I: If A and B are both greater than 1 and C is between them, B must be less than the square root of A and C must be greater than the square root of A. An example is $4 \div \frac{3}{2} = \frac{8}{3}$.

Case II: If A is between zero and one, then the square root of A is larger than A. So, B must be greater than the square root of A and C must be less than the square root of A. Therefore C is between A and B. An example of this case is $\frac{1}{4} \div \frac{3}{4} = \frac{1}{3}$.

7.1 • Fractions in Fund-Raising

The intent of this problem is to use contexts to help students begin to think about division when fractions are involved. The sequence of problems is deliberately organized to provide scaffolding for more challenging problems. In Problem 7.1, the students work with a whole number divided by a fraction; in Problem 7.2 they work with a fraction divided by a whole number; and finally, in Problem 7.3, they work with a fraction divided by a fraction.

Because the goal in Problems 7.1, 7.2, and 7.3 is for students to understand and be able to divide fractions, we suggest that students not use calculators. Rushing to division on the calculator, which may produce a decimal answer, does not promote deep analysis of why division is appropriate, how to compute an answer, and what an answer, including the remainder, means.

Students are often asked to write problems that fit a given computation expression. How a student responds will tell a great deal about his understanding of different kinds of division situations and whether he can make sense of what the answer to a division problem, with any fractional part, means. The goal of Problems 7.1, 7.2, and 7.3 is to help students develop an efficient algorithm for division of fractions. Although every student may not get to the "invert and multiply" algorithm, each should have efficient ways of tackling problems that call for divisions with fractions.

Discussion of Problem 7.1

What students know about whole number division should be used to help stimulate their thinking about division situations that involve fractions. To help review their experiences with whole numbers and division, Problem 7.1 provides a substantive Think About This! focusing entirely on whole numbers.

There are many kinds of situations that call for division with whole numbers or fractions. Here the problems are designed to allow you to have a conversation with the students about two major types of division problem situations— sharing and grouping.

In a sharing situation, some known quantity is <u>shared</u> equally among a known number of entities. What is not known in a sharing situation is the <u>amount</u> of the given quantity per share. For example, in the Think About This!, 24 members are raising money by collectively swimming 120 miles. The question is how many miles should each team member swim to meet the goal. In this problem you know the amount to be shared—120 miles—and the number of entities who will share the miles—24 members. So we are looking for the "share" for each person. This would be structurally the same as sharing 120 cookies among 24 scout members. This kind of the problem may be solved using division to find the fair share. In the swim team example, the quotient from the division means "miles per swimmer." In the scout situation—120 cookies and 24 scout members—the quotient would mean "cookies per scout." To summarize, in a sharing situation you know the <u>amount</u> to be shared and the <u>number</u> of entities that will receive a share. The answer to the division, the quotient, tells the amount per share.

In a grouping situation, the size of the groups being formed and the total quantity available to make those groups are known. The unknown is the <u>number of groups</u> of the given size that can be made. In the third part of Think About This! the total number of students is 360, and the group size is 30 students. Students are asked to find the number of groups that can be made with each group representing a busload. This is a grouping problem much like having 24 students and making teams of four. How many groups (teams) can you make? In each kind of problem, grouping or sharing, division may be used to determine the numerical answer, but the context tells what that answer means. In this example, the quotient means "number of buses needed." In the "making teams" example, the answer to 24 ÷ 4 is 6. Adding a label helps clarify what the answer means. In this case it means 6 <u>teams</u>. In a grouping situation, the answer tells how many groups of the specified size can be made from the given quantity.

Continue to use this language of "sharing" and "grouping" and asking for analysis in the fraction division problems as well. This language is very helpful in understanding when division is an appropriate operation.

Launch of Think About This!

Pose a whole number division situation to help students review what they already know about division.

> Tell me some situations where we use division. (*Various answers.*)

> Here is a problem to think about and get us started.

> Emily and three friends go on a hike together. Emily's dad sends along a small bag with 12 candy bars in it. How many candy bars does each get if they share them equally?

> I would like you to draw some kind of diagram that helps explain why your answer to this problem makes sense.

Give the students a minute to think about the problem and then call on someone to present his or her diagram and solution to the problem. Let other students share any different approaches to the problem.

> Sam, tell us how you solved the problem and what your answer tells you.

> What does your answer tell you?

> Did anyone think about this problem in a different way?

Here are some possible diagrams that students might produce for this problem.

Diagram 1

This diagram shows the 12 candy bars arranged in one row and distributed one by one to the circles representing the four friends—like dealing out the candy bars one by one until they are all gone.

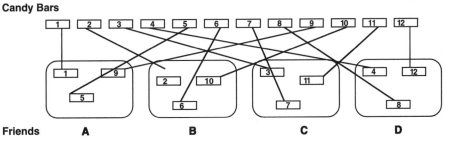

Diagram 2

This diagram has an array with four columns to represent the four friends with as many rows of four candy bars as possible. Then each friend's share is circled.

Candy Bars

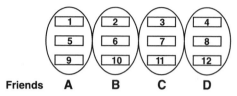

Friends   **A**   **B**   **C**   **D**

Diagram 3

Some students may use repeated subtraction to find the answer. They might reason something like this:

We have 12 candy bars and four friends, so it takes four bars to give each person one candy bar. And we can just keep subtracting four until we have nothing left. So it is

12 (bars) − 4 (one for each person) = 8 (bars left)   8 − 4 = 4   4 − 4 = 0
We subtracted three groups of four so each person gets three candy bars.

In the class discussion, focus on how you recognize when division is an appropriate operation to use and how the numerical answer should be interpreted in the given situation. Many students will recognize that division will help solve the problem because it is a sharing problem. Since $12 \div 4 = 3$, we just have to figure out what the 3 means. Here it means 3 candy bars for each friend or 3 candy bars per friend.

It is also a good time to remind students that a fraction can be interpreted as an implied division. Hence $\frac{12}{4}$ is another way to represent $12 \div 4$.

Now read with the class the directions for the Think About This! Be sure that students remember to include an explanation for each problem.

Explore

Have students work alone for a few minutes so that each student has an opportunity to make sense of the given situations before pairing with a partner to share thoughts and proposed strategies. As they work, circulate to determine which pairs are ready to offer ideas for recognizing that each of these problems can be solved using division. If needed, offer an example of how to record a number sentence and explain the justification for the sentence.

The discussion of the problems is crucial in setting the stage for division of fractions.

Summarize

Share explanations of solutions, number sentences, strategies, and drawings and how each helped students to make sense of the problem. If they did not draw pictures, show a diagram and say that this is one that makes sense to you, and you want to see if it makes sense to them. Samples are shown on page 162e for the bus problem referred to earlier.

Method 1

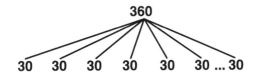

Method 2

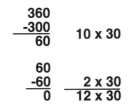

$$\begin{array}{r} 360 \\ -300 \\ \hline 60 \end{array}$$ 10 x 30

$$\begin{array}{r} 60 \\ -60 \\ \hline 0 \end{array}$$ $$\dfrac{2 \times 30}{12 \times 30}$$

makes 12 buses

Method 3

Imagine drawing circles to represent the 360 students. Since drawing 360 circles is tedious and time-consuming, draw enough to see why division will give the numerical answer

STUDENTS IN GROUPS OF THIRTY	BUSES
O O O O O O O O O O O O O O O O O O O O O O O O O O O O O O	1
O O O O O O O O O O O O O O O O O O O O O O O O O O O O O O	2
O O O O O O O O O O O O O O O O O O O O O O O O O O O O O O	3
⋮ ⋮	⋮
O O O O O O O O O O O O O O O O O O O O O O O O O O O O O O	12

Discuss the problems with an eye toward what is coming in Problem 7.1. In the first problem, for instance, you are given two quantities and asked to find a third. You are given 24 swim team members and 120 miles. You are to find a quantity that represents miles per swim team member.

With the class, notice such things as the kinds of quantities in the problems. These whole number counts are setting the stage for the more complicated world of fractions.

What kind of numbers (quantities) are given or implied in the problem?

What do you need to know?

What will your answer tell us?

Be sure that students can interpret their answer in the context of the Thinking About This! situation, miles per swim team member in the first part, boxes per member in the second, number of buses in the third, and apples per person in the last part.

After a discussion of each situation, discuss the two kinds of division problems illustrated in the introductory paragraphs on sharing and grouping. Review each problem and ask if it is a sharing or a grouping problem and why.

All are sharing problems with the exception of the third situation. In the first problem, each swimmer's share is five miles. In the second, each band member's share is 30 boxes. The third part is a grouping problem. Finding that you can create 12 groups of 30 students means you need 12 buses. The number of groups is 12. In the final Think About This! situation, 15 students share 125 apples. So each student's share is $8\frac{1}{3}$ apples.

Use the summary to segue into the launch of Problem 7.1.

Launch of Problem 7.1

Now that our heads are back into what kinds of questions division can help us answer, we are going to tackle problems with a new challenge. Some counts or measures in Problem 7.1 involve fractions. Use what you know about whole number computation and about fractions to find ways to solve these problems. Even though you have not been taught a particular method for solving such problems, you know enough to make sense of how to think about these situations. Let's read the problem statement and make sure you understand what you are expected to do.

Call on a student to read the problem.

What kinds of numbers will you deal with in the first two parts of Think About This? *(Whole numbers and fractions.)* Let's do a think–pair–share. Work alone for five minutes. Then pair with your partner and share what you have done so far. Then, work together until I call you back to share with the whole class. Remember that drawing a picture or a representation can help you think through each situation.

Explore

Circulate, as the class works, paying attention to how students are thinking about the problems and where they are having difficulty. Encourage the students to draw pictures or diagrams to help them think about the problems. Encourage the students to also write number sentences that reflect how they solved the problem. Ask questions about whether the problems seem to be about sharing something equally or about how many groups or things of a certain kind can be made. In the first problem, you are making pizzas with different amounts of cheese. In each case, you know how much cheese you have and how much is needed for each group (pizza). You do not know how many pizzas you can make. This is a form of grouping. The second problem is also a form of grouping. Here you are making groups of a given amount of coffee. You know the total amount of coffee and the amount per group (bag) in each case.

Summarize

As you go over the problems, have any students who drew diagrams to help them share their drawings. The problems with unit numerators are easy once the students draw diagrams.

STUDENT ONE:

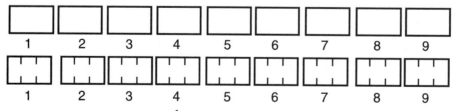

I need to find out how many $\frac{1}{3}$s are in 9. This will tell me how many pizzas I can make. I need to divide 9 by $\frac{1}{3}$ to find how many pizzas. So $9 \div \frac{1}{3} = 27$ which means that I can make 27 pizzas with 9 cups of cheese.

Students also drew the above diagram and said "I have 9 cups of cheese. Since each cup has three thirds, I can multiply 9×3 to find how many thirds in 9. So 27 pizzas can be made with 9 cups of cheese when each pizza takes $\frac{1}{3}$ cup of cheese."

STUDENT TWO:

Students who use common denominators may reason like this:

$9 \div \frac{1}{3}$ is the same as $\frac{27}{3} \div \frac{1}{3}$. This means how many $\frac{1}{3}$s are in 27 thirds. The answer is 27.

Drawing a diagram for Problem A, Part 4 is different because the numerator of the divisor is not 1.

STUDENT THREE:

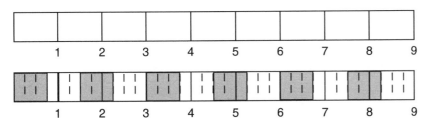

I need to find out how many $\frac{3}{4}$s are in 9. This will tell me how many pizzas I can make. I need to divide 9 by $\frac{3}{4}$ to find how many pizzas. I need to mark off $\frac{3}{4}$ size groups on the 9 bars of cheese and count to see that there are 12, which means that I can make 12 pizzas with 9 cups of cheese. (Some students may write this as $9 \times 4 \div 3 = 12$.)

Others will rewrite the 9 as $\frac{36}{4}$ and think of the problem as $\frac{36}{4} \div \frac{3}{4} = 12$.

Discuss each problem and ask questions that help students to develop a shortcut for each of the situations encountered—dividing a whole number by a unit fraction or dividing a whole number by a non-unit fraction. Discuss part A 1, 2, 3 and part B 1, 3 together. Students must verbalize that they must find the number of the fractional parts that are in the whole number, for example, $\frac{1}{3}$s in 9. Then find how many in one whole and multiply by that number—multiply by 9 in this example.

To summarize the data,

A. 1. $9 \div \frac{1}{3} = 27$ 2. $9 \div \frac{1}{6} = 54$ 3. $9 \div \frac{1}{4} = 36$

B. 1. $12 \div \frac{1}{5} = 60$ 3. $12 \div \frac{1}{8} = 96$.

The pattern is clear. In each case, the answer is the same as these products.

A. 1. $9 \times 3 = 27$ 2. $9 \times 6 = 54$, and   3. $9 \times 4 = 36$

B. 1. $12 \times 5 = 60$ 3. $12 \times 8 = 96$

This makes sense because there are three $\frac{1}{3}$s in 1, six $\frac{1}{6}$s in 1, and so on.

After the students have articulated the pattern (multiply by the denominator or some equivalent expression), ask a few questions of the same type for practice.

> Let's use the pattern you have seen to do a couple of additional problems of the same type. What would the answer to each of these be?
> $6 \div \frac{1}{2}$ $5 \div \frac{1}{9}$ $7 \div \frac{1}{3}$

> Now let's look at the rest of the problems and see whether we can find a pattern that makes sense. Let's do the same kind of arrangement for the other three problems.

A. 4. $9 \div \frac{3}{4} = 12$ B. 2. $12 \div \frac{3}{5} = 20$ B. 4. $12 \div \frac{5}{8} = 19\frac{1}{5}$

Let's think about why these answers make sense. Look back at our reasoning when the numerator was one. If the problem were $9 \div \frac{1}{4}$, we would say that there are 4 fourths in each whole. So we would multiply 9×4 to get 36.

But the problem is $9 \div \frac{3}{4}$. It takes three $\frac{1}{4}$s to make a pizza. How will this affect the answer? (*We will have to divide by three to get the final answer since it takes three times as many $\frac{1}{4}$s to make a pizza.*) So we can make $36 \div 3 = 12$ pizzas.

Let's look at the other two and see if the same reasoning works.

Call on students to talk about each problem, guiding the discussion toward these explanations:

For part 2 of B, $12 \div \frac{3}{5} = 20$.
We can think of the problem this way. We need to find how many $\frac{3}{5}$s there are in 12 wholes. We can first find the number of $\frac{1}{5}$s in 12 which is $12 \times 5 = 60$. Because it takes 3 of the $\frac{1}{5}$s to make a pizza, we can divide by 3 and get 20 pizzas, the same result as multiplying 12 by $\frac{5}{3}$. $12 \times \frac{5}{3} = 20$.

For part 4 of B, we need to divide 12 by $\frac{5}{8}$. We find how many eighths in a whole and multiply by the 12 wholes. Then we have to divide by the number of eighths needed for each pizza. This is the same as multiplying by the denominator and dividing by the numerator of the divisor. So if we are dividing by $\frac{5}{8}$ we can get the answer by multiplying by $\frac{8}{5}$. Remember that this is the same thing as multiplying by 8 and dividing by 5.

The students should now do the Follow-Up either individually or in pairs or as homework. When the Follow-Up is done, discuss the results with the class. In part 1, discuss student strategies. Ask what kind of situation each problem represents, sharing or grouping. Ask students to justify their answers and share any diagrams they drew to make sense of the problem.

For part 2, some students may see that you multiply by the reciprocal. Others may feel more comfortable with saying that you multiply the dividend by the denominator of the divisor and then divide the product by the numerator of the divisor.

For part 3, students can exchange the problems they created with other students and then work each other's problems. Ask the writers of some of the problems to show their drawings and explain what type the problem is.

7.2 • Share and Share Alike

This problem builds on the experiences students have dividing a whole number by a fraction in Problem 7.1. However, in Problem 7.2, the students will encounter dividing a fraction by a whole number. The problems are organized to help students build on their ideas from 7.1 to see a pattern that will lead to an algorithm for division of fractions if either the dividend or the divisor is a whole number. In Problem 7.3, students will deal with a fraction divided by a fraction and see that their ways of thinking and their algorithms can be expanded to include all cases.

Problem 7.2 has two parts, each of which gives a different situation. In part A, each problem involves a unit fraction (a fraction with one in the numerator and a non-zero whole number in the denominator) divided by a whole number. In part B, each problem involves dividing a non-unit fraction by a whole number.

The Follow-Up for this problem is essential to translate the students' experiences to an algorithm. The students reinforce their understanding by actually writing problems that fit the computation $\frac{8}{3} \div 4$.

Launch

Let's review some things we have studied.

Who can tell me how to change $\frac{3}{5}$ into a decimal? *(Divide the 5 into the 3.)*

Why does that make sense? *(Because $\frac{3}{5}$ means 3 ÷ 5.)*

So we learned that $\frac{2}{3}$ can be thought of as another way to show division. This means that $\frac{2}{3}$ can be thought of as 2 ÷ 3. If you divide 2 by 3 you get $\frac{2}{3}$.

Now give me a situation in which this would be an appropriate interpretation of a fraction. *(Three people order two pizzas to share equally. How much does each get? The answer can be obtained by computing 2 ÷ 3 which is $\frac{2}{3}$. Another situation is converting a fraction to a decimal. Dividing 2 by 3 with or without a calculator gives you the decimal approximation for $\frac{2}{3}$.)*

In an earlier part of this unit we looked at products of two numbers that give exactly 1 as the answer. Some examples are $\frac{1}{2} \times 2 = 1$; $3 \times \frac{1}{3} = 1$; $\frac{2}{3} \times \frac{3}{2} = 1$. What did we call these pairs of numbers whose product is exactly 1? *(We called them reciprocals.)*

So what is the reciprocal of $\frac{3}{5}$? $(\frac{5}{3})$
How about 7? What is its reciprocal? $(\frac{1}{7})$

How about a mixed number such as $4\frac{1}{3}$? What is its reciprocal? *(First write $4\frac{1}{3}$ as a fraction. This is $\frac{13}{3}$. So the reciprocal is $\frac{3}{13}$ because $\frac{13}{3} \times \frac{3}{13} = 1$)*

I would like someone to summarize what kinds of problems we solved in Problem 7.1 and what we learned. *(Look for "dividing a whole number by a fraction" leading to a statement of an algorithm such as "Multiply by the reciprocal" or "Multiply by the denominator and divide by the numerator." Be sure to ask for an explanation of why these explanations make sense.)*

Today we have a problem about jellybeans with several parts to solve. As we read it, notice what is different from the problems you've already solved.

Call on a student to read the problem.

> Let's review some things you might think about as you work on the problem.
> Remember that drawing a diagram is often very helpful.
> What are the numbers (quantities) given in the problem? Remember to label
> each so you know what the number means.
> What do you need to find?
> What does the answer tell you?
> Remember to label your answer so that we know what the number you get
> tells us about the situation.

Explore

Have the students work on parts A and B individually and then in pairs to compare solutions and strategies.

As they work, walk around and ask questions to make sure that the students notice the types of problems that make up parts A and B. Ask a pair to make up another problem that fits the kind of problem requested in part A or part B. Encourage them to think about shortcuts.

You may need to help students share their ideas and drawings for these problems. The drawings are related to those done earlier, but now we are working with a fractional part of something and we need to share it equally among a whole number of entities. Ask students what kinds of problems these are—grouping or sharing.

Summarize

Review the work of parts A and B with the students. Call on students to illustrate how they did the divisions called for in parts A and B.

> Who can give me an answer for part A, question 1? Explain why you think
> you are correct.

Some students may draw diagrams such as the following.

STUDENT ONE:

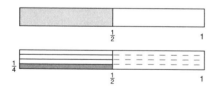

I drew a fraction strip to show $\frac{1}{2}$. Then I divided the half into four parts. This is the same as finding $\frac{1}{4}$ of the amount. Then I had to name the small part that shows $\frac{1}{4}$ of $\frac{1}{2}$. The drawing shows that $\frac{1}{4} \times \frac{1}{2} = \frac{1}{8}$. Since we have eight equal parts in the whole, each person gets $\frac{1}{8}$ of a pound of jellybeans.

Capitalize on this response to point out that the problem called for the computation $\frac{1}{2} \div 4$, and this diagram shows that $\frac{1}{2} \div 4$ is the same as $\frac{1}{2} \times \frac{1}{4}$ which is $\frac{1}{8}$.

Some students will draw a diagram that looks like this one.

STUDENT TWO:

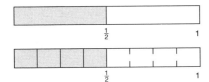

I first made a drawing of $\frac{1}{2}$. Then I divided $\frac{1}{2}$ into four parts because there are four people to share. Now I can see that each person gets $\frac{1}{8}$ of a pound of jellybeans. The diagram shows that $\frac{1}{2} \div 4 = \frac{1}{8}$. This makes sense because you will have smaller portions than the original $\frac{1}{2}$, and they will be $\frac{1}{4}$ as large. I guess we could do this by seeing that $\frac{1}{2} \div 4 = \frac{1}{2} \times \frac{1}{4} = 8$.

Each of these diagrams helps students move from the division problem to multiplying the dividend by the reciprocal of the divisor. Since the first one also suggests the model we used for multiplication of fractions, it may be even more helpful for students.

Finish part A before progressing to part B in which the fractional parts are not unit fractions.

> Who can tell me how these problems in part B are different from those in part A? *(They have non-unit fraction parts to be shared.)*
>
> So who can tell me how they thought about question 1 in part B?
> *(I thought about the problem just like those in part A. First I worked it for $\frac{1}{4}$ of a bar and then multiplied my answer by 3. Here were my steps: $\frac{1}{4} \div 2 = \frac{1}{4} \times \frac{1}{2} = \frac{1}{8}$. But I have 3 $\frac{1}{4}$s to share so each person gets $3 \times \frac{1}{8} = \frac{3}{8}$ of a bar of candy.) (I found common denominators, so I wrote $\frac{3}{4} \div 2 = \frac{3}{4} \div \frac{8}{4} = \frac{3}{8}$ of a candy bar.)*
>
> Did anyone think about question 1 in a different way? *(I drew a picture like I did before but the amount I started with was $\frac{3}{4}$. Each person would get half of the $\frac{3}{4}$.)*

A whole candy bar

Three - fourths of a candy bar

Person 1
Person 2

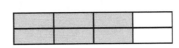

Each person gets $\frac{3}{8}$ of a candy bar. This is the same as $\frac{3}{4}$ x $\frac{1}{2}$ = $\frac{3}{8}$.

> Who can tell me whether the answer to question 2 is more or less than $\frac{1}{4}$ of a candy bar?
> How can you tell this without actually doing the exact computation? *(Since the amount you have is almost a whole, each of the four persons will get a little less than a fourth.)*

So exactly how much will each person get? ($\frac{7}{32}$ *of a candy bar.*)
Is this less than $\frac{1}{4}$? *(Yes, $\frac{1}{4}$ is equal to $\frac{8}{32}$. So each person gets $\frac{1}{32}$ less than a fourth.)*

Who can estimate how much each person will get in question 3? *(Each person will get less than a half because you have three halves altogether to share among four people.)*

Please explain your strategy for finding the answer to question 3. *(You have $\frac{3}{2}$ to share among four people. So we need to find $\frac{3}{2} \div 4$. I drew a diagram and found that each person gets $\frac{3}{8}$ of a candy bar.) (I got common denominators and wrote $\frac{3}{2} \div 4 = \frac{3}{2} \div \frac{8}{2} = \frac{3}{8}$.)*

Is $\frac{3}{8}$ less than $\frac{1}{4}$? *($\frac{1}{4}$ is equal to $\frac{2}{8}$, so $\frac{3}{8}$ is more.)*

If any students write this one as $\dfrac{1\frac{1}{2}}{4}$, help them to see that this is

equivalent to $1\frac{1}{2} \times \frac{1}{4}$. Then we can write $1\frac{1}{2}$ as $\frac{3}{2}$, and we have $\frac{3}{2} \times \frac{1}{4} = \frac{3}{8}$.

As a class, work on verbalizing an algorithm for division involving fractions and whole numbers. Build on what the students have found out in Problems 7.1 and 7.2. By this time, they should have reasonable ways of thinking about the computations. Some will see that multiplying the dividend by the reciprocal of the divisor makes sense and works in both kinds of problems they have studied so far. Others will see this as multiplying by the denominator and dividing by the numerator of the divisor. Some may need to draw pictures to help think through a problem.

You can do the Follow-Up in class or assign it for homework. In either case, discuss it in class focusing on developing an efficient algorithm or procedure for division of fractions.

Solutions with Sample Drawings for Problem 7.2

A.

2. $\frac{1}{4} \div 3 = \frac{1}{12}$ lb of jellybeans each

    Step one shows a representation of the whole.

    Step two shows $\frac{1}{4}$ of the whole.

    Step three shows each fourth divided into three equal parts resulting in $\frac{1}{12}$, which is each student's share.

    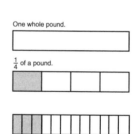

3. $\frac{1}{3} \div 3 = \frac{1}{9}$ lb of jellybeans each

    When we divide $\frac{1}{3}$ by 3 we get $\frac{1}{3}$ divided into three equal parts.
    If we mark the rest of the whole, we can see that one part is $\frac{1}{9}$ of the whole.

    So, the answer is $\frac{1}{3} \div 3 = \frac{1}{9}$.

7.3 • Summer Work

Problem 7.3 takes the students into the final case in developing an efficient strategy for dividing with fractions, dividing a fraction by a fraction. While this is conceptually and procedurally harder for students, the basis for understanding has been built through Problems 7.1 and 7.2. Continue to remind the students that they have ways of thinking about these problems even though they are a bit different.

Launch

We have already learned to divide fractions with a whole number dividend or a whole number divisor. Now we are going to look at problems that involve two fractions.

Suppose you have half of a large chocolate bar, and your cookie recipe uses $\frac{1}{8}$ of a bar. The chocolate you have is enough for how many batches of cookies? Think about this for a minute.

What are we trying to find in this problem? *(How many $\frac{1}{8}$s there are in $\frac{1}{2}$.)*

Is it a sharing or a grouping problem? To decide, think about what the quantities in the problem are. What are you given and what are you trying to find? *(The quantities given are the amount of chocolate bar that you have and the amount needed per recipe. You are trying to find how many batches (groups) you can make that are of the size given. So, this is a grouping problem.)*

Who has an idea about how to do this? *(Let's get common denominators. We can write the $\frac{1}{2}$ as $\frac{4}{8}$ and see that there are four $\frac{1}{8}$s in $\frac{1}{2}$. So the answer is 4 batches of cookies.) (I think we should draw a diagram. First draw a fraction strip to show $\frac{1}{2}$ and then mark off parts equal to $\frac{1}{8}$. Or, mark the bar into eighths—that is like finding a common denominator.)*

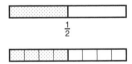

(The bar is marked into eight equal pieces. Each is $\frac{1}{8}$. Now we can count to see that there are 4 eighths in the part of the bar that the cook has. So the cook can make four batches of cookies.)

Now I would like you to work individually on question 1 in part A. Then share your strategies with your partners. For each of the remaining problems, try to solve each alone and then talk about what you did with your partner. Be prepared to explain your reasoning in each case.

Explore

Circulate, looking for students who need help and for those who have an idea that should be shared in the summary. Remind them that diagrams can help them make sense of the situation.

Ask students:

> What are the quantities? What do you know and what are you trying to find?
> Is this a sharing or a grouping problem? Why?
> What kind of diagram might help?
> Did you find a shortcut for doing the problem?

When the students have done most or all of the problems, have the class discuss what they found.

Summarize

> Which part was harder, part A or part B? Why? *(B seemed harder because it took $\frac{2}{3}$ to make one bow. Unit fractions seem easier.)*
>
> Did your strategies have to change a lot for part B? *(No, actually the same ideas seemed to work.)*
>
> Are these grouping or sharing problems? *(They are all grouping problems.)*
>
> O.K. let's look at some of the problems. Describe the strategy used to solve question 1 in part A. *(We need to find $\frac{1}{2} \div \frac{1}{6}$. We have $\frac{1}{2}$ yard and we need $\frac{1}{6}$ per badge. This means we need to find how many $\frac{1}{6}$ are in $\frac{1}{2}$. I drew a diagram and counted.)*

> *(Mark off sixths on the whole.*

> *We could mark off in the other direction. Either way shows that there are three $\frac{1}{6}$ in $\frac{1}{2}$ This means we can make three badges.)*
>
> How do you know that each of the parts of the second diagram is $\frac{1}{6}$ of the whole? *(You can see that each part is $\frac{1}{2} \times \frac{1}{3}$ which is $\frac{1}{6}$ or you can just count the equal sized pieces and get 6.)*
>
> Does anyone have another way to think about this one? *(I got a common denominator. So, I wrote $\frac{1}{2}$ as $\frac{3}{6}$. Then I had to find how many $\frac{1}{6}$ are in $\frac{3}{6}$. This is the division problem $\frac{3}{6} \div \frac{1}{6}$ which equals 3.)*

Who can tell us about the second problem? What is different about this problem? *(You have a non-unit fraction amount of ribbon.)*

So do the same strategies work? *(Yes. You can still ask the question, "How many $\frac{1}{6}$ are in $\frac{3}{4}$?" You can still draw a diagram. And you can still use common denominators.)*

Play out your strategy for us. *(I used a common denominator to write the $\frac{3}{4}$ as $\frac{9}{12}$ and the $\frac{1}{6}$ as $\frac{2}{12}$. So I just had to divide 9 by 2 and got $4\frac{1}{2}$ badges.) (I drew a picture.)*

(I drew the three fourths of the whole and then divided the strip in thirds to make twelfths. But it takes two twelfths to make a sixth. So I have $4\frac{1}{2}$ badges. You can see them on the diagram below.)

Some of you used the "Multiply by the denominator and divide by the numerator of the divisor" reasoning. Does that still work here? *(Yes. $\frac{3}{4} \div \frac{1}{6} = (\frac{3}{4} \times 6) \div 1 = \frac{18}{4} = 4\frac{2}{4} = 4\frac{1}{2}$ badges.)*

What is the answer for Problem 3? *(I got $\frac{30}{8} = 3\frac{6}{8} = 3\frac{3}{4}$ badges.)*
Any problem with this one?

If the students are having trouble with the remainder, go through the common denominator approach and draw a picture to help them see.

Let's have a volunteer to talk about question 4 in part A. What is the answer and how did you find it? *(We need to find the number of one-sixths in $\frac{8}{3}$. It is easy if we find a common denominator. $\frac{8}{3}$ is equivalent to $\frac{16}{6}$, so we can make 16 badges.)*

Now let's look at part B. Here we need $\frac{2}{3}$ yard for each bow. In question 1 we are making bows from a piece of ribbon measuring $\frac{4}{5}$ yard. What is the question we are trying to answer? *(How many $\frac{2}{3}$ are in $\frac{4}{5}$?)*

Are these grouping or sharing problems? *(They are all grouping problems because you are given a quantity to work with and how much each bow takes. You have to find the number of bows which is like finding the number of groups.)*

Tell me how you found the answer. *(I tried common denominators. I wrote both of the given fractions as fifteenths. This gave me $\frac{10}{15}$ as the amount of ribbon each bow needed and $\frac{12}{15}$ as the amount of ribbon I have. I have 12 parts, and it takes 10 parts to make a bow. I can make 1 bow and have $\frac{2}{10}$ left over for another bow. This means I can make $1\frac{2}{10}$ bows.)*

Anyone do it differently? *(I tried multiplying by the denominator and dividing by the numerator. This gave me $(\frac{4}{5} \times 3) \div 2$ which is $\frac{12}{5} \div 2$. This is the same as $\frac{12}{10}$ which is $1\frac{2}{10}$ bows.)*

Ask similar questions for the remaining problems and ask for drawings as needed to help students make sense of the problems.

The Follow-Up is essential. Whether they are assigned as class work or homework, the problems must be discussed.

Investigation 7

1. Mary's scout troop is learning to tie knots. Each scout needs $\frac{5}{8}$ of a yard of cord to practice tying knots. How many of the required lengths can be cut from a 6-yard length of cord? Explain your answer.

2. How is the answer to $14 \div \frac{1}{3}$ related to the answer to $14 \div \frac{2}{3}$? Explain.

3. Mrs. Brown bought 120 kg of whole-wheat flour for her bakery. She sold $\frac{2}{5}$ of the flour to a friend and packed the remainder equally into five storage containers. Find the weight of the flour in each of the five containers.

4. Every morning Mrs. Brown makes cinnamon rolls in her bakery. Each cinnamon roll requires $\frac{2}{3}$ cup of sifted flour. She has a 20-pound bag of flour and knows that one pound of this particular flour yields about 3 cups of sifted flour. How many cinnamon rolls can she make from this bag of flour?

5. Compute the following and explain why your answer makes sense.

    a. $\frac{1}{4} \div 3$ b. $4 \div \frac{2}{5}$

    c. $\frac{2}{3} \div \frac{1}{6}$ d. $2\frac{3}{5} \div 1\frac{1}{2}$

Answer Keys

1. $6 \div \frac{5}{8} = 9\frac{3}{5}$

   This means 9 of the required lengths can be cut from the cord with $\frac{3}{5}$ of another as the remainder.

2. The answer to $14 \div \frac{1}{3}$ is 42.

   The answer to $14 \div \frac{2}{3}$ will be half as large. Since it takes two $\frac{1}{3}$s to make $\frac{2}{3}$, the answer is half of 42 or 21.

3. $\frac{2}{5} \times 120 = 48$

   She sold 48 kg and kept $120 - 48 = 72$ kg. Each container would have $72 \div 5 = 14\frac{2}{5}$ kg flour.

4. 90 cinnamon rolls

   There are $20 \times 3 = 60$ cups in the bag of flour, and $60 \div \frac{2}{3} = 90$ cinnamon rolls.

5. **a.** $\frac{1}{12}$ Since $3 = \frac{12}{4}$, think of the problem as $\frac{1}{4} \div \frac{12}{4} = \frac{1}{12}$.

   b. 10 Since there are 20 fifths in 4, there are 10 $\frac{2}{5}$ in 4.

   c. 4 Use a common denominator to rewrite the problem as
   $\frac{4}{6} \div \frac{1}{6} = 4$, or use the fact that dividing by $\frac{1}{6}$ is the same thing as multiplying by 6. This gives
   $\frac{2}{3} \times 6 = 4$.

   d. $2\frac{3}{5} \div 1\frac{1}{2} = \frac{13}{5} \div \frac{3}{2} = \frac{13}{5} \times \frac{2}{3} = \frac{26}{15}$ or $1\frac{11}{15}$. We could also draw a strip model.

Looking Back and Looking Ahead

Unit Reflections

*R*ational numbers can be expressed in several forms—*fractions*, *decimals*, and *percents*. In this unit, you learned how to choose the form that will be most useful in a given situation and how to draw *diagrams* or *pictures* to make sense of those situations. You learned how to identify situations that call for *computation* with rational numbers. You developed *algorithms* for adding, subtracting, multiplying, and dividing fractions and decimals, and you have learned how to compute and solve problems with percents.

Using Your Quantitative Reasoning—To test your understanding and skill in using rational numbers, consider the following examples of ways that fractions, decimals, and percents occur in everyday situations.

① *A local department store offered a scratch-off coupon to attract customers. Shoppers received a discount of 5%, 10%, 15%, and 25% off the list prices of any collection of items in the store. (Typically, sales tax and discounts are computed on the original price and rounded up to the nearest cent.)*

a. What were the least and the greatest possible costs, including 6% sales tax, for a shirt listed at $24.99?

b. Joey decided to buy the shirt in part a in three different colors. At the checkout, he scratched the coupon, and 15% appeared. How much did he actually pay for the shirts?

c. The store conducted a survey to find out whether the scratch-off coupons had influenced customers to buy. At the end of the day, they tallied these results.

- Would have purchased the items without the coupon—556
- Were strongly influenced by the coupon—378
- Were somewhat influenced by the coupon—137

i. What percent of customers was influenced by the coupon?

ii. Make a graph to show the percent of customers in each category.

Using Your Quantitative Reasoning

Answers may have slight variations due to rounding. Answers reflect tax, discount, etc. computed on the original price. All money answers are rounded up to the nearest cent to fit the reality of commerce and the context of money.

1a. Highest is $25.16 and lowest is $19.87.

b. The total cost is $67.55.

c. i. 48%. This is the sum of both the strongly influenced and the somewhat influenced categories.

ii. The percents for the graph are approximately 52% would buy without the coupon, 35% were strongly influenced by the coupon, and 13% were somewhat influenced by the coupon.

Percent of Customers in Each Category

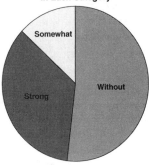

How to Use
Looking Back and Looking Ahead: Unit Reflections

The first part of this section includes problems that allow students to demonstrate their mathematical understandings and skills. The second part gives them an opportunity to explain their reasoning. This section can be used as a review to help students stand back and reflect on the "big" ideas and connections in the unit. This section may be assigned as homework, followed up with class discussion the next day. Focus on the *Explaining Your Reasoning* section in the discussion. Encourage the students to refer to the problems to illustrate their reasoning.

2a. $10.16

b. $\frac{1}{2}$ pound of cinnamon apple is 25% of the total. $\frac{1}{3}$ pound of lemon is approximately 17% of the total. $\frac{1}{4}$ pound of licorice is 12.5% of the total. $\frac{1}{6}$ pound of bubble gum is 8% of the total. $\frac{3}{4}$ pound of coconut is 37.5% of the total.

c.

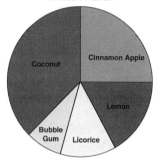

Percent of Jellybeans of Each Flavor

d. $6.35

e. i. $12.04

   ii. ≈ 56.9% or 57%

Explaining Your Reasoning

1. The least percent discount is 5% and the greatest is 25%. Therefore, the costs computed using each of these two discounts determine the greatest and least costs possible. Two possible computation strategies are shown at the right.

---

2 *The Sweet Shop sells jellybeans in many different flavors. One day Jane asked for this mix:*

   $\frac{1}{2}$ pound of cinnamon apple $\frac{1}{6}$ pound of bubble gum

   $\frac{1}{3}$ pound of lemon $\frac{3}{4}$ pound of coconut

   $\frac{1}{4}$ pound of licorice

a. What was Jane's bill, including sales tax, if jellybeans cost $4.98 per pound? There is a 2% tax on candy and snack food in her state.

b. What percent of Jane's mix did each flavor of jellybean represent?

c. Make a graph to show the percent of each flavor of jellybean in Jane's order.

d. Sammy hates coconut jellybeans, so he asked for Jane's mix without the coconut. What was his bill?

e. Shaquile likes fruit flavors. He wanted a mix of peach, mango, blueberry, and strawberry. The following chart shows how much the Sweet Shop still had of each flavor and how much Shaquile ordered.

Sweet Shop's Stock	Shaquile's Order
$1\frac{1}{2}$ pounds of peach	$\frac{1}{3}$ of what is left
$\frac{2}{3}$ pound of mango	$\frac{1}{2}$ of what is left
$\frac{3}{4}$ pound of blueberry	$\frac{1}{4}$ of what is left
$2\frac{1}{4}$ pounds of strawberry	$\frac{3}{5}$ of what is left

   i. What was the bill for Shaquile's mix?

   ii. What percent of his mix was strawberry?

Explaining Your Reasoning—When you use mathematical calculations to solve a problem or make a decision, it is important to be able to justify each step in your reasoning.

1. Explain how you found the least and greatest possible costs for a shirt in Problem 1.

2. How did you find the percent of customers in each category in Problem 1c? Explain why you chose the particular type of graphic display that you used. Explain how you constructed that display.

3. What operations did you use to find the cost for Jane's jellybeans?

4. How did you find the percent of the mix for each flavor in Jane's order?

5. Do you agree with these computations: $4 \div \frac{1}{3} = 12$ and $4 \div \frac{2}{3} = 6$? If so, why is the second answer half of the first?

- Find the new cost after the discount: $24.99 × 0.95 = $23.74. Then compute the cost with the tax: $23.74 × 1.06 = $25.16.

- Or, find the regular price including the tax: $24.99 × 1.06 = $26.49. Then take the discount, $26.49 × 0.95 = $25.16.

Notice that in both cases you multiply by 0.95 to show the 5% discount and by 1.06 to include the sales tax. This means that each computation is essentially $24.99 × 0.95 × 1.06 = $25.16. This cost is the greatest because this discount is the least.

The greatest discount gives the least cost. The shirt would cost $24.99 × 0.75 × 1.06 = $19.87.

2, 3. See page 167.

4, 5. See page 168.

6. Use the following problems to show the steps involved in algorithms for adding, subtracting, multiplying and dividing fractions and decimals. Be prepared to explain your reasoning in each case.

a. $\frac{5}{6} + \frac{1}{4}$ **b.** $\frac{3}{4} - \frac{2}{3}$ **c.** $\frac{2}{5} \times \frac{3}{8}$ **d.** $\frac{3}{8} \div \frac{3}{4}$

e. $23.4 + 17.42$ **f.** $43.09 - 17.62$ **g.** 350.5×12.4 **h.** $15.6 \div 9$

7. Explain the general procedures you use to answer these questions about percents. Give specific numerical examples that illustrate your answers.

a. How do you find the percent equivalent to a given decimal number?

b. How do you find what percent one number is of another?

c. How do you find a given percent of a number?

The ideas and techniques you've used in this unit will be applied and expanded in many future units of *Connected Mathematics* and in other mathematics work on problems that lie ahead in school and in your future work. Fractions, decimals, and percents are used in measuring and calculating quantities of all kinds—from length, area, and volume to time, money, test scores, and weights.

2. The total number of customers surveyed is 556 + 378 + 137 = 1071. To find the percentage for each category, divide the number of customers in each category by the total. The percent of customers in each category is without the coupon: 556 ÷ 1071 ≈ 0.5191 or about 52%; strongly influenced: 378 ÷ 1071 ≈ 0.3529 or about 35%; somewhat influenced: 137 ÷ 1071 ≈ 0.1279 or about 13%. Explanations for completing the graph are given below at the left.

3. Adding all of the fractional parts gives a total of 2 pounds of jellybeans. Multiply the total number of pounds by the price per pound. Multiply this result, $9.96, by 1.02 to find that the total cost with tax is $10.16.

The amount of tax could be computed by multiplying the total cost of the beans by 0.02 and then adding this tax amount to the total cost of the jelly-beans. Multiplying by 1.02 does both operations in one step.

4–6f. See page 168.

6g–7. See page 169.

2. (*Continued from above right.*)

A circle graph is one good choice of graphic display. A graphing program could be used to draw it. By hand, the angle measure from the center of the circle must be computed for each category. For example, the 52% who were not influenced would be represented by a wedge of the circle with an angle of 0.52 × 360° = 187.2°. For the other categories, the angle measures are 0.35 × 360° = 126° and 0.13 × 360° = 46.8°.

Draw a radius of the circle for your graph, measure a 187.2° angle from that radius, and draw another radius. This wedge of the circle represents those who would buy the shirt without the coupon. Then measure an angle of 126° from the new radius. This gives the wedge for those strongly influenced, and the remaining wedge represents those somewhat influenced.

Looking Back and Looking Ahead

Possible Answers

4. Find what fraction of the total each flavor of jellybean represents and then express each as a percent. For example, the fractional part of the total that is cinnamon apple is $\frac{1}{2} \div 2 = \frac{1}{4}$ or 25%. This makes sense because there are four $\frac{1}{2}$s in the total of 2 pounds. So, the cinnamon apple portion is $\frac{1}{4}$ of the total or 25%. Similarly, since $\frac{1}{3} \div 2 = \frac{1}{6}$, the lemon is 0.166667 or about 17% of the total. Licorice is $\frac{1}{4} \div 2 = \frac{1}{8}$ or 12.5%; bubble gum is $\frac{1}{12}$ or about 8%, and coconut is $\frac{3}{8}$ or 37.5%.

5. Yes, $4 \div \frac{1}{3} = 12$. Since there are three thirds in each whole, and $3 \times 4 = 12$, there are twelve thirds in four wholes. The second part is $4 \div \frac{3}{4}$ or one-half of the first answer. Since it takes two $\frac{1}{3}$ to make $\frac{2}{3}$, the answer is one-half of 12 or 6.

6a. To add $\frac{5}{6} + \frac{1}{4}$, write each fraction in equivalent form using a common denominator. If 12 is the common denominator, the addition becomes $\frac{10}{12} + \frac{3}{12}$ which equals $\frac{13}{12}$. This improper fraction can be rewritten as $1\frac{1}{2}$.

b. For subtraction, the fractions must be expressed in equivalent form with a common denominator. For the problem $\frac{3}{4} - \frac{2}{3}$, 12 is a common denominator so the problem can be rewritten as $\frac{9}{12} - \frac{8}{12}$, which equals $\frac{1}{12}$.

c. To multiply fractions, multiply the numerators and the denominators. For $\frac{2}{5} \times \frac{3}{8}$ this gives $\frac{2}{5} \times \frac{3}{8} = \frac{6}{40}$. The final answer has many equivalent forms. $\frac{6}{40} = \frac{3}{20}$, so $\frac{3}{20}$ is another form of the answer. In fact, $\frac{3}{20}$ is the simplest form of the answer.

d. To divide fractions, multiply the dividend by the reciprocal of the divisor. So $\frac{3}{8} \div \frac{3}{4} = \frac{3}{8} \times \frac{4}{3} = \frac{12}{24}$, which is equivalent to $\frac{1}{2}$. This makes sense because $\frac{3}{8} \div \frac{3}{4} = \frac{3}{8} \div \frac{6}{8}$. There are three $\frac{1}{8}$ in $\frac{3}{8}$. This is only $\frac{1}{2}$ of a $\frac{6}{8}$ because six $\frac{1}{8}$ are needed to make $\frac{6}{8}$.

e. To add decimals, add the value of the place the number is in. This means that the decimal points must be aligned so that numbers with the same place value are in the same column.

$$\begin{array}{r} 23.4 \\ +\ 17.42 \\ \end{array}$$

To make this clearer, rewrite the 23.4 as 23.40. Annexing zero does not change the value of the number. So, we now have

$$\begin{array}{r} 23.40 \\ +\ 17.42 \\ \hline 40.82 \end{array}$$

f. Subtraction requires the same column alignment as addition so only numbers with the same place value are subtracted. So,

$$\begin{array}{r} 43.09 \\ -\ 17.62 \\ \hline 25.47 \end{array}$$

6g. There are many ways to understand what is going on when one decimal number is being multiplied by another decimal number. The form of the numbers can be changed to fractions so the problem can be written as $\frac{3505}{10} \times \frac{124}{10}$. The product resulting from multiplying the numerators and the denominators is $\frac{434,620}{100}$.
Complete the computation by dividing 434,620 by 100. The result is 4346.20.
A short way to do this is to multiply as for whole numbers and adjust the "answer" by matching the total number of decimal places in the two factors to the number of decimal places in the product. Therefore, first multiply 3505 × 124 = 434,620. Because there is a total of two decimal places in the original problem, the product must have two decimal places to the left as well. This answer is 4346.20. This is the same as multiplying the numerators and then dividing by the denominator of 100 which is 10 × 10 and which moves the decimal point two places to the left.

h. To divide decimals, change the form of the problem as for multiplication. Since $15.6 = \frac{156}{10}$, the problem can be rewritten as $\frac{156}{10} \div 9 = \frac{156}{10} \times \frac{1}{9}$. This equals 156 ÷ 90 which is approximately 1.73.

To complete the standard long division algorithm, the problem is written as $9\overline{)15.6}$. Multiply the dividend and the divisor by 10 to get an equivalent form of the problem with no decimal places and rewrite the problem.

$$90\overline{)156}$$

Write a decimal point after the 6 in 156 and annex as many zeros as necessary to get the required accuracy. Complete the division.

```
         1.73
  90)156.00
      90
      66 0
      63 0
       3 00
       2 70
         30
```

7a. Since percent means "out of 100," (for example, 35% means 35 out of 100), using the "%" symbol means "divide the given number by 100." So to find the percent equivalent of 0.145, multiply by 100 and write "%" to keep the expressions equal but to change the form. Now we have 14.5/100 which is 14.5 out of 100 or 14.5%. To express 1.256 as a percent we would think of 1.256 as $\frac{125.6}{100}$. This means the percent is 125.6% or 125.6 out of 100.

b. Suppose the problem is what percent of 20 is 5, or 5 is what percent of 20.
The equation 5 = ?% of 20 can be used to find what percent to multiply by 20 and get 5. To solve the equation, divide 5 by 20 and get 0.25 which is 25%. The solution checks because 20 multiplied by 0.25 equals 5.

c. To find a percent of a number, multiply by the percent number and divide by 100. For example, to find 17% of 155, write (17 × 155) ÷ 100 which equals 26.35. An alternative is to write the percent as a decimal and then multiply. Since 17% = $\frac{17}{100}$, this would be 0.17 × 155 = 26.35.

algorithm An algorithm is a set of rules for performing a procedure. Mathematicians invent algorithms that are useful in many kinds of situations. Some examples of algorithms are the rules for long division or the rules for adding two fractions. The following algorithm was written by a middle-grades student:

To add two fractions, first change them to equivalent fractions with the same denominator. Then add the numerators and put the sum over the common denominator.

base ten number system The base ten number system is the common number system we use. Our number system is based on the number 10 because we have ten fingers with which to group. In a number like 253, each place represents ten of the previous groups, we can write numbers efficiently. By extending the place-value system to include places that represent fractions with 10 or powers of 10 in the denominator, we can represent quantities less than 1. Below is a graphic representation of the number 253 in the base ten number system.

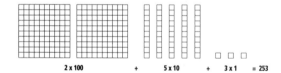

2×100 + 5×10 + 3×1 = 253

benchmark A benchmark is a "nice" number that can be used to estimate the size of other numbers. For work with fractions, 0, $\frac{1}{2}$, and 1 are good benchmarks. We often estimate fractions or decimals with benchmarks because it is easier to do arithmetic with them, and estimates often give enough accuracy for the situation. For example, many fractions and decimals—such as $\frac{37}{50}$, $\frac{5}{8}$, 0.43, and 0.55—can be thought of as being close to $\frac{1}{2}$. We also use benchmarks to help compare fractions such as $\frac{5}{8}$ and 0.43. For example, we could say that $\frac{5}{8}$ is larger than 0.43 because $\frac{5}{8}$ is larger than $\frac{1}{2}$ and 0.43 is smaller than $\frac{1}{2}$.

decimal A decimal, or decimal fraction, is a special form of a fraction. Decimals are based on the base ten place-value system. To write numbers as decimals, we use only 10 and powers of 10 as denominators. Writing fractions in this way saves us from writing the denominators because they are understood. When we write $\frac{375}{1000}$ as a decimal—0.375—the denominator of 1000 is understood. The digits to the left of the decimal point (period) show whole units, and the digits to the right of the decimal point show a portion of a whole unit. The diagram below shows the place value for each digit of the number 5620.301.

5	6	2	0	3	0	1
Thousands	Hundreds	Tens	Ones	Tenths	Hundredths	Thousandths

denominator The denominator is the number written below the line in a fraction. In the fraction $\frac{3}{4}$, 4 is the denominator. In the part-whole interpretation of fractions, the denominator shows the number of equal-size parts into which the whole has been split.

equivalent fractions Equivalent fractions are equal in value but have different numerators and denominators. For example, $\frac{2}{3}$ and $\frac{14}{21}$ are equivalent fractions. The shaded part of this rectangle represents both $\frac{2}{3}$ and $\frac{14}{21}$.

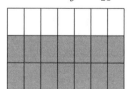

Descriptive Glossary

fraction A number (a quantity) of the form $\frac{a}{b}$ where a and b are whole numbers. A fraction can indicate a part of a whole object or set, a ratio of two quantities, or a division. For the picture below, the fraction $\frac{3}{4}$ shows the part of the rectangle that is shaded: the denominator 4 indicates the number of equal-size pieces, and the numerator 3 indicates the number of pieces that are shaded.

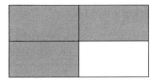

The fraction $\frac{3}{4}$ could also represent three of a group of four items meeting a particular criteria; the ratio 3 to 4 (for example, when 12 students enjoyed a particular activity and 16 students did not); or the amount of pizza each person receives when three pizzas are shared equally among four people, which would be $3 \div 4$ or $\frac{3}{4}$ of a pizza per person.

numerator The numerator is the number written above the line in a fraction. In the fraction $\frac{5}{8}$, 5 is the numerator. When you interpret fractions as a part of a whole, the numerator tells the number of parts in the whole.

percent Percent means "out of 100." A percent is a special decimal fraction in which the denominator is 100. When we write 68%, we mean 68 out of 100, $\frac{68}{100}$, or 0.68. We write the percent sign (%) after a number to indicate percent. 68 of the 100 squares in this rectangle are shaded, so we say 68% of the rectangle is shaded.

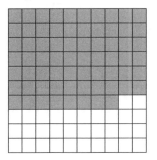

reciprocal A factor by which you multiply a given number so that their product is 1. For example, $\frac{3}{5}$ is the reciprocal of $\frac{5}{3}$ and $\frac{5}{3}$ is thr reciprocal of $\frac{3}{5}$ because $\frac{3}{5} \times \frac{5}{3} = 1$. Note that the reciprocal of $1\frac{2}{3}$ is $\frac{3}{5}$ because $1\frac{2}{3} \times \frac{3}{5} = 1$.

unit fraction A unit fraction is a fraction with a numerator of 1. For example, in the unit fraction $\frac{1}{13}$, the part-whole interpretation of fractions tells us that 13 indicates the number of equal-size parts into which the whole has been split and that the fraction represents the quantity of 1 of those parts.

Index

Index

Index